Comments on *The Tobin Tax: Coping* *Financial Volatility*

"Policy ideas must rest on good logic and good analysis—especially in international financial and monetary matters, which in my opinion are of such importance. That's why this book on the Tobin tax is so useful. It provides a thorough and balanced review of four major themes: the potential of the Tobin tax as an instrument of monetary policy; its feasibility, both technical and political; what one can learn so far from comparable measures applied by individual countries; and finally, how to use the proceeds, and what their possible economic effects could be."
Jacques Delors, President
European Commission, 1985–1994

"Many governments around the world—including mine—have become interested in the Tobin tax as a revenue source for global cooperation in the UN and elsewhere, to support among other things peace building and peacekeeping activities, which are presently under-funded. This pioneering book demonstrates that the Tobin tax, whether for this purpose or as an instrument of global monetary policy, or both, has a real chance of being proved feasible. As such, it takes an intriguing idea a significant step closer to realisation."
Gareth Evans, Foreign Minister of Australia, 1988–1996

"This book is overdue. It is 24 years since James Tobin first presented his proposal to throw sand in the wheels of international finance and make some money as a by-product. It does not reflect well on the profession that for all those years we have been content to write dismissive footnotes. The editors are to be congratulated for forcing us to think seriously about this proposal at long last."
John Williamson, Senior Economist
Institute for International Economics, Washington, D.C.

"To keep the United Nations relevant to a rapidly changing world, the Commission on Global Governance recommended a number of possible reforms, urging also serious consideration of additional funding mechanisms. This book offers serious consideration of the "Tobin" tax, one of the most intriguing potential ways to stabilize UN financing without damaging sovereignty or distorting market flows. Those who worry about the future of cooperative peacekeeping would do well to inform themselves herein."
Barber Conable, President and Executive Director
The World Bank, 1986–1991

Contributors

Manuel Agosin, Universidad de Chile, Santiago, Chile

Michael Dooley, University of Santa Cruz, California

Barry Eichengreen, University of California at Berkeley

David Felix, Washington University, Saint Louis, Missouri

Ricardo Ffrench-Davis, Economic Commission for Latin America and the Caribbean, Santiago de Chile

Jeffrey Frankel, University of California at Berkeley

Peter Garber, Brown University

Stephany Griffith-Jones, Institute of Development Studies, Brighton, Sussex, UK

Isabelle Grunberg, United Nations Development Programme

Mahbub ul Haq, Human Development Centre, Islamabad, Pakistan

Inge Kaul, United Nations Development Programme

Peter Kenen, Princeton University

John Langmore, MP, Member of Parliament, Australia

Yung-Chul Park, Korea Institute of Finance, Seoul, Korea

Ranjit Sau, New Jersey Institute of Technology

James Tobin, Yale University

Charles Wyplosz, Graduate Institute for International Studies, Geneva, Switzerland

THE TOBIN TAX

Coping with Financial Volatility

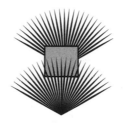

Edited by

Mahbub ul Haq
Inge Kaul
Isabelle Grunberg

Oxford University Press
New York   Oxford

Oxford University Press

Oxford   New York

Athens   Auckland   Bangkok   Bogotá
Bombay   Buenos Aires   Calcutta   Cape Town
Dar es Salaam   Delhi   Florence   Hong Kong
Istanbul   Karachi   Kuala Lumpur   Madras
Madrid   Melbourne   Mexico City   Nairobi
Paris   Singapore   Taipei   Tokyo   Toronto

and associated companies in
Berlin   Ibadan

Published by Oxford University Press, Inc.,
198 Madison Avenue, New York, New York 10016

Oxford is a registered trade mark of Oxford University Press

Library of Congress Cataloging-in-Publication Data

Haq, Mahbub ul, 1934–
    The Tobin tax: coping with financial volatility/Mahbub ul Haq, Inge Kaul,
    Isabelle Grunberg, eds.
        p.   cm.
    Includes bibliographical references and index.
    ISBN 0–19–511180–X (cloth).—ISBN 0–19–511181–8 (paper)
    1. Foreign exchange futures—Taxation. 2. Tobin, James, 1918–. I. Kaul,
    Inge. II. Grunberg, Isabelle. III. Title.
    HG3853.H37   1996
    332.4'5—dc20   96–17533
                                                                          CIP

9 8 7 6 5 4 3 2 1
Printed in the United States of America on acid-free paper.

Cover: Gerald Quinn, Quinn Information Design, Cabin John, Maryland

Editing, design, desktop composition and production management: Ilyse Zable, Glenn
McGrath and Laurel Morais, with American Writing Corporation, Washington, D.C.

Contents

Lessons from Individual Country Experiences

Revenue Raised by the Tobin Tax

Conclusion

Acknowledgements

This book would not have been possible without the many valuable contributions, comments and suggestions we received from a large number of individuals and organizations. Special thanks are due to Barry Eichengreen, who has served as lead consultant and contributed so generously to the design and review of the studies included in this book. We are most appreciative of the support provided for this project by the United Nations Development Programme, as well as various member states and independent foundations. The views expressed here, however, do not in any way reflect the positions of these institutions.

The first drafts of these studies were presented at an expert group meeting held on 10 October 1995. We are grateful to the participants who shared their ideas with us, in particular those who acted as discussants of the drafts: Paul Armington of the World Bank, Keith Bezanson of the International Development Research Council of Canada, Andrew Cornford of the United Nations Conference on Trade and Development, Albert Fishlow of the Council on Foreign Relations in New York, Arminio Fraga of the Soros Fund, Carmen Reinhart of the International Monetary Fund, James Tobin of Yale University and John Williamson of the Institute for International Economics in Washington, D.C. Laura MacQuade was invaluable in the organization and planning of this meeting.

Special thanks are also due to the readers of the final manuscript, including Patricia de Mowbray, Richard Jolly, John Langmore, Maggie McMillan and Almud Weitz.

Sophie Trémolet and Almud Weitz provided outstanding assistance in the preparation and review of the manuscript and its statistics. The volume has also benefited from the design work of Gerald Quinn and the editing and prepress production work by American Writing's Ilyse Zable, Glenn McGrath, Laurel Morais and Meg Tilton.

We also wish to acknowledge with thanks the efforts of Flora Aller, Rocio Kattis and Zipora Vainborg-Rogg who provided valuable administrative support.

Prologue

James Tobin

The publication of this book and the holding of the conference that preceded it testify to an active interest in my proposal for an international tax on foreign exchange transactions—the so-called Tobin tax. Bob Haq, once a student of mine, Inge Kaul and their colleagues deserve great credit for their initiative in organizing this project—they assembled leading experts in international economics, development, global finance and world politics. They have certainly earned my gratitude. I appreciate immensely the serious consideration the authors of these excellent papers have given the proposal. Their research and analysis have certainly advanced understanding, mine in particular, of the issues raised by the proposal, while pointing out the need for further study.

The proposal and its cool reception, 1972–95

I dropped the idea of a currency transactions tax into the pool almost a quarter of a century ago—in my Janeway Lectures at Princeton in 1972 (published in Tobin 1974). The tax was on my list of measures to enhance the efficacy of macroeconomic policy. In 1977, I was emboldened to devote my presidential address to the Eastern Economic Association entirely to it (Tobin 1978). It did not make much of a ripple. In fact, one might say that it sank like a rock. The community of professional economists simply ignored it. The interest that occasionally arose came from journalists and financial pundits. It was usually triggered by currency crises and died out when the crisis passed from the headlines.

The idea was anathema to central bankers. The most recent currency crises led reporters to ask Ottmar Issing, the economic brain of the Bundesbank, about the Tobin tax. He replied with some asperity, "Oh, that again. It's the Loch Ness Monster, popping up once more!" When I next encountered Issing, whom I like and respect, I said, "Well here I am, the Monster still."

Another source of recent and current interest in the proposal (for example, shown by President Mitterand at the World Social Summit in Copenhagen in 1994) is its potential as a generator of revenue—revenue that could be dedicated to multilateral purposes, given the probable necessity of having a tax that is implemented internationally. I had suggested this use in Tobin (1978) as a by-product of the proposed tax, not as its principal purpose.

Some of the interest in the tax at the Social Summit and on the fringes of the 1995 Halifax G-7 meeting arose from motivations in a sense similar to my own—to improve the macroeconomic performance of economies trapped by external financial pressures. These sympathizers, though their interest and support were welcome, often seemed to expect more from the Tobin tax than it could deliver.

As for economists, my friend John Williamson, himself a sceptic, remarked at the conference that only now was the idea emerging from the dismissive footnotes where it had long been consigned. I was naturally disappointed by the proposal's summary rejection. Usually, those of my professional colleagues who took any notice of it at all rejected it on the same general grounds that incline economists to dismiss out of hand any interferences with market competition, including, of course, tariffs and other barriers to international trade in goods and services. They seemed to presume that the same reasoning extends to trade in financial assets. Those who did make specific objections said the tax would damage the liquidity of currency markets. They said it would move the world's currency markets to tax-free jurisdictions, like Indonesia or the Cayman Islands. They said it wouldn't keep exchange rates from fluctuating; it wouldn't save overvalued currencies from speculative attacks and devaluations. And they said these things as if I had overlooked them.

Most disappointing and surprising, critics seemed to miss what I regarded as the essential property of the transactions tax—the beauty part—that this simple, one-parameter tax would automatically penalize short-horizon round trips, while negligibly affecting the incentives for commodity trade and long-term capital investments. A 0.2% tax on a round trip to another currency costs 48% a year if transacted every business day, 10% if every week, 2.4% if every month. But it is a trivial charge on commodity trade or long-term foreign investments. I am glad to see that this essential feature was emphasized by Eichengreen and Wyplosz, Frankel and other authors here.

An important general trend in the practical economics of regulation—in particular, the handling of environmental externalities and the safety of workers and products—has been the substitution of taxes and other quasi-price incentives and disincentives for arbitrary and absolute quantitative constraints, whether prohibitions or quotas. The transactions tax is proposed in this spirit. It handles, with built-in flexibility, problems that were formerly tackled by rigid quantitative exchange controls or financial regulations. On this score, it deserves the sympathy of modern economists.

Recognizing the problems of frictionless markets

The tax especially deserves their sympathy in the light of recent changes in the climate of opinion regarding the desirability of completely unfettered mobility of financial capital across currencies. Throughout the Bretton Woods era and for a decade afterwards, official restrictions were common, even among industrial countries with sophisticated domestic financial institutions and markets. In retrospect, those years look pretty good compared with the volatilities and crises of the past 10 years (see the papers in this volume by Eichengreen and Wyplosz, and by Felix and Sau). The "Bretton Woods Commission" chaired by Paul Volcker recently expressed anxiety about world monetary turmoil.

At the annual meetings of the American Economic Association in San Francisco in January 1996, worries about excessive volatility were the main concerns of participants in a session on exchange rates, and the Tobin tax was seen as a potentially useful measure if enforcement problems could be solved (IMF 1996). Stanley Fischer, First Deputy Managing Director of the IMF and thus the Fund's chief economist, agreed. He observed that exchange rate systems would still need to allow flexibility. I certainly agree with that. I have never believed that the transactions tax could make an adjustable peg system like Bretton Woods viable; the masses of private funds that can move across currencies overwhelm the funds available to central banks to defend parities.

Before 1995, the Managing Director of the IMF was promoting the idea of amending the Articles of Agreement to require complete convertibility of all members' currencies—not just of current account transactions but of all transactions, not just for foreigners but for residents too. The Mexican crisis may have convinced the IMF that there are times when some kind of sand in the wheels may be desirable. In my opinion, this, along with Fischer's willingness to consider a Tobin tax, is a fortunate change of heart. The IMF is in a good position to develop ways in which a transactions tax could work.

Objectives: Reducing short-term speculation and increasing national policy autonomy

My main objectives for the tax are two. The first is to make exchange rates reflect to a larger degree long-run fundamentals relative to short-range expectations and risks. While I always recognized that "fundamentalists" would be taxed too, I thought that they were likely to have longer horizons than "Keynes-beauty-contest" speculators and therefore would be less discouraged by the tax. Consequently, I thought the tax would strengthen the weight of regressive expectations relative to extrapolative expectations. Volatility—in particular detours from fundamentals (of which Eichengreen and Wyplosz provide several examples)—would be diminished. I am glad to see this common-sense conjecture confirmed by theoretical models (see Frankel) and empirical evidence.

Evidently, 80% of foreign exchange transactions involve round trips of seven days or less. Most occur within one day. An undergraduate student of mine, upon graduating, got a job in the Chicago mercantile exchange and became assistant and apprentice to an active trader who had been an economics professor. After a few weeks the young man made bold to ask his mentor about the long-run calculations that must—necessarily he thought—govern his trades. The reply was "Sonny, my long-run is the next ten minutes."

My second objective is to preserve and promote autonomy of national macroeconomic and monetary policies. I realize that here, as is often the case, I am opposed by a powerful tide. A widespread orthodoxy holds that financial markets know best, that the discipline they exert on central banks and governments is salubrious. Adverse capital movements should be taken as a correct judgment that internal fiscal and monetary policies are unsound and need to be changed. The example of Mexico, which is suffering cruel and painful punishments for crimes of fiscal and monetary policy it did not commit, should suffice to raise doubts about the "markets-always-know-best" proposition. The conference papers, that by Eichengreen and Wyplosz in particular, cite other cases.

Will the tax work in fixed- and floating-rate regimes?

My articles of the 1970s were written in the aftermath of the demise of Bretton Woods. By 1978, there was already considerable discontent with the floating-rate regime that had replaced Bretton Woods and considerable nostalgia for fixed rates. I thought that this debate was misplaced. For one thing, the Bretton Woods system could not be restored. In the circumstances, floating rates were an improvement, certainly among the G-3 currencies—the dollar, yen and deutsche mark. At the same time, floating rates were not going to restore domestic monetary and macroeconomic policy autonomy—contrary to the more enthusiastic claims of its proponents, notably Milton Friedman.

The reasons were the increasing international mobility of massive amounts of financial capital, abetted by deregulation and by revolutions in the technologies of communication and computation. I thought that international interest rate arbitrage among money markets would be increasingly efficient and increasingly beyond the capacities of national central banks and governments—individually and in concert—to control. Yet sometimes the exchange rates brought about by these financial movements, or the interest rates necessary to prevent them, would be damaging to the affected countries. An important contribution of the Eichengreen and Wyplosz paper, and the Felix and Sau paper is that they document the relationship of intercurrency interest rate differentials to various forms of sand in the wheels—exchange controls, transactions taxes and deposit requirements.

I still do not favour restoring Bretton Woods. Adjustable pegs are not feasible. When they have to be changed, one-way speculation against a misaligned currency is bound to prevail. Devaluation is inevitable, but the process is politically and economically traumatic. Floating rates among the deutsche mark, the yen and the dollar allow economies differing in cyclical phase and in appropriate macroeconomic policies to coexist much more painlessly than pegged rates could.

The transactions tax could be helpful in either regime—fixed or floating, or in hybrids like floating bands. The numerical tax costs cited above are margins by which money market interest rates in two currencies can differ without provoking movements of funds. They provide the two central banks with some freedom to manoeuvre. The tax would not be necessary or possible within a single-currency area, whether the European Union or the whole world.

Will financial activity migrate to the Cayman Islands?

There are two issues on which I have been quite uncertain and inconstant. One is the danger that the tax can be evaded by moving transactions to tax-free jurisdictions. The other is evasion by substituting untaxed transactions. On the whole, I found the papers reassuring. The studies in this volume are particularly informative on these points.

Regarding the shifting of transactions to tax-free jurisdictions, Kenen's devices seem to be feasible protections. One is to consider transfers of funds to or from such locations as taxable transactions—at penalty rates. The other is to tax at the site where the deal is made rather than at the site where the transaction occurs.

Anyway, I suspect that the danger of pushing transactions to the Cayman Islands is overblown. The already existing attractions of low-cost sites for financial dealings do not seem great enough to drive activity away from London, New York and Tokyo. I doubt that the transactions tax would move them, either. Perhaps agreement on the tax among the G-7 countries and a few other financial centres—the sites of big bank foreign exchange dealers—would suffice.

If not, the administration of a transactions tax could be assigned to the IMF, as I suggested in a recent paper. Each IMF member would be required, as a condition of membership and of borrowing privileges, to levy a tax in compliance with IMF specifications. The carrot would be that most members, all but the jurisdictions of the major financial centres, would keep for themselves the taxes they collected. Implementing this measure would require amending the Fund's Articles of Agreement. In any case, the IMF or the Bank for International Settlements (BIS), or the two together, would be the logical administrators of other details of the transactions tax: the rate of taxation, the definition of taxable transactions and the exemption of some currencies from the tax.

Must all derivatives and non-cash asset exchanges be taxed?

Defining those currency transactions that would be subject to a Tobin tax presents some difficulties. I first thought that the tax could be confined to spot transactions. I thought that derivatives need not be taxed, except at the time and to the extent that they are settled by spot transactions in currencies. The purpose of the levy, after all, is to tax transactions that affect the demand for and supply of currencies and thus the spot exchange rate. If you and I bet on the baseball World Series, the bet is a derivative of the game and does not affect the game's outcome. (When it did, as in the Black Sox scandal of 1919, there was hell to pay.) The analogy applies to future contracts and options, which are settled entirely by payments in the currency in which the value of the contract is expressed.

Thanks to Peter Kenen, I see that forwards and swaps are so much like spots that they also must be subject to the tax. For simplicity, the spot contents of such contracts could be taxed all at once.

Peter Garber points out that transactions could be settled in Treasury bills or in agreed mutual exchanges of other assets instead of in bank deposits. He warns that if the definition is broadened to extend the reach of the tax, this process could be never-ending. I am not as worried about this possibility as he is. Widening the range to cover the loophole of mutual deliveries of Treasury bills should not be too difficult. Beyond that, I am consoled by the likelihood that these exchanges can be transformed into exchanges of liquid means of payment only at costs that would probably be no less than the tax itself. If Professor Garber would like to trade his home in Providence for an Oxford don's abode for an academic year, I wouldn't cry over the loss of tax revenue that would have been collected, had the equivalent trade involved two opposite dollar-sterling conversions. I don't think such barters would become routine speculations or hedges. What is important is to tax transactions that make the exchange rates for trade in goods and services volatile and transactions that perfect the arbitrage between the interest rates relevant to monetary policies. The objective is not to maximize revenue.

Should we tax only customer-originated transactions?

Most currency transactions are made between banks and dealers. Three or four such transactions occur for every one transaction initiated by an outsider. Generally, banks and dealers are engaging in these secondary transactions in order to maintain balanced positions. If so, those transactions are not affecting exchange rates. The margins in such deals are very small, so that there is little room for a tax.

Retail transactions with customers, both non-financial individuals and businesses and other financial institutions, are a different matter. They move exchange rates, and the margins are much bigger. They could be taxed, while leaving the secondary transactions tax-free. Recognized bankers and dealers could instead be taxed on the changes in their daily net positions in currencies.

Revenues will be lower than expected

In Tobin (1978), I recognized that a universal transactions tax would raise substantial revenues, and I observed that it would be appropriate to devote the proceeds of an international tax to international purposes. My specific suggestion was to augment the resources of the World Bank, but it was only an example. Raising revenue has never been my main motivation.

In recent years, the burdens on the United Nations and other international organizations have multiplied, while fiscal and political circumstances have caused national governments to curtail their financial support. As a result, the Tobin tax has been seen as a possible source of funds for international purposes. For some advocates of the tax, this is the principal motivation.

The volume of foreign exchange transactions worldwide reached $1,300 billion a day in 1995—$312 trillion in a year of 240 business days.

With this volume, it seems at first that even a small tax would yield mammoth revenues, for example $312 billion a year from every 0.1% of tax. I have learned from the conference papers to expect much more modest yields, for several reasons.

First, the tax rate must be lower than I originally thought. It should not exceed 0.25% and perhaps should be as low as 0.1%. Otherwise, the tax would swamp the normal commission charged.

Second, allowance must be made a for tax-induced reduction in the volume of transactions. After all, the primary purposes of the tax, in my mind, depend on just such shrinkage. As Frankel and other authors suggest, the present bank-centred organization of the market, which entails three to eight interbank transactions for every customer-bank transaction, might give way to arrangements that entail fewer taxed transactions. A market organized like securities markets would enable non-bank transactors to make deals directly with each other.

Third, if my suggestion that banks and dealers be taxed only on changes in their end-of-day open positions were adopted, only 30% of the gross volume of transactions cited above would be taxable, plus the unknown volume of taxable open positions. This is roughly the same number as would be taxable if an organized market replaced the present institutional arrangements. The revenue yield would be $94 billion a year for a 0.1% one-way tax, and perhaps as little as half of that because of the tax-induced reduction of transactions volume.

Fourth, the actual collection of the tax could be the job of the tax authorities of member nations. In order to obtain their agreement and cooperation, it would be desirable to let the various jurisdictions retain shares of the collected revenues. For small countries, the shares could be 100%—the purpose of requiring them to levy the tax is not to gather revenue but to prevent them from setting up tax-free facilities, while undermining the tax base of the major market centres. These centres could be expected to dedicate larger shares to international purposes.

Clearly, there are difficult political problems in any international agreement under which sovereign nations levy a tax tailored to international specifications and turn over part or all of the revenues collected. It might sweeten the pill if each nation were allowed to retain at least 50% of the proceeds and to choose—among internationally agreed alternatives—where the tax revenues would go.

Several of the papers argue that the currency transactions tax is not the only possible source of revenue dedicated to international purposes, or necessarily the most appropriate source. I agree that a range of alternatives should be considered. A carbon tax, for example, makes a great deal of sense. I do believe that a well-functioning international monetary and payments system is a public good to which national members could legitimately be expected to contribute.

In summary, the authors of the papers differ in their verdicts on the Tobin tax; many of them are still uncertain. I am neither surprised nor dismayed. I am just pleased that the proposal is finally being seriously evaluated.

References

IMF (International Monetary Fund). 1996. "International Issues Prominent at AEA Meeting." *IMF Survey* (January 22, 1996):32.

Tobin, James. 1974. "The New Economics One Decade Older." The Eliot Janeway Lectures on Historical Economics in Honour of Joseph Schumpeter, 1972. Princeton: Princeton University Press.

———. 1978. "A Proposal for International Monetary Reform." *Eastern Economic Journal* 4(July-October):153–9.

Overview

Inge Kaul, Isabelle Grunberg and Mahbub ul Haq

M ost good ideas take years, sometimes centuries to be recognized.
The future of the Tobin tax may be larger than its modest
beginnings.

It was in 1972 in his Janeway Lectures at Princeton that James Tobin,
the 1981 Nobel prize winner for economics, submitted a proposal for
a levy on international currency transactions. His argument then:

> It is clearly desirable to preserve some possibilities of autonomy in
> national or continental monetary policies and to defend them
> against the growing internationalization of money markets. Our
> economies and governments are not sufficiently unified in other
> respects—goods, labour and capital markets, taxes and fiscal poli-
> cies—to live with a single area-wide monetary policy.
>
> How can some national monetary autonomy be preserved?
>
> Stronger measures are needed to drive a wedge between short-
> term interest rates in different national markets. One possible
> measure would be an internationally agreed uniform tax, say 1%,
> on all spot conversions of one currency into another. This would

The views expressed here are those of the authors and do not necessarily reflect
those of the organizations with which they are affiliated.

mean that a three-month Treasury bill in pounds sterling would have to bear an interest rate eight points higher than a dollar Treasury bill before it would be worthwhile for an American who wants dollars in three months to shift. (Tobin 1974, pp. 88–9)

As Tobin writes in his Prologue here, the idea was not received with much enthusiasm. Born in the 1970s, during a period of optimism and confidence in floating exchange rates, it was at odds with the spirit of its time. Yet since then, whenever currency crises erupted, the proposal for a levy on international currency transactions tended to resurface. And so it has recently: in response to Europe's exchange rate mechanism (ERM) crises in 1992 and 1993 and the Mexican peso crisis at the end of 1994.

In the 1990s, two additional facts have sharpened interest in the Tobin tax proposal. One is the growing volume of foreign exchange trading. While the global daily turnover in foreign exchange markets amounted to about $18 billion in the early 1970s—when the proposal was first submitted—its volume is now $1.3 trillion. The other is that interest is coming not only from policy-makers and experts concerned with the smooth functioning of financial markets. It is shared by those concerned with public financing of development—the fiscal crisis of the state as well as the growing need for international cooperation on problems such as the environment, poverty, peace and security. This coincidence of interests—the tax's incentive side and its revenue side— has brought Tobin's proposal back into the political debate.

While many commentators have hastily dismissed the idea, some have endorsed it, and others have adopted a wait-and-see attitude. Hence the need for a more systematic analysis. This is the central objective of this volume: it offers a critical and scholarly study of the proposal for a foreign exchange transactions levy. Its chapters examine the economic desirability of such a levy, its technical and political feasibility, its revenue potential, the possible uses of that revenue and related administrative and institutional aspects. This is the first occasion that a panel of outstanding scholars has applied analytical rigour to a systematic evaluation of the proposal.

This study reaches some reliable findings and conclusions. But all questions have not been answered definitely—yet. Much research still needs to be done, and many areas have been identified for further work.

The main conclusions and policy messages emerging from these studies can be summarized in the following five points.

Today's foreign exchange markets do not always function optimally. They are marked by excessive, destabilizing volatility.

Up fourteenfold since 1972, the \$1.3 trillion in daily foreign exchange trading registered in 1995 has grown by 50% since 1992, and by 30% if the dollar's depreciation is taken into account. Whatever the statistic chosen, foreign exchange trading is of tremendous proportion. By comparison, the annual global turnover in equity markets in 1995 was \$21 trillion—equivalent to just 17 days of trading on the foreign exchange market. The annual global trade in goods and services was a mere \$4.3 trillion—or 3.5 days of trading on the foreign exchange market (Gawith 1995).

Chief among the reasons for this stupendous growth was the breakup in the early 1970s of the Bretton Woods system of fixed parities among major currencies—and the move to floating exchange rates. This increased the variability of exchange rates. The result: opportunities to bet on the incessant movements of currencies. It also increased the demand of market participants for hedging operations. The result: derivatives. Foreign exchange futures were introduced in 1972. Foreign currency swaps appeared in 1981, and foreign currency options as well as futures options in 1982 (Kregel 1992, p. 39). Similar instruments now manage interest rate risk.

Moreover, greater emphasis on economic liberalization led to ever-freer movements of capital. Some industrial countries already had full capital account convertibility in the 1960s, and others followed in the 1970s and 1980s. Many developing countries lifted controls on capital movements in the 1990s. But even where these controls still exist, they are applied less strictly. Economic liberalization also diversified and broadened the community of institutional investors—private pension funds, insurance companies, mutual funds, hedge funds and corporate treasurers engaged in cross-border financial trading (IMF 1995b). Not surprisingly, the latest Federal Reserve survey (as reported in Frankel's chapter) shows that in the United States, trade with financial customers grew fastest between 1992 and 1995—by 100%. That with non-financial customers grew by 78%. And only one in every five transactions in London and New York markets is with non-financial customers—those actually engaged in international trade and capital investment.

These facts also explain the high proportion of short-term trading. Data from the Bank for International Settlements (BIS) indicate that about 80% of all transactions involve round trips of seven days or less—

and more than 40% of two days or less (see the Statistical Appendix to this volume, table A.5).

Much of this increased volume, as well as the increased volatility, may have little to do with fundamentals, and can even lead to misleading price signals—a reason that the efficiency of foreign exchange markets has been put in doubt.

Moreover, the sheer volume of this market increasingly dwarfs the stabilizing capacities of central banks. Central banks' reserves now barely amount to one day of foreign exchange trading—hence a reduced ability to intervene in markets in times of crises or misalignments.[1]

More than short-term volatility, it is the instability and unpredictability of foreign exchange rates that make it harder and harder to manage national economies. Yet the leverage that financial markets have over governments can have beneficial effects. As Eichengreen and Wyplosz argue, it was probably beneficial for the UK economy to have been moved off an unsustainable peg in 1992. The pressure of foreign exchange markets incites governments to stay on a financially sustainable course. Sometimes, however, "getting the fundamentals right" is no guarantee that a country will avoid currency crises. Take the run on the French franc in 1993. And while the Mexican peso crisis in 1994 was in part due to policy failures, herd behaviour made it worse—by spurring a crisis out of proportion with the scale of the initial mistakes.

Today's foreign exchange markets are thus beset with speculation and volatility, inflicting unnecessary costs—policy disruptions, resource loss, credit curtailments, production declines and unemployment. The Bretton Woods Commission Report convened by former US Federal Reserve Board Chairman Paul Volcker, for example, stated that: "Since the early 1970s long-term growth in the major industrial countries has been cut in half, from about 5 percent a year to about 2.5 percent a year. Although many factors contributed to this decline in different countries at different times, low growth has been an international problem, and the loss of exchange rate discipline has played a part." (Bretton Woods Commission 1994, p. 4.)

The studies here once again show the existence of the "Impossible Triad". As Frankel notes, a country can have any two of financial openness, currency stability and monetary independence—but it cannot have all three. Countries that aim at stabilizing their exchange rates will thus have to sacrifice a lot of policy independence.

The question is whether this must be so—or whether, by slowing down the international mobility of capital, the Tobin tax can restore some compatibility between the three objectives.

4

The Tobin tax has an efficiency rationale—on second-best grounds. It would reduce short-term trading and strengthen the defensibility of the exchange rate regime. But only modestly, if at all, would it widen the scope of national policy autonomy.

Interfering in markets always leads to a loss of efficiency. Yet there is one important proviso—this is true only if these markets are proven to be efficient to start with. Where markets do not function the way they should, we have no proof that intervention leads to a loss of efficiency—indeed, intervention may enhance efficiency. Hence the conventional warning about a possible loss of welfare brought about by taxation (raised at times in Dooley's study) may not be applicable to the foreign exchange market as it operates in the real world.

The objective of the Tobin tax is to improve the efficiency of financial markets in allocating resources by discouraging short-term capital flows (or providing an incentive for longer-term capital flows), by reducing exchange rate volatility and by restoring some of the monetary and fiscal autonomy policy-makers have lost in the process of economic and financial liberalization. Can the tax deliver on all these?

Several of the articles here try to answer this question—notably those by Eichengreen and Wyplosz, Dooley, Felix and Sau and Frankel, as well as the synthesis paper on lessons learned by Eichengreen. The authors agree that the tax would certainly deter traders with a short-term horizon because it would make the movement of large sums of money quickly in and out of a country more costly. An example: the yearly cost of a 0.2% round trip tax would amount to 48% of the value of the traded amount if the round trip were daily, 10% if weekly and 2.4% if monthly.

Frankel uses modeling and empirical evidence to argue that such discouragement of short-term trading would bring more stability to foreign exchange markets. He warns, however, that the foreign exchange market could become a centralized, transparent market, with drastically fewer operators, and that there is no proof that such a market is economically more efficient than the current decentralized, dealer-driven type. Others hold the view that reducing the volume of short-term trading would reduce liquidity and possibly increase volatility. In balance, however, the empirical evidence does not seem to support a correlation between more trading and more stable markets. Just the opposite. Over the past two decades there has been a parallel

5

increase in both the size and the instability of the foreign exchange market.

Would less short-term trading and greater stability really enhance, as Tobin assumed, the autonomy of governments in conducting macro-economic policies? Most authors seem to suggest that the tax's effect in enhancing autonomy, if any, would be modest. Consider the tax rate: most authors stress (for reasons discussed under the next point) that the tax rate should not exceed 0.25% and should preferably be 0.1% or lower. And at a level of 0.1%, the Tobin tax would likely offer policy-makers only minuscule additional space for manoeuvre.

Here's why. The margins by which money market interest rates in two countries could differ without provoking movements of funds would be equal to the tax costs. As Frankel, and Eichengreen and Wyplosz point out, the dealers who sold pounds, lira and francs en masse, pushing against the limits of the ERM in September 1992 and August 1993, were seeking returns greater than the 48% annual cost of a 0.1% Tobin tax. And as Eichengreen notes, investors speculating about a 15% devaluation of the peso within weeks of a new govern-ment's installation would hardly have been discouraged by a Tobin tax, even one of 0.25%. Eichengreen and Wyplosz nevertheless stress that in a crisis, the tax could slow down the depletion of foreign exchange reserves and thus give the authorities more breathing space to nego-tiate orderly realignments.

The Tobin tax thus seems likely to produce some of the desired effects. But are there alternatives, and what are their costs and bene-fits? Eichengreen and Wyplosz examine the evidence from both indus-trial and developing countries. Agosin and Ffrench-Davis add to this Chile's experience with capital controls, and Park to the Republic of Korea's. They agree that capital controls helped by giving governments some scope for autonomous policy-making. But Eichengreen and Wyplosz suggest that compulsory deposit requirements could be more doable than the Tobin tax, because they require the decision of one country, not all. Yet because deposit requirements also have the con-siderable drawback of applying to all flows, short and long, it might be desirable to consider the Griffith-Jones proposal—to aim at a combi-nation of a Tobin tax with, if the need arises, temporary individual country measures (such as those described by Agosin and Ffrench-Davis, and Park).

Since the Tobin tax could have desirable effects, it is worth examin-ing its feasibility.

The feasibility issues raised by the Tobin tax are more political than technical.

All taxes—income, value-added, property and inheritance—suffer some evasion, but this has never been a reason not to have them. For the Tobin tax too, the right question is not whether there will be evasion (with the implication that the proposal should be abandoned if it proves to exist). It is what scope of evasion to expect and what kind: through trade in non-participating jurisdictions or through trade in substitute assets. Garber and Kenen address these issues, and Eichengreen and Griffith-Jones provide additional points.

To minimize the migration of foreign exchange trade to non-participating jurisdictions, it would, as Kenen suggests, be important to collect the tax on a market basis and at the dealing site. Ideally, the geographical coverage of the tax should be universal, achievable through an international agreement in which all countries would commit themselves to levying the tax. Failing that, one could avoid the emergence of "Tobin tax havens" by levying a penalty on transactions with tax havens of, say, twice the normal tax rate. Then it would suffice to secure the collaboration of the major eight or nine foreign exchange markets. No mean feat, as Eichengreen points out, considering that these markets are as diverse as Hong Kong (soon China), Singapore, the United Kingdom and the United States.

Kenen and Garber argue that to reduce the problem of asset substitution, the tax should apply to forwards, futures, swaps and possibly other contracts. Eichengreen and Wyplosz hold the view that a tax restricted to spot transactions could capture enough of the underlying transactions to be effective economically. Griffith-Jones describes how, in the case of the stamp duty, British authorities were able to respond effectively to observed leakages into other markets as and when they occurred. Frankel adds that computer trading makes the tax technically more feasible.

In addition, some authors argue that the cost of the tax to market operators—if 0.1% or lower—would be too low for evasion to be profitable, either through migration (because of the costs of relocating trading rooms) or through asset substitution (because few other instruments are perfectly substitutable for foreign currency deposits). For this reason, Kenen suggests a tax rate of 0.05%. Higher levels, such as the 0.25% suggested by Felix and Sau, would enhance the economic effects of the tax, especially of policy autonomy. But they could also, as Frankel points out, change the market structure—from decentralized to more centralized. So, the tax rate will have to be established carefully—balancing economic considerations, feasibility aspects and revenue concerns.

If the feasibility of the tax depends primarily on whether countries participate in its implementation, the key issue becomes political will: why would governments support a Tobin tax? Governments might feel that financial markets have come to constrain their freedom to manoeuvre—a belief voiced in various recent debates on this issue (*The Economist* 1995; *The International Economy* 1995). Or, governments might be attracted by its revenue potential, which could be quite substantial, as the discussion in the next point will show. This revenue could be important for them because financial markets place high demands on governments for meeting "credibility" criteria, including those for low public expenditures, low national tax rates and balanced budgets. As Kaul and Langmore underline, governments might, under these conditions, welcome additional resources from a Tobin tax.

It appears more and more likely that the national sovereignty individual countries have lost as a result of the internationalization of markets can be recaptured only through more policy coordination among states. What holds true for more efficient management of the global environment also holds for more efficient management of the financial markets. For example, it makes little sense for only two or three countries to put a carbon tax in place if other countries try to get a "free ride". Similarly, no country alone can limit "noise" trading in foreign exchange without putting in place heavy-handed controls and thus losing the benefits of financial openness. All countries would thus be better off if they were to cooperate to put into place a price-based mechanism (an ad valorem tax like the Tobin tax) with a view to enhancing the manageability of national economies.

Taxes are not popular, however. In some countries, efforts are under way to cut back tax revenues. In others, if not most, there is recognition that market-led development requires a competent state—whether the objective is economic growth alone or economic growth for sustainable human development.

Yet, as Kaul and Langmore show, in some countries the additional revenues could make it possible to cut taxes that are unpopular or economically less efficient. The Tobin tax proposal has already attracted considerable political attention. Heads of state and governments have called for its study both at the World Summit for Social Development in Copenhagen, Denmark in 1994 and in connection with the Fiftieth Anniversary celebrations of the United Nations in 1995. The issue was also considered during the preparatory process for that year's G-7 Summit in

Halifax, Canada. With many uncertainties surrounding the proposal, references to it have been understandably cautious. But there seems to be interest, which will become amplified once more reliable information on the desirability and feasibility of the tax becomes available.

The Tobin tax would not create a supranational taxation power. Instead, governments would levy it nationally.

Some express concern that the Tobin tax would entail the creation of a supranational tax authority.[2] From what is described here, this would not be the case. Kenen proposes collection of the tax on a market basis and at the dealing site. This can only be done by national authorities. Since all authors see the implementation of the tax as resulting from an international agreement, participating can be a decision of only sovereign governments. The formula for splitting revenue between national and international purposes would be subject to intergovernmental negotiation and agreement. Similarly, governments would decide on the use of the international portion of the revenue. Kaul and Langmore suggest that existing forums (such as the United Nations and/or the World Bank) could be used for this purpose or that a new mechanism could be established, such as an international cooperation fund. The advantage would be that such a fund could better harmonize agreed-on policy objectives with global expenditure priorities (a task for which the international community is hardly equipped at present).

Tobin has proposed that if there was political will to introduce the tax, we could consider amending the IMF's Articles of Agreement to stipulate that implementation of the tax is a condition for Fund membership and borrowing privileges. He and Griffith-Jones have furthermore proposed that the IMF and/or the Bank for International Settlements play a role in harmonizing tax implementation—for example, setting the rate of taxation, defining taxable transactions, determining exemptions from the tax and undertaking monitoring and auditing tasks.

The Tobin tax's considerable revenue potential adds to its overall desirability.

So far, analyses of the economic desirability of the Tobin tax have usually centred on its effects on foreign exchange markets. Only passing attention, if any, has been devoted to revenue. This is changing for two main reasons. First, as discussed by Kaul and Langmore (and alluded to above), nation-states are having to adjust to the fact that the internationalization of production and wealth is eroding their taxation power, creating revenue shortfalls. And it is changing the game: without coordination, the factors most mobile internationally are more able to circumvent taxes, while those least mobile are asked to make up for the shortfall. Governments are recognizing that international coordination will be needed to resist shedding the fiscal burden onto income earners. The Tobin tax would thus not necessarily increase the national tax burden—it would enable more equitable sharing of this burden among all segments of society.

Second, more problems are becoming global—the environment, poverty, security. Yet the international community has few resources for addressing them. Countries recycle on average 30% of their income through the government budget, but international public spending amounts to a mere 0.3% of the budgets of a small number of donor countries. As Kaul and Langmore suggest, it might be necessary and desirable to tap international economic activities to generate funds for international cooperation, especially cooperation in support of global public goods.

Despite all the rhetoric on the breakdown of international cooperation, governments are resorting more to joint action—from the Montreal Protocol banning chlorofluorocarbons, to the Uruguay Round of multilateral trade negotiations that created the World Trade Organization. The Tobin tax would fit well as another part of this emerging framework of cooperation—as a global incentive policy and as a funding source for global initiatives.

On splitting the revenue from the Tobin tax, Griffith-Jones and Kaul and Langmore suggest that most of the revenue be retained nationally—for example, some 80%, with up to 100% for low-income countries. Based on a 0.1% tax rate and a revenue yield of $148 billion, this breakdown would raise about $27 billion a year for international purposes. Since the tax would be collected by governments, the formula for sharing (or not sharing) the proceeds between the national and the international levels would also be a decision of governments. Similarly, governments would be involved in negotiating the international uses of the revenue, just as they are involved today in negotiating and coordinating the uses of aid.

Could governments take a stand that all of the revenue be retained nationally? Kaul and Langmore believe this would be untenable. The

Tobin tax can be implemented effectively only as a collective effort of the international community. If no revenue went to multilateral initiatives of common interest, countries that expected very little revenue from participating, or no revenue at all, would surely defect.

Frankel and Felix and Sau attempt to project the amount of revenue the Tobin tax could generate, making different estimates for pre-tax transaction costs and the price elasticity of demand for foreign exchange. Frankel predicts that a 0.1% tax would raise some $166 billion, and Felix and Sau arrive at a comparable figure of about $148 billion. Felix has also calculated the revenue from taxes of 0.25% and 0.05%. The findings are $290 billion and $90 billion, respectively.

But raising revenue should not be the primary concern. Nor should it outweigh other aspects of the tax, such as its likely market impact. But it is important and should thus be part of any evaluation of the costs and benefits of the measure.

In conclusion, the Tobin tax is an idea that deserves careful analysis. It cannot be dismissed as "too idealistic" or "too impractical", since continuing and excessive instability in foreign exchange markets will call for many policy responses, both at the national and international level. Unless some reasonable proposals are identified, we are all taking the risk of unreasonable and unpredictable policy responses. At the same time, one cannot yet pretend that the Tobin proposal has been thrashed out so fully that it is both technically fool-proof and politically attractive enough. Much spade work must be done before the international community develops such confidence. By publishing the first set of scholarly papers on the topic, we hope to contribute to a more rational, enlightened dialogue and to more efficient and effective policy-making.

Notes

1.   See Statistical Appendix table A.2. Daily turnover, however, may not matter as much as the willingness of operators to change their foreign exchange positions at the day's closure. Central Banks' reduced capacities to deal with foreign exchange crises are documented in the chapter by Eichengreen and Wyplosz.

2.   The term "global" may have led to the misunderstanding by some commentators that a supranational taxation authority would levy the Tobin tax.

References

Bretton Woods Commission. 1994. Bretton Woods: Looking to the Future, Commission Report, Staff Review, Background Papers. Washington: The Bretton Woods Commission.

The Economist. 1995. "Who's in the Driving Seat? A Survey of the World Economy." October 7.

Gawith, Philip. 1995. "Forex Surge Masks Maturing Market." *Financial Times,* October 25, 1995.

The International Economy. 1995. "Have Global Markets Become Too Powerful? A Symposium of Views." July-August, pp.32–7.

IMF (International Monetary Fund). 1995a. "Capital Account Convertibility; Review of Experience and Implications for IMF Policies." Occasional Paper 131 by staff team headed by Peter J. Quirk and Aven Evans. Washington, D.C.

———. 1995b. *International Capital Markets: Developments, Prospects and Policy Issues.* Washington, D.C.

Kregel, Jan A. 1992. "Globalisation of Financial Markets, Capital Flows and Economic Policy." Paper prepared for the United Nations Committee for Development Planning, Working Group on World Economic Outlook, September 29–October 2. New York.

Tobin, James. 1974. "The New Economics One Decade Older." The Eliot Janeway Lectures on Historical Economics in Honour of Joseph Schumpeter, 1972. Princeton: Princeton University Press.

The Tobin Tax as an Instrument of Global Monetary Policy

1

Taxing International Financial Transactions to Enhance the Operation of the International Monetary System

Barry Eichengreen and Charles Wyplosz

M̲ost economists are instinctively sceptical about taxing international financial transactions as a way to enhance the operation of the international monetary system. Holders of the union card are taught to prize the efficiency of the market and to regard intervention through taxation and controls as welfare reducing. They are trained to anticipate the incentive of market participants to evade taxes and circumvent administrative restrictions. These instincts are evident in the debate over the Tobin tax (see, respectively, Obstfeld 1995 and Garber and Taylor 1995).

Yet, when the question is posed differently—as, what policies towards capital imports should developing economies pursue?—the professional consensus is different. Early confidence in the optimality of immediate and complete capital account liberalization has given way to a more nuanced view that international capital markets should be freed only gradually.[1] In the wake of the 1994–95 Mexican crisis, even the International Monetary Fund (IMF), traditionally a proponent of immediate and full liberalization, has cautiously endorsed limited reliance on taxes and restrictions on selected international financial transactions.[2]

The authors thank Chang-Tai Hsieh for research assistance and Andrew Rose for permission to draw on joint work.

The goal of this article is to confront this professional schizophrenia. We suggest that many widely accepted arguments for restricting capital imports to developing countries carry over to taxes or restrictions on international financial transactions in industrial economies. We show that the successful application of restrictions on capital imports is inconsistent with more extreme arguments about the potential ineffectiveness of such measures. And, finally, we argue that taxes on international financial transactions could enhance the operation of the international monetary system.

Along with weighing the case for and against these measures, it is useful to consider the merits of alternative approaches to implementation. Thus, even though we prepared this article for a conference on the Tobin tax, we consider other ways of stabilizing foreign exchange markets. These include dual exchange rates, administrative prohibitions and compulsory deposit requirements on bank lending and borrowing from non-residents.

The limits of alternative exchange rate regimes

The basic choice confronting a country's international economic policy-makers is whether to peg or float the currency. Intermediate arrangements, such as crawling pegs and target zones, can, for our purposes, be considered hybrids of these extremes. The case for taxing international financial transactions must rest, therefore, on theory and evidence that neither pegging nor floating in the absence of taxes and controls perform better than restrictions on international capital flows.

The limits of pegged exchange rates

There is obvious appeal to simply pegging the exchange rate and leaving international capital transactions unregulated. This, of course, has long been the view of advocates of the gold standard. A credible peg would eliminate the uncertainties and costs associated with floating exchange rates. It would provide a nominal anchor for domestic policy. But in practice, exchange rate pegs in the presence of high capital mobility are exceedingly fragile. They leave countries vulnerable to foreign disturbances. Except for limited periods, pegging the exchange rate in the presence of open capital markets is not a viable option.

Typically, exchange rates are pegged by governments seeking to lock in programmes of economic liberalization and stabilization.[3] Economic reform, macroeconomic retrenchment and exchange rate stabilization initiate a surge of capital inflows as investors seek to exploit newly attractive production and investment opportunities. Banks borrow abroad in order to lend domestically to customers who are attracted by new investment projects. But because the exchange rate is pegged, the government and the central bank are unable to control the money supply, and inflation and real overvaluation result. This problem, in turn, leads to poor international competitiveness, deteriorating trade performance, and a profit squeeze on sectors producing tradable goods.

At some point, the capital flow reverses direction. To defend the exchange rate, the central bank is forced to raise interest rates. But higher interest rates aggravate the squeeze on the tradables sector. They give rise to loan defaults, which threaten the stability of the banking sector. They increase the cost of servicing the public debt. They impose hardship on homeowners with indexed mortgages and others with interest rate–sensitive liabilities. Currency traders force the issue, anticipating that the government has an incentive to cut interest rates and relax credit conditions to avoid destabilizing the domestic economy and antagonizing its constituency. The surge of capital inflows gives way to a surge of outflows, bringing down the currency peg.

These dynamics are evident in a wide variety of historical cases, including Germany in the second half of the 1920s, the Republic of Korea in the 1960s, Chile in the 1970s, Italy in the 1980s and Mexico in the 1990s, to name a handful of prominent examples. In each case, domestic financial markets were opened to capital inflows from abroad. In each case, it proved impossible to defend the currency peg when flows turned around. And in each case, the interlude of prosperity was succeeded by a costly and extended "morning after" of depression.

The limits of floating exchange rates

Since the breakdown of the Bretton Woods system of pegged but adjustable exchange rates, an increasing number of countries have floated their currencies. For countries like the United States and Japan, which are relatively closed to international trade and large relative to international capital markets, this condition is bearable. Surges of foreign investment are not large enough to swamp domestic financial markets. Domestic and foreign disturbances still lead to marked exchange rate swings, but the costs are tolerable for economies less dependent on international transactions.

The situation is different in smaller, developing countries with thinner financial markets. Admittedly, increasing numbers of small, open countries have gravitated towards greater exchange rate flexibility as they relaxed restrictions on international capital transactions, for want of an alternative. But the vast majority believe that this regime is unsatisfactory. The increase in nominal exchange rate variability translates into an almost proportionate increase in real exchange rate variability, even after controlling for other determinants of the real exchange rate. Surges of capital inflows, by pushing up the nominal exchange rate, lead to dramatic real appreciation. The swing in relative prices can be highly disruptive to production and investment in an economy open to international commodity transactions.

The limits of intermediate arrangements

If neither pegged nor floating exchange rates are desirable and feasible for most countries, what about intermediate arrangements like crawling pegs and target zones? If these arrangements involve an explicit limit on the value of the exchange rate that the authorities seek to defend, they are subject to the same objections as pegged rates. Once the currency has crawled to the edge of its band or moved to the limit of its zone, it must be defended and is subject to the same pressures as a pegged rate. Adjusting the central parity each period by adopting a crawling peg does not ease this problem. Mexico, after all, operated a crawling peg prior to the end of 1994. What could better illustrate the fact that such arrangements are susceptible to the same instabilities as a simple peg?

If, however, the authorities are not prepared to defend their crawling peg or are prepared to shift the target zone before its limit is reached, then the performance characteristics of these regimes will not differ significantly from those of a floating system. A credible target zone will reduce the variability of the exchange rate for a given variability of fundamentals only as long as the markets believe that the authorities are credibly committed to whatever measures are required to keep the currency within the band.[4] But if market participants anticipate that the authorities will shift the band when the limits are approached, the variability of the exchange rate may be exacerbated relative to the variability of fundamentals (see Bertola and Caballero 1990).

Reasons for restricting capital flows

That the performance of exchange rate regimes has been less than ideal is not necessarily an argument for sand in the wheels of international finance. Friedman (1953) argues that problems in foreign exchange markets are properly attributable to inconsistent domestic policies. In this view, floating rates are unstable because underlying monetary and fiscal policies are unstable. Pegged rates are fragile because domestic policy-makers do not show the discipline required for their maintenance. The implication is that the performance of the exchange rate system can be enhanced not by tinkering with its institutional characteristics—throwing sand in its gears or otherwise—but by improving the formulation of domestic policy.

The implications of domestic distortions

Without question, erratic policy is sometimes responsible for episodes of exchange rate instability. But examining a random sample of such episodes, rather than picking them selectively, reveals that the association between exchange rate crises and policy imbalances is far from universal. Whether one considers the European Monetary System (EMS)—the one part of the industrialized world that has made a persistent effort to peg exchange rates—or a broader range of industrial and developing countries, there is only weak evidence of more expansionary monetary and fiscal policies in the periods leading up to currency crises.[5]

If not ill-advised policies, what are the distortions that give rise to instability in the foreign exchange market? One is asymmetric information and herd behaviour on the part of investors. This is, of course, the basis for the Keynes (1936)-Tobin (1978) case for sand in the wheels of international finance. It derives from the assumption that incompletely informed investors display, successively, excessive optimism and excessive pessimism. Investors follow the lead of other investors, committing funds to fashionable emerging markets. Eventually, bad news or simply a change of sentiment provokes a reaction. Everything that was gold turns to dross overnight. Under fixed rates, the sudden shift puts excruciating pressure on the monetary authorities. Under floating rates, surges of capital inflows amplify the appreciation and depreciation of both the nominal and real exchange rates.

The literature on the efficiency of markets is too extensive to be usefully surveyed here.[6] Suffice it to say that there is an accumulation of historical and episodic evidence consistent with the notion that distortions of this sort characterize international financial markets.[7] Swings in sentiment not obviously associated with the arrival of economic or political news occur often in capital markets. There is reason to think that problems of incomplete information conducive to herd behaviour are particularly prevalent in international markets, which require the transfer of capital and transmission of information over long distances. The fact that the mode of intermediation has changed repeatedly—from bond finance to bank finance to equity finance—means that the agents at the centre of the process have little institutional memory.

A second distortion that gives rise to excess capital flows, emphasized by McKinnon and Pill (1995) and Felix and Sau (1996), is moral hazard in the banking system. Assume that regulators are unwilling or unable (for political reasons, perhaps) to allow domestic banks to fail—those banks will be bailed out in the event of a bad realization of the stochastic process governing the returns on bank lending. In this case, the distribution of returns will be truncated downwards, reinforcing the incentive for banks to borrow abroad in order to lend domestically. The standing bailout offer acts as a distortion leading to excessive capital inflows. Under flexible rates, the injection of domestic credit will exacerbate exchange rate swings over the cycle. Under pegged rates, the government will eventually be forced to abandon its currency peg in order to provide the liquidity required to stabilize the banking system.[8]

A third distortion includes anything that gives rise to multiple equilibria in foreign exchange markets. Most economists take for granted the assumptions of the Arrow-Debreu model, which guarantee the existence of a unique equilibrium. But other, equally plausible assumptions can support the existence of multiple equilibria. If the assumptions of the Arrow-Debreu model fail, then speculative attacks may succeed in the absence of underlying macroeconomic imbalances.[9]

For illustrative purposes, imagine a government that values output and price stability now and in the future. It is prepared to defend a fixed exchange rate and to endure the costs of austerity now in return for acquiring a reputation for valuing exchange rate and price stability in the future. If it has a sufficiently low discount rate, it may be prepared to raise interest rates to defend its currency peg in response to speculative pressures. But in the presence of political distortions that cause the government's discount rate to exceed the social discount rate (because, for example, the government attaches no value to future reputational benefits, given that it may be voted out of office), the government may no longer be prepared to bear that cost. Authorities may be willing and

able to maintain the prevailing currency peg in the absence of a speculative attack. However, if such an attack occurs, they will be forced to
raise interest rates, increasing the costs of austerity now relative to the
benefits of an enhanced reputation in the future. As a result, they may
be induced to shift to a more accommodating policy. Aware of this possibility, currency traders have an incentive to attack. Thus political distortions can give rise to multiple equilibria and self-fulfilling attacks.[10]

These distortions are particular problems for countries undergoing
liberalization, stabilization and reform. Government stability is especially precarious in such countries, raising discount rates. Banking systems are fragile, and there are few counterweights to financial interests
lobbying for bailouts. Information relevant for assessing investment
opportunities is particularly scarce.

But it is important to emphasize that such distortions also afflict
industrial economies. They too can be on the receiving end of foreign
capital surges. They too find it difficult to resist the pressure to bail out
the banking system. Their governments also face intertemporal trade-
offs that can give rise to self-fulfilling attacks.[11] Recent experience and
analysis have amply documented the infeasibility of pegged exchange
rates in an environment characterized by such distortions.

The rationale for restraints

These market imperfections provide an efficiency rationale, on second-
best grounds, for foreign exchange market intervention. This rationale
should be applied with caution, however. Restrictions on capital mobility are denigrated by mainstream economists (who instinctively assume
the absence of other distortions) not only because they seem to con-
tradict the principles of good economics, but also because they have
been used to prevent good economics from functioning. They have
been associated with distortionary policies designed to divert domestic
savings towards domestic investment, irrespective of market rates of
return on domestic and foreign projects. They have been put in place
by governments eager to blame markets for the consequences of their
own ineptitude. Like all good measures, restrictions on capital
movements can be misapplied.

But they can also be used to achieve respectable ends. With floating
rates, restrictions work by limiting the tendency for markets to push
exchange rates away from the underlying equilibrium. For example, currency traders betting on a rational bubble must be able to liquidate their
positions quickly when the bubble bursts.[12] With restrictions on foreign

exchange transactions in place, such quick reactions will be difficult or costly, discouraging them from placing such bets in the first place.

In the case of fixed exchange rates, restrictions on capital movements operate in two ways. By limiting the flow of speculative capital, they leave the authorities the breathing space needed to prepare orderly realignments. An orderly realignment entails more than setting the new parity; it requires the adoption of supporting macroeconomic policies, which in turn requires consultations with opposition parties and social partners. A second function of taxes and administrative restrictions is to reduce the cost of defending the peg. Because they increase the cost to market participants of shifting funds between currencies, they limit the resources the authorities must commit to the exchange rate's defence. An extended defence gives observers time to distinguish fundamental-based crises from self-fulfilling attacks.

Principles of effective restrictions

Whether the problem is capital inflows or outflows, the room that officials have for manoeuvre is limited by the small size of their balance sheets relative to the size of the market. One way of gauging "smallness" is to compare reserves and Treasury bill holdings with foreign exchange market turnover. In the United States, the sum of the Federal Reserve's domestic and foreign assets is about $400 billion. In Japan, the value of domestic and foreign assets is also about $400 billion. In Germany, it is about $150 billion. These amounts are dwarfed by annual daily turnover on foreign exchange markets, which exceeds $1 trillion.[13]

Another way of gauging the intervention required to counter speculative pressure is to recall that when a currency is declared convertible, the central bank pledges to buy or sell it in unlimited amounts. When the exchange rate is pegged, this commitment is extended to guaranteeing the price. If sellers suddenly insist on being paid in foreign currency, that commitment will necessarily be abrogated, because foreign exchange reserves are always smaller than the monetary base.[14] An all-out attack can be repelled only if the central bank is prepared to reset the exchange rate to a level at which the domestic currency value of foreign exchange reserves is at least as large as the base. Examining the ratio of foreign exchange reserves to the monetary base for several countries, we see that, apart from the special case of Switzerland, the required depreciation would be between 75% and 1,000% (table 1.1).[15]

Even if reserves are not exhausted, the economic and political costs of defending the currency may still be prohibitive, as argued in the

Table 1.1 Foreign exchange reserves as a percentage of the monetary base, May–June 1994

Country	Percent
Switzerland	90.5
Mexico	76.3
United Kingdom	57.2
Germany	39.7
Argentina	30.4
Japan	9.8

Source: IMF, *International Financial Statistics* (various years).

previous subsection. If one assumes that the interest semi-elasticity of money demand is 0.1, then purchasing 50% of the monetary base would result in a 500 percentage point rise in the domestic interest rate—a rate that most governments could not sustain for any length of time. Even before the stock of international reserves is exhausted, the authorities would be forced to abandon the currency peg.

The implication is that restrictions on international capital mobility should not be seen as protecting the stock of foreign exchange reserves in the face of capital outflows, as commonly assumed, but simply as slowing down its rate of depletion.[16] Speculative attacks are generally preceded by an extended period of moderate sales of domestic currency and by the gradual depletion of foreign reserves, which only picks up speed as the final denouement approaches.

Restrictions on international capital flows cannot prevent this attack. Their contribution is simply to slow the rate at which reserves are depleted, giving the authorities time to implement the requisite monetary and fiscal adjustments and to alter the exchange rate peg if necessary. A few hours may make the difference between the collapse of a pegged rate arrangement and an orderly realignment.[17] Moreover, controls do not have to be watertight to be effective. Although monetary authorities can do little to prevent the conversion of foreign holdings of the domestic currency (in cash or in offshore bank deposits), for example, controls are still useful.[18] Excess reserves can be used to mop up offshore sales of domestic currency, at which point the latter no longer constitute a threat.

Types of restrictions

We can distinguish two basic categories of restrictions on capital mobility. The first uses administrative measures to prohibit transactions. The second uses taxes or tax-like measures to regulate the volume of international capital flows.

We can make another distinction between restrictions targeting inflows and those targeting outflows. Capital outflows threaten to depreciate the exchange rate and, by exhausting reserves, force the authorities to abandon their currency peg. Inflows are problematic if they jeopardize competitiveness and monetary control. To limit the appreciation of the exchange rate, the authorities must purchase foreign exchange with fresh supplies of domestic currency. To avoid increasing the money supply, they must then sterilize their intervention by buying back the newly issued money for other domestic assets, chiefly Treasury bills. The risk is that the stock of Treasury bills in the central bank's portfolio will be exhausted, leaving the central bank no means of sterilizing its intervention.

There is thus a need for other measures to buttress the defensibility of the exchange rate commitment. We consider a range of alternatives in ascending order of practicality.

Administrative controls

Administrative controls, although widely used in the past, are not very practical or attractive in today's world of sophisticated trading technologies and liberalized domestic financial markets.[19] They require an extensive bureaucracy to track, register, evaluate and authorize capital transfers. Such an apparatus cannot be put in place promptly or dismantled easily. In addition, prohibitions create especially severe distortions and provide particularly strong incentives for evasion. And new methods of evasion, in turn, encourage the authorities to widen the coverage of administrative controls, compounding the initial distortions. For example, when controls are initially implemented, they typically regulate capital movements but exempt trade credits. Yet, a standard technique of evasion is to use leads and lags in commercial transactions. Eventually, therefore, administrative restrictions on capital flows interfere with international trade.

Dual exchange rates

Several countries have used dual exchange rates—Belgium until 1989 and South Africa until 1995, for example. This system separates the commercial exchange market for current account transactions from the financial market for capital account transactions. A pegged exchange rate is typically adopted to protect trade from disruptions arising from exchange rate variability. But fixing the exchange rate may be impossible given unlimited international capital flows. By fixing the commercial rate and allowing the financial rate to vary, the central bank attempts to obtain the best of both worlds.

The Achilles heel of this approach is leakages between the two markets. The incentive to disguise capital account transactions and funnel them through the commercial market grows with the gap between the commercial and financial rates. Experience suggests that dual exchange rates work well only when the gap between the commercial and financial rates is small—meaning that they work least well during crises.

Other forms of sand in the wheels

Alternatives to administrative controls are taxes and tax-like instruments that increase the cost of international financial transactions but leave them otherwise unrestricted. The simplest variant of this approach is the Tobin tax. A modest ad valorem tax on all spot transactions falls most heavily on short round trips. In contrast, the impact of the tax on long-term investments should be minimal because it can be amortized over many years. The tax is unlikely to hamper international trade, since the impact of a modest ad valorem tax on costs will be small compared with transportation costs. The cost to importers and exporters of a modest Tobin tax would not exceed that of using forward and futures markets to hedge against currency fluctuations.

Alternatively, the effect of the Tobin tax can be replicated by increasing the cost to financial institutions of borrowing or lending to foreigners. Variants of this approach include negative interest rates (as in Switzerland) and special reserve requirements on foreign bank deposits (as with the German Bardepot). They take the form of special deposit requirements for banks on their net foreign currency deposits (as in Italy and Spain) or on their foreign borrowing (as in Australia, Chile and Colombia).[20] Although such measures provide considerable disincentive to engage in short-term speculative transactions, their distortionary effects should be minimal for trade and long-term foreign investments. They are easily imposed when needed and then removed. New information processing technologies are likely to make them even easier to implement. They could be administered by adding a few lines of code to banks' computerized trading programmes. Compliance could be monitored by periodic inspection of banks' computer records.

Evidence on the effects of controls

To review the evidence on the effects of capital controls and allied measures on the operation of foreign exchange markets, we start with the Bretton Woods system, since it was under this pegged rate regime that controls played an especially prominent role. We then turn to the post-Bretton Woods float, a panel of industrial countries and the recent Mexican crisis.

Evidence from Bretton Woods

Controls were integral to the operation of the Bretton Woods system of pegged but adjustable rates. In the 1950s, countries experiencing balance of payments deficits and reserve losses tightened capital controls as well as exchange restrictions and licensing requirements for importers, or at least slowed the rate at which they were relaxed, in order to strengthen the trade balance. Following the restoration of current account convertibility at the end of 1958, restrictions on capital account convertibility were maintained. When payments pressures mounted, controls on capital movements could be tightened. The United States employed the Interest Equalization Tax, which discouraged residents from investing in foreign bonds.[21]

One measure of the effectiveness of controls is the size of covered interest differentials (interest rate differentials adjusted for the forward discount on foreign exchange) as computed by Obstfeld (1993) for the 1960s. Obstfeld found that they were as large as two percentage points for the United Kingdom and larger than one percentage point for Germany.[22] Differentials of this magnitude, which cannot be attributed to expected exchange rate changes, confirm that capital controls mattered. Similarly, Marston (1993) compared covered interest differentials between Eurosterling (offshore) rates and British (onshore) rates. The advantage of this comparison is that it eliminates country risk—the danger that one country is more likely to default on its interest-bearing obligations. Between April 1961, when Eurosterling interest rates were first reported by the Bank of England, and April 1971, the beginning of the end of the Bretton Woods system, the differential averaged 0.78%. Marston concludes that controls "clearly . . . had a very substantial effect on interest differentials".

Such differences suggest that, despite the fixed exchange rate constraint, the authorities had leeway for conducting independent monetary policies. This suggestion is confirmed by Kouri and Porter (1974), who found that in the cases of Australia, Italy and the Netherlands, only 50% of changes in domestic credit were offset by international capital flows. (The offset ratio rose to between two-thirds and three-quarters in the case of Germany.) Their results suggest that although international capital flows responded to changes in credit conditions, there was still scope for autonomous monetary policy.

Evidence for the post–Bretton Woods period

In the heyday of the Bretton Woods system, national financial markets were tightly regulated. Perhaps controls on international financial transactions retained their effectiveness only because they were buttressed by domestic financial restrictions that prevented leakages. It is noteworthy, therefore, that studies of the post-Bretton Woods period confirm the continued effectiveness of controls.

Various types of controls were deployed to support the limited flexibility of exchange rates in the 1970s. The Japanese government supported the yen in 1973–74 by revising capital controls to favour capital inflows and discourage outflows. In 1977, it imposed 50% reserve requirements on most non-resident deposits, and in 1978 it raised these to 100% and prohibited foreigners from purchasing most domestic securities from the over-the-counter market. In 1977–78, as an alternative to more inflationary policies, the German authorities revoked the authorization for non-residents to purchase certain classes of German bonds. They also raised reserve ratios on non-resident deposits with German banks in order to limit capital inflows into Germany and prevent further appreciation of the mark.

Marston (1993) compares his results for onshore-offshore differentials during Bretton Woods and during the post–Bretton Woods float. As he notes, comparisons are complicated by the fact that the 1970s saw both a shift from pegged to floating exchange rates and changes in the prevalence and stringency of controls. If the shift from pegged to floating rates occasioned further divergences in national economic policies but little immediate change in the stringency of capital controls, then we might expect controls to have a larger impact on onshore-offshore differentials. This seems to have been true for the United Kingdom, where controls were maintained through the middle of 1979. The Eurosterling-domestic interest differential widened significantly, almost doubling between 1961–71 and 1973–79.

The United States offers another illuminating example. Although controls on US capital exports had been removed by the end of 1973, onshore-offshore differentials persisted because US banks were required to hold reserves against deposits, but Eurodollar deposits were exempt. The onshore-offshore US interest gap averaged more than one half of a percentage point over 1974–89 and reached much higher levels during periods such as the Herstatt crisis of 1974–75 and in the early 1980s.

Controls were also pervasive in the EMS until the Single European Act in 1987 mandated their removal. Giavazzi and Giovannini (1987) and Giovannini (1989) studied onshore-offshore differentials during various EMS realignment episodes. In the period surrounding the EMS realignment of April 7, 1986, for example, when the Italian lira and the French franc were devalued relative to the deutsche mark, large interest differentials opened up between onshore and offshore interest rates. Although the onshore deutsche mark–franc interest differential was constant or narrowed slightly over the period, the Euro–deutsche mark/Euro-franc rate jumped up at the beginning of 1986 from 7 to 13 percentage points. In the case of the Italian lira, the widening of the onshore-offshore differential was less dramatic but still significant: it rose from about 2 to 6 percentage points. Again, this evidence suggests that capital controls under the EMS provided domestic markets with significant insulation from the pressures of foreign exchange markets, reducing the cost to policy-makers of defending their pegged exchange rates.

Evidence from a panel of industrial countries

Eichengreen, Rose and Wyplosz (1995b) compared the behaviour of macroeconomic variables in periods of tranquillity and speculative crisis. Rather than relying on case studies, we considered a panel of 22 countries and covered a long period during which currencies were explicitly pegged under the provisions of, among others, the Bretton Woods system, the Snake and the EMS.

Specifically, we investigated the behaviour of macroeconomic variables during speculative crises and periods of tranquillity, asking whether the presence of controls made a difference.[23] Although we found no evidence that the budget balance, the real exchange rate, interest differentials or the evolution of foreign exchange reserves behaved differently during the speculative crises that occurred when capital controls were in place, other variables were significantly affected. The presence or absence of controls made a difference for inflation (which was higher and more variable when controls were in place), the trade balance (which tended towards deeper deficit when controls were in place) and the growth of domestic credit and money supply (which was higher in the presence of controls). The effect of controls was even more noticeable in tranquil periods. Only reserves and, possibly, budget deficits behaved similarly when controls were present and when they were absent. Rates of growth of money and credit were faster, real overvaluation was greater and budget and trade deficits were larger for countries not experiencing speculative attacks, but with capital controls in place.

These findings are consistent with the view that controls made a difference. Countries with controls in place followed more expansionary monetary policies and experienced larger trade deficits. One might have expected to see lower interest rates and smaller reserve losses in the presence of controls. In fact, interest rates were higher rather than lower, which could be explained by a higher inflation trend and the existence of a political risk premium (the risk that it becomes difficult to repatriate investments in countries that have a tradition of using controls).

The behaviour of foreign exchange reserves was no different in countries experiencing currency crises, depending on whether or not they had capital controls in place. This observation may provide the key to understanding how countries use controls. It suggests that controls do not allow countries that pursue inconsistent policies to keep their exchange rates unchanged forever. Controls do not prevent speculative attacks, nor do they permit countries to avoid reserve losses or interest rate increases when attacks occur. They do, however, render limited monetary policy independence compatible with a fixed exchange rate regime for a longer period than would be feasible otherwise.

Evidence from emerging markets in 1995

To evaluate the role of restrictions on capital movements in developing countries at the time of the 1995 Mexican crisis, we examined interest rates in two groups of countries: those with some type of controls on capital inflows—Brazil, Chile, Colombia, Indonesia, Malaysia and the Philippines—and those with no controls—Argentina, Mexico, Venezuela, Thailand, Singapore and Hong Kong.[24] The average change in interest rates was small in both the third and fourth quarters of 1994, and it differed insignificantly between countries with and without capital controls. In the first quarter of 1995, however, interest rates rose significantly in countries without controls, while remaining flat in countries with controls. The difference in the average change in interest rates in the two subgroups was significant at the 95% confidence level. Again, this result is evidence that countries with controls in place gained insulation for domestic policy.[25]

Although the subsamples are small, we can use these observations to verify that the effects of controls are concentrated in crisis rather than non-crisis periods. We distinguish "crises" (quarters in which the decline in reserves is greater than a critical threshold, taken here to be 5%) and "periods of tranquillity or strength" (quarters in which the rise in reserves is greater than the threshold value) within each subsample, comparing the behaviour of the change in reserves and the trade balance.[26] Although the level of statistical significance varies with the precise threshold used to define crises, the results tell a consistent story. Although there is no discernible difference in tranquil periods between countries with and without controls, the average percentage loss of reserves in crisis periods was significantly larger in countries without controls. The deterioration in the trade balance was also significantly larger during crises if controls were absent.

Recapitulation

Identifying the effects of capital controls is notoriously difficult because the stringency of controls and other aspects of the macroeconomic environment differ over time and across countries. It is noteworthy, therefore, that all the evidence points in the same direction. Whether it derives from the history of the Bretton Woods system, the post–Bretton Woods float, the EMS or the 1995 Mexican crisis, and whether it is drawn from the experience of industrial or developing countries, the evidence suggests that restrictions on international financial transactions have had statistically significant and economically important effects. It is still difficult to leap from this conclusion to an appraisal of the likely effects and effectiveness of a foreign exchange transactions tax. But the evidence provides little support for the sceptical view.

Enforcement and evasion

Issues of enforcement and evasion fall into two classes: evasion through substitution among financial instruments and evasion through substitution between national markets. We start by considering them in the context of the Tobin tax before providing a comparative analysis of compulsory deposit requirements.

Which transactions should be subject to taxation?

Kenen (1996) argues in favour of taxing spots, forwards, futures and swaps. The complexity of his argument is telling of the difficulty of selecting a dividing line between instruments subject to and exempt from taxation. Taxing forwards is deemed unavoidable because there is no clearly delineated border between spots and forwards. With a two-day delivery lag on spots, a three-day forward is a close substitute, providing a low-cost way of evading a tax limited to spot transactions. Since futures are similar to forwards, there is also a case for taxing futures. But then, options and swaps that incorporate futures should be taxed as well. Kenen is reluctant to tax options for fear that financial engineers will develop new derivative instruments in response to the tax.

A counter-argument for limiting the tax to spot transactions runs as follows. Banks and other financial institutions actively manage their risk positions. When a foreign currency asset is sold to a non-bank customer, a bank takes a foreign exchange position. Standard risk management practices dictate closing that position by purchasing that same asset from another bank. As in a game of musical chairs, the bank that finds itself without a chair will make a purchase on the spot market. Hence authorities can affect the entire chain of transactions by imposing a tax on spot market transactions.

Consider the case of a German exporter to the United Kingdom who expects to be paid in sterling in three months. To cover his exchange risk, the exporter purchases a matching deutsche mark forward against sterling from his bank. The bank, now long in sterling and short in deutsche marks, passes on the position to other wholesale market participants. In the aggregate, however, this exposure is only shifted, not eliminated. At some point, a market participant seeking to close the position will buy a deutsche mark spot, and someone will sell a sterling spot in three months' time as an indirect consequence of the forward transaction. Similar logic applies to options, swaps and other derivatives—which is why they are called derivatives, after all.[27] The incidence of a tax on spot transactions will be shifted to other instruments so as to discourage their use for short-term round-tripping as well.

Is universal coverage necessary?

A tax on spot foreign exchange transactions poses no greater conceptual difficulties than an excise tax on any well-defined good or service. But national authorities can only impose the tax in domestic markets.

This restriction has led many (such as Goldstein and Folkerts-Landau 1993) to conclude that the Tobin tax is impractical unless all countries agree to implement it. Since universal agreement is unlikely, the effectiveness of the tax would be vitiated, it is believed, through the international migration of the foreign exchange market.[28] Given the incentives for individual countries to free ride in the effort to gain business for their foreign exchange markets, implementation may be impractical.

This conclusion may be too simple, however. Felix and Sau (1996) note that the international transfer of trading operations entails both the fixed cost of moving the trading room and the variable costs of paying compensating differentials to employees who relocate abroad. Kenen notes that this type of avoidance can be countered by taxing the trading room, not the head office, and that the incentive for banks to relocate their trading operations in tax havens can be further reduced by applying the tax at penalty rates to transactions with banks and other dealers in tax-free jurisdictions.

Are deposit requirements an alternative?

Compulsory deposit requirements for financial intermediaries borrowing or lending to non-residents have effects similar to a Tobin tax.[29] An advantage of this approach is that implementation does not require international agreement. The experiences of a wide variety of countries, from Germany and Switzerland to Chile and Malaysia, demonstrate that countries can unilaterally moderate inflows (and subsequent outflows) by raising the cost to banks of borrowing abroad and reducing the returns to foreign investments.

Avoidance can nonetheless be a problem. In the case of an expected depreciation, domestic-currency loans can be disguised as intrafirm transfers channelled through "mailbox operations". These subsidiaries can then arrange with foreign banks to sell short positions. Although it may be possible to identify such behaviour on the basis of its paper trail, this can only be done after the crisis—presumably, too late.

Working in the other direction is the fact that banks and governments are engaged in building long-term relationships. Banks and other financial intermediaries will incur serious penalties if they have violated deposit requirement laws by setting up disguised subsidiaries. Anticipation of such penalties will limit their resort to such devices.

That it may not be necessary to maintain compulsory deposit requirements permanently, but only to impose them during periods of speculative pressure, reduces the incentive to incur the fixed costs of shifting business to other markets. In addition, certain activities may be impossible to shift offshore. For example, offshore institutions can lend domestic currency—whether to finance short sales or for other reasons—only in quantities that can be financed by their previously accumulated balances of domestic currency. Once these balances have been mopped up, the role of offshore banks is finished: they can obtain additional domestic currency to finance short sales only from onshore banks. Even if offshore banks are beyond the purview of the regulators, the regulators' oversight of onshore banks will limit the ability of their offshore counterparts to finance speculative activity.

It is sometimes argued that one difference between the Tobin tax and deposit requirements is that the Tobin tax is a source of revenue. But this argument is not strictly correct. In the case of compulsory deposit requirements, implicit tax revenues accrue to the central bank in the form of interest-free deposits. The central bank is free to invest the corresponding sums in fixed-term assets and to transfer the receipts to the appropriate fiscal authorities. In principle, there is no reason on revenue-raising grounds to prefer a Tobin tax to deposit requirements.

Conclusion

Our case for the Tobin tax rests on the fact that distortions prevent the efficient operation of foreign exchange markets. Foreign exchange markets suffer from asymmetric information and herd behaviour, moral hazard when players are too big or powerful to fail and policy distortions that produce multiple equilibria. The consequences include persistent misalignments and unstable exchange rate regimes. The social costs, in the form of trade distortions, disruptions of governments' economic policy strategies and even threats to political stability, can be substantial.

Although these points have long been acknowledged, policy-makers have been reluctant to embrace a Tobin tax in response. In part, the explanation lies in the difficulties of implementation: officials worry that the tax would be circumvented unless adopted worldwide and despair over the prospects for international agreement.

But a Tobin tax is just one of several instruments available to achieve these ends. The novelty of Tobin's proposal was its cost-based approach, in contrast to the then-prevailing tendency to invoke administrative restrictions on capital flows. Pursuing Tobin's logic further, it is possible to imagine other instruments that also raise the cost of cross-border capital movements and affect mainly short- rather than long-term flows, but which can be implemented unilaterally.

We have in mind deposit requirements on bank borrowing or lending to non-residents. These can target particular assets (liabilities to non-residents, as in Brazil and Chile, or loans to non-residents, as in Italy and Spain). Alternatively, they can be applied to all open positions in foreign exchange (as described in Eichengreen, Tobin and Wyplosz 1995). Implementation is simplified by the information revolution, which makes possible continuous monitoring of trading activities. Certainly, these measures have their own costs and limitations. But their study should be pursued more vigourously than has been the case to date.

Notes

1. A clear statement of this increasingly conventional wisdom is McKinnon (1993).

2. See Folkerts-Landau and Ito (1995). This statement that the Fund has traditionally been an advocate of immediate and complete liberalization refers to the IMF of the 1980s and 1990s. The Articles of Agreement made provision for the indefinite maintenance of controls on capital account transactions, and the early IMF was a proponent of their retention.

3. We have in mind the situation in developing and transition economies, although many of the same arguments apply to industrial countries, like the United Kingdom and Scandinavia in the 1980s, which reduced their inflation rates and liberalized their economies.

4. The reference here is to the seminal target zone model of Krugman (1991).

5. We provided evidence to this effect for the 1992 EMS crisis in Eichengreen and Wyplosz (1993). We have documented it more generally in a series of papers with Andrew Rose (Eichengreen, Rose and Wyplosz, 1995a, b and c). We return to this evidence in the third section.

6. See Frankel (1996) for a concise survey of the relevant literature.

7. See, for example, Kindleberger (1978), Eichengreen and Lindert (1989) and Eichengreen (1991) and the references cited therein.

8. As always, the first-best intervention would take place as close to the distortion as possible. If moral hazard in the banking system is the source of the problem, then the optimal policy response would be to remove the guarantee

of a bailout. Hence, moving from this distortion to the case for restrictions on capital inflows requires adding the assumption that a promise to resist pressure to extend a bailout is not credible or time consistent.

9. This possibility has been well known since the seminal work of Flood and Garber (1984) and Obstfeld (1986). The problem with such models is that they fail to pin down the timing of the potentially self-fulfilling attack. This problem is nothing but a pegged-rate analog to the indeterminacy of rational self-fulfilling bubbles in currency prices under floating rates. On the theory of self-fulfilling bubbles, see Frankel (1996).

10. Under floating rates, multiple equilibria become an additional source of exchange rate volatility: not only does the exchange rate exhibit wide swings when the fundamentals change, but it can jump from one equilibrium to another even when fundamentals remain unchanged. The volatility of exchange rates relative to fundamentals is perhaps best documented by Rose (1994). Frankel (1996) presents a catalog of theoretical models in which results of this sort can obtain.

11. This is documented in the now-ample literature applying self-fulfilling attack models to EMS countries. See Eichengreen and Wyplosz (1993), Svensson (1994), Obstfeld (1994) and Rose and Svensson (1994).

12. Frankel (1996) discusses the literature on rational bubbles.

13. Comparing these magnitudes to average daily foreign exchange market turnover is potentially misleading, however. First, the $1.3 trillion figure typically cited represents gross turnover. A transaction initiated by a final purchaser, say the customer of a bank, sets in motion a chain of subsequent transactions through which banks pass along the "hot potato" and rebalance their portfolios. Net turnover and, more to the point, transactions initiated by non-financial entities, are significantly less. Frankel's (1996) estimates suggest that non-financial customers account for a mere 12% of foreign exchange market transactions. Working in the other direction, and more important for our purposes, is the fact that in periods of intense speculative pressure, the volume of foreign exchange transactions rises to a multiple of that observed on a normal day.

14. The exception is the case of a currency board, where, by definition, the domestic currency is fully backed with foreign reserves.

15. The special case of Switzerland is grounded on the unusual stability of its currency. Requiring the base to be fully backed with foreign reserves is excessive, it might be argued, because this assumes that currency speculators will demand that the entire base be converted into foreign exchange. This is unrealistic: even during periods of speculative crisis, some domestic currency is still required for transactions.

16. The same argument holds in reverse for capital inflows.

17. This, it can be argued, was the situation in Italy in August 1992. Folkerts-

Landau and Ito (1995) overlook this point: they claim that controls are superfluous because "the time that is bought is likely to be only a few months, and possibly less" (1995:103). Frankel (1996) also minimizes this point.

18. We return to this point below in the context of enforcement and evasion.

19. Such measures were widely used after World War II, when it took 16 years for most European countries to return to convertibility. Ninety-eight of the 179 members of the IMF had accepted current account convertibility by early 1995. In 1955, only nine countries (all located in the Western Hemisphere) had adopted full current account convertibility; their number was still only 50 at the beginning of 1980. See IMF (Various years).

20. The experiences of these countries are described in Folkerts-Landau and Ito (1995), Agosin and Ffrench-Davis (1996) and Park (1996).

21. The Interest Equalization Tax was followed by voluntary restraints on banking and corporate transfers of funds abroad, as described above. These were tightened in 1965, coincident with the escalation of US involvement in Viet Nam, and again in 1966. In 1968, controls were made mandatory.

22. Aliber (1978) and Dooley and Isard (1980) undertake similar analyses and reach similar conclusions.

23. Doing so required first constructing an index of speculative pressure. Our index combined exchange rate changes, reserve changes and interest rate changes. The three components were weighted to equate their conditional volatilities.

24. Short-term interest rate data are from *International Financial Statistics,* except for Hong Kong, Thailand, Indonesia and Malaysia, which are quarterly averages of weekly observations reported in *The Economist.*

25. The contrast is not due entirely to the inclusion of Mexico in the sub-sample of countries without controls. Our measure of the change in interest rates was negative in the first quarter of 1995 for every country with controls, except Colombia, and positive for every country without controls.

26. Since we are pooling data for 12 countries and three quarters surrounding the Mexican crisis, we have about 30 observations, following adjustments for missing data.

27. This eliminates a problem identified by Kenen: that it is desirable to tax options only when they are in the money. It is only when they are in the money, of course, that they will generate a matching spot market transaction.

28. Other than the treaties binding the members of the European Union, there is no compulsory tax treaty under whose provisions governments could be compelled to adopt the Tobin tax.

29. In the case of Chile, the authorities explicitly considered the choice between deposit requirements and a front-loaded tax (Agosin and Ffrench-Davis 1996).

References

Aliber, Robert Z. 1978. "The Integration of National Financial Markets: A Review of Theory and Findings." *Weltwirtschaftsliches Archiv* 114(3):448–80.

Agosin, Manual R. and Ricardo Ffrench-Davis. 1996. "Managing Capital Inflows in Latin America." This volume.

Bertola, Guiseppe and Ricardo J. Caballero. 1990. "Target Zones and Realignments." CEPR Discussion Paper 398. London.

Dooley, Michael and Peter Isard. 1980. "Capital Controls, Political Risk, and Deviations from Interest-Rate Parity." *Journal of Political Economy* 88(2):370–84.

Eichengreen, Barry. 1991. "Trends and Cycles in Foreign Lending." In Horst Siebert, ed., *Capital Flows in the World Economy.* Tübingen: Mohr.

Eichengreen, Barry and Peter Lindert, eds. 1989. *The International Debt Crisis in Historical Perspective.* Cambridge, Mass.: MIT Press.

Eichengreen, Barry, Andrew Rose and Charles Wyplosz. 1995a. "Exchange Market Mayhem: The Antecedents and Aftermath of Speculative Attacks." *Economic Policy* 21(2):251–312.

———. 1995b. "Is There a Safe Passage to EMU? Evidence from the Markets." In Jeffrey Frankel, Giampaolo Galli and Alberto Giovannini, eds., *The Microstructure of Foreign Exchange Markets.* Chicago: University of Chicago Press.

———. 1995c. "Speculative Attacks on Pegged Exchange Rates: An Empirical Investigation with Special Reference to the European Monetary System." In Matthew Canzoneri, Paul Masson and Vittorio Grilli, eds., *Transatlantic Economic Issues.* Cambridge, U.K.: Cambridge University Press.

Eichengreen, Barry, James Tobin and Charles Wyplosz. 1995. "Two Cases for Sand in the Wheels of International Finance." *Economic Journal* 105(1):162–72.

Eichengreen, Barry and Charles Wyplosz. 1993. "The Unstable EMS." *Brookings Papers on Economic Activity* 1:51–143.

Felix, David and Ranjit Sau. 1996. "On the Revenue Potential and Phasing in of the Tobin Tax." This volume.

Flood, Robert P. and Peter Garber. 1984. "Gold Monetization and Gold Discipline." *Journal of Political Economy* 92(1):90–107.

Folkerts-Landau, David and Takatoshi Ito. 1995. *International Capital Markets: Developments, Prospects and Policy Issues.* Washington, D.C.: International Monetary Fund.

Frankel, Jeffrey. 1996. "How Well Do Foreign Exchange Markets Function: Might a Tobin Tax Help?" This volume.

Friedman, Milton. 1953. "The Case for Flexible Exchange Rates." In *Essays in Positive Economics*. Chicago: University of Chicago Press.

Garber, Peter and Mark Taylor. 1995. "Sand in the Wheels of Foreign Exchange Markets: A Skeptical Note." *Economic Journal* 105 (January):173–80.

Giavazzi, Francesco and Alberto Giovannini. 1987. "Models of the EMS: Is Europe a Greater Deutsche-Mark Area?" In Ralph C. Bryant and Richard Portes, eds., *Global Macroeconomic Policy: Conflict and Cooperation*. London: Macmillan.

Giovannini, Alberto. 1989. "How Do Fixed Exchange Rate Regimes Work? Evidence from Bretton Woods and the EMS." In Marcus Miller, Barry Eichengreen and Richard Portes, eds., *Blueprints for Exchange Rate Management*. New York: Academic Press.

Goldstein, Morris and David Folkerts-Landau. 1993. *International Capital Markets*. Washington, D.C.: International Monetary Fund.

IMF (International Monetary Fund). Various years. *International Financial Statistics*. Washington, D.C.

Kenen, Peter. 1996. "The Feasibility of Taxing Foreign Exchange Transactions." This volume.

Keynes, John Maynard. 1936. *The General Theory of Employment, Interest and Money*. London: Macmillan.

Kindleberger, Charles. 1978. *Manias, Panics and Crashes*. New York: Norton.

Kouri, Pentti J.K. and Michael G. Porter. 1974. "International Capital Flows and Portfolio Equilibrium." *Journal of Political Economy* 82(3):443–67.

Krugman, Paul. 1991. "Target Zones and Exchange Rate Dynamics." *Quarterly Journal of Economics* 106(3):669–82.

McKinnon, Ronald. 1993. *The Order of Economic Liberalization*. Second edition. Baltimore: Johns Hopkins University Press.

McKinnon, Ronald and Huw Pill. 1995. "Credible Liberalizations and International Capital Flows: The 'Over-Borrowing Syndrome'." Department of Economics. Stanford University. Processed.

Marston, Richard. 1993. "Interest Differentials under Bretton Woods and the Post-Bretton Woods Float: The Effects of Capital Controls and Exchange Risk." In Michael Bordo and Barry Eichengreen, eds., *A Retrospective on the Bretton Woods System*. Chicago: University of Chicago Press.

Obstfeld, Maurice. 1986. "Rational and Self-Fulfilling Balance-of-Payments Crises." *American Economic Review* 76(1):72–81.

———. 1993. "The Adjustment Mechanism." In Michael D. Bordo and Barry Eichengreen, eds., *A Retrospective on the Bretton Woods System*. Chicago: University of Chicago Press.

———. 1994. "The Logic of Currency Crises." NBER Working Paper 4640. Cambridge, Mass.

————. 1995. "International Currency Experience: New Lessons and Lessons Relearned." *Brookings Papers on Economic Activity* 1:119–220.

Park, Yung Chul. 1996. "The Republic of Korea's Experience with Managing Foreign Capital Flows." This volume.

Rose, Andrew. 1994. "Are Exchange Rates Macroeconomic Phenomena?" *Federal Reserve Bank of San Francisco Economic Review* 19(1):19–30.

Rose, Andrew and Lars Svensson. 1994. "European Exchange Rate Credibility Before the Fall." *European Economic Review* 38(5):1185–1216.

Svensson, Lars. 1994. "Fixed Exchange Rates as Means to Price Stability: What Have We Learned?" *European Economic Review* 38(3–4):447–68.

Tobin, James. 1978. "A Proposal for International Monetary Reform." *Eastern Economic Journal* 4(July–October):153–9.

2

How Well Do Foreign Exchange Markets Work: Might a Tobin Tax Help?

Jeffrey Frankel

Many observers have concluded that the international monetary system is not working well, particularly the foreign exchange market. The conclusion is fed by some recent developments in international financial markets, on the one hand, and by a number of academic findings on the other. This chapter examines the foreign exchange markets as they currently operate and then considers the arguments over the desirability of a Tobin tax. Misgivings regarding how well the markets are working arise from recent misalignments and crises, on the one hand, and from a set of seven academic findings, on the other.

A review of the structure and size of the foreign exchange market draws on the most recent central bank surveys released in September 1995. The Bank for International Settlements (BIS) figure for the worldwide total is $1,230 billion of trading per day in April 1995. Importantly, less than one in five transactions is made with a non-financial customer (0.18 in London and New York).

The author thanks Richard Lyons and the Harvard University International Economics Seminar for useful discussions. He also thanks the Bank of England, the Bank of Japan and the Federal Reserve Bank of New York for making available the latest statistics.

The case in favour of the Tobin tax features two major arguments. First, such a levy might reduce exchange rate volatility. A simple model giving this result is presented in appendix C. The starting point is a calculation showing that even a small tax would be a large disincentive to short-term transactions. The disincentive to long-term capital flows would be much smaller. This property does not extend to other forms of capital controls—thus the beauty of the Tobin tax proposal. The crucial proposition then becomes that short-term speculation is (on average) destabilizing. Some support for this claim is cited by market participants, in the form of tests on survey data of exchange rate forecasts. Second, the Tobin tax would raise a lot of revenue more efficiently than alternative taxes such as tariffs. Some possible flaws in earlier revenue estimates are pointed out in this chapter. The relevant base of transactions to which the tax would apply is larger than some have assumed, but the possible drop in trading volume in response to the tax is larger as well. A tax large enough to alter the structure of trading could conceivably collapse trading volume to as little as $151 billion a day. I do not support a tax of this magnitude. Nevertheless, it is clear that even a more reasonable tax rate of 0.1% would raise a great deal of revenue—$166 billion a year in one estimate. Whether raising this amount of revenue would be desirable depends on the use to which the funds were put or the alternative sources of tax revenue for which they are substituted.

The case against the Tobin tax also has two major components. First, it might create distortions and inefficiencies. As noted, it is even conceivable that the fundamental structure of the foreign exchange market could change, from decentralized and dealer-driven to centralized and customer-driven. Whether this would constitute a loss or gain in efficiency is difficult to say. Second, the Tobin tax would be extremely difficult to enforce. Along these lines lie my greatest doubts.

How well do foreign exchange markets function?

In the 1970s, the majority view among economists was that floating exchange rates were the right way to avoid undervaluations and overvaluations, such as the overvaluation to which the dollar had become increasingly subject in the 1960s. The market usually knows the true value of the currency better than do governments. Most economists had been persuaded by the argument that Milton Friedman made as far back as 1950: that speculators would on the whole be stabilizing rather than destabilizing, because any who increased the magnitude of exchange rate fluctuations could only do so by buying high and selling low, which is a recipe for going out of business pretty quickly.

The pendulum began to swing back in the 1980s. The decade began with Robert Mundell and a few supply-siders arguing for some version of a return to the gold standard. Concerns about floating rates became much more widespread with the sharp appreciation of the dollar in the early 1980s, culminating in what some viewed as a dollar bubble in 1984–85. The market sometimes got it wrong. (We may have seen another bubble more recently, with the appreciation of the yen in 1994 and early 1995). In the 1980s, a variety of proposals appeared, with the aim of stabilizing exchange rates among the major currencies. Some economists argued that going to a target zone or fixed rate would eliminate speculative bubbles (see, for example, Williamson 1985).

Rational speculative bubbles

The notion that financial markets might suffer from excessive volatility has been boosted by the theory of rational speculative bubbles. The initial motivation for the theory was purely mathematical curiosity. But the theory of speculative bubbles also showed that speculators could be destabilizing without losing money. In a rational speculative bubble, the price goes up each period, because traders expect it to go up further the next period, and in this expectation they are correct. Even though the price becomes increasingly far removed from the value justified by economic fundamentals, individual traders know that they would lose money if they tried to buck the trend on their own. These rational speculative bubbles disprove Milton Friedman's theory that destabilizing speculators would lose money.

The main problem with the theory of rational speculative bubbles is that it fails to explain what gives rise to bubbles (or what causes them to burst). Under the theory, the exchange rate is simply indeterminate. The theory also offers no particular grounds for thinking that such destabilizing speculation would disappear with government action. Episodes such as the 1984–85 dollar and 1994–95 yen may be better understood by models with small deviations from rational expectations. Some models have two classes of actors: technical analysts, or "noise traders", on the one hand, and traditional fundamentalists (whose expectations would be rational, if not for the existence of noise traders) on the other. The result can be a speculative bubble developing on the back of a movement that originated in fundamentals. I call it over-shooting of the overshooting equilibrium.

Recent fixed-rate experiments and the yearning for a "third way"

A further reason that the pendulum swung part way from floating to fixed in the 1980s was the emergence of the nominal anchor argument, especially for smaller countries. This argument is a prescription to peg exchange rates firmly, as a credible precommitment on the part of the monetary authorities not to inflate. It became popular for both southern European countries joining the European Monetary System (EMS) and developing countries that were adopting stabilization programmes based on fixing the exchange rate. This shift in sentiment was due in large part to the high inflation rates of the 1970s and the high output costs of reversing them in the early 1980s. (Even the IMF rethought its previous emphasis on devaluation-based country programmes and began to look favourably on exchange rate–based stabilization programmes.)

Since 1992, the disenchantment with pure floating seems to have given way to a renewed disenchantment with fixing, because a number of disruptive crises occurred when countries tried to fix their rates. It is true that many of these exchange rate crises have been the result of governments trying to defend parities that were no longer justified by fundamentals. Prominent examples include the pound and the lira in 1992 and the peso in December 1994. (Among the many precursors were the UK crises of 1931, 1949 and 1967; the dollar crisis of 1973; and the Chilean collapse of 1982.) The mainstream economist's view holds that these crises were the fault of governments, not of markets.

But unwarranted speculative attacks can occur under fixed rates or target zones, too—for example, the French franc in 1993. The theory has been supplied in "second-generation" models of speculative attacks, which feature multiple equilibria.[1] Judged according to macroeconomic fundamentals such as inflation and interest rates, the franc was not overvalued against the mark in 1993 and yet was forced by speculative attack to abandon its 2.25% margins. These speculative attacks are the fixed-rate analog of the speculative bubbles that arise under floating rates. Concluding that unwarranted speculation bedevils both floating rates and fixed rates, some observers have suggested a third way, along the lines of the tax on all foreign exchange transactions that was proposed by James Tobin in 1978.[2]

The nature of foreign exchange trading

It is important to understand the market for currencies at a level of detail that is at least somewhat less abstract than standard macroeconomic theories. Let us begin by noting that the foreign exchange market is not a centralized location—it is the sum-total of transactions in which national currencies are traded for one another.

The size of the market

The most salient aspect of the foreign exchange market is its size. Our information comes from the surveys that are conducted every three years by major central banks and aggregated by the BIS in Basle. Transactions volume increased more than fourfold between 1977 and 1980. The volume of trading in the US market, corrected for double-counting, increased another 44% between 1980 and 1983 (figure 2.1). Trading roughly doubled between 1983 and 1986, and again between 1986 and 1989 (among the four major markets). It then increased by 42% between 1989 and 1992 globally (BIS 1993). The BIS survey of April 1992 produced a total figure (after eliminating double-counting) of $880 billion of trading a day. This number, perhaps with an allowance for the growth in trading that had presumably taken place since 1992, has often been cheerfully rounded off to a trillion dollars.

Figure 2.1 Daily turnover in the US foreign exchange market
(billions of US dollars per day)

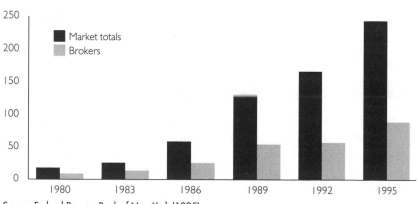

Source: Federal Reserve Bank of New York (1995).

We now have a much better idea of current trading volume. The April 1995 surveys have been conducted. As in the past, the Federal Reserve, Bank of Japan and Bank of England announced the results in their markets (the three largest) in September 1995. The subsequent BIS report on the total adjusts for double-counting across the largest markets and adds in the other, smaller markets for a total of 26 countries.

The latest surveys show a 60% increase in volume between April 1992 and April 1995, to $464 billion a day in London; a 46% increase, to $244 billion in New York; a 34.3% increase, to $161.4 billion in Tokyo; a 43% increase, to $105 billion in Singapore; a 50% increase, to $90 billion in Hong Kong; and a 32% increase, to $86 billion in Switzerland. (These figures have been adjusted for internal double-counting.) The total for the six markets is $1,150 billion, a 48% increase. The final BIS total for the larger set of central banks, adjusting for international double-counting, shows a new worldwide figure of $1,230 billion a day (BIS 1995a). (This figure excludes trading in derivative contracts. If derivatives are included, the total would probably reach about $1,300 billion a day.)

The increases in trading volume would not look quite as large when measured in yen, deutsche marks or other foreign currencies. The reason, of course, is that the dollar has depreciated against those currencies since 1992.

There had been a fear that trading may have been unrepresentatively low in April 1992 and unrepresentatively high in April 1995. April 1992 was a period of relatively low volatility in the foreign exchange market, while April 1995 was a period of high volatility, particularly in the yen-dollar market—and trading volume is known to be correlated with volatility.[3] If so, the rate of growth over the past three years is overstated. It turns out that in the 1995 New York survey, only 7% of the participants viewed trading activity in April to be above normal that month, while 48% viewed it to be below normal. Still, it is likely that volume in Tokyo was unusually high.

The structure of the market

As noted, the foreign exchange market is decentralized. It is dealer-driven, over-the-counter, and non-transparent. The New York Stock Exchange (NYSE), by contrast, is centralized. When a stock broker executes a trade on behalf of a client, the price and quantity are public information. Foreign exchange dealers are under no obligation to disclose this information; to the contrary, their ability to earn a living hinges on their skill at gleaning more information from other traders, particularly in the form of trades, than they reveal.

According to the 1992 BIS survey, roughly one in three transactions were executed in the traditional way, by speaker phone (typically at prices with narrower spreads than the indicative prices quoted over computer screens). Roughly one in three was settled by automated dealer systems, in which no voice contact is necessary. Finally, as had long been true, about one in three was settled through brokers. Brokers simply match buy and sell orders from dealers without taking a position themselves.

The 1995 survey reports that the split between direct interdealer trading and brokerage is broadly similar to that in 1992: the brokers' share is 30% now compared with 35% then (figure 2.2). The survey also reports a new phenomenon, the growth of automated brokerage (electronic order-matching), as distinct from automated systems for direct trading, to 6% of the total market volume from virtually nothing in 1992. The two automated brokerage systems operating in the United States are Electronic Brokerage System and Reuters Dealing 2000–2. The older automated trading system is Reuters Dealing 2000–1.[4] The brokerage share was similarly steady in London, at 35%.

The number of firms that trade a given currency in a given market is relatively small. Nevertheless, the survey suggests that the foreign exchange market is highly competitive. Among the top ten dealers, only four dealers' rankings remained unchanged between 1992 and 1995, and three of the 1995 top ten were not among the top ten in 1992. Among

Figure 2.2 Trading methods

(percentage of total market volume)

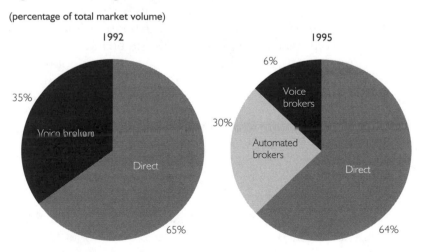

Source: Federal Reserve Bank of New York (1995).

the top ten dealers in either 1992 or 1995, four saw their ranking fall by five places or more, while four saw their ranking rise by five places or more. Moreover, there was a gain in the market share of the second tier of dealers in the top 20 firms. The Bank of England survey reports similar statistics (1995, p. 6). It should be noted that some of this shuffling of rankings may be due to individual traders switching employers.[5]

These indicators of competition say little about whether the brokers or Reuters feel free to compete with the dealers by offering an alternative market altogether, in which customers could trade directly. The distinction is competition *within* a market versus competition *between* market structures.

The composition of the market

The surveys decompose total trading along a number of dimensions: location, currency, type of contract and counter-party.

Location
London has long been the largest market. The latest survey now shows that London is larger than New York and Tokyo combined, as the *Financial Times* trumpeted ("London Keeps Forex Supremacy," September 20, 1995). Growth in the Japanese market, which was very rapid in the early 1980s as the result of liberalization, has slowed down sharply. Instead, it is Singapore and Hong Kong that have gained rapidly in the East Asian time zone. The relative shares for April 1995 garnered by the four largest markets are: 0.476 for London, 0.25 for New York, 0.166 for Tokyo and 0.108 for Singapore. Singapore attained the number four slot in 1992, but Hong Kong and Switzerland are close behind.

The list of 26 central banks reporting to the BIS includes such small "offshore" countries as Bahrain and Luxembourg. It does not include such "off-offshore" centres as the Cayman Islands or the Isle of Man, which are ready to provide a comfortable home for currency traders should the established centres become less hospitable.

Currency composition
The shares of currencies in foreign exchange trading add up to 200%, since each trade involves two currencies. Until relatively recently, the dollar was used in almost 99% of trades, serving as the "vehicle currency" when customers wanted to go from one lesser currency to another. The dollar's share has declined, however. According to the 1995 survey of the US market, the dollar appeared in 86% of trades—13% featured the

deutsche mark against third currencies, and less than 1% featured third currencies against each other. Figure 2.3 shows the currency distribution in the US market. The total share of the deutsche mark was 43% (of which about 29% is against the dollar). In third place was the yen, with 23%, followed by the pound sterling, Swiss franc, and French franc. A large increase in French franc trading is attributed to the aftermath of the 1992 and 1993 crises in the European exchange rate mechanism (ERM).

According to the Bank of Japan, the US dollar share in Tokyo trading in 1995 remained high at 93.7%, followed by the yen at 81.1%, and the deutsche mark at a distant 15.4%. As the London market is by far the biggest, its currency composition figures prominently in the worldwide total. The aggregation of 21 financial centres in the 1992 data showed the pound sterling in the number four position, followed by the Swiss franc, French franc, Canadian dollar and ECU.

Spot versus forward transactions
The decomposition by foreign exchange products has changed little in 1995 from earlier surveys, though a gradual downward trend in the

Figure 2.3 Comparison of foreign exchange daily turnover, 1992 and 1995

(percentage share by currency pair)

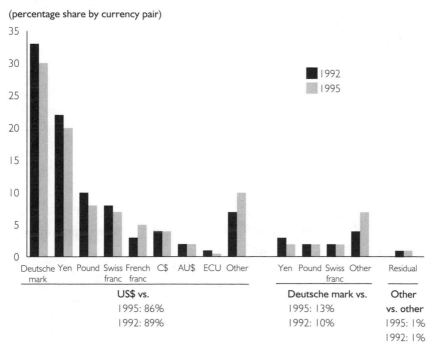

Source: Federal Reserve Bank of New York (1995).

share of spot transactions has continued. The turnover volume in New York was 55% in spot transactions. The rest can be broadly described as forward transactions (34% swaps and 11% actual forward contracts). The trend within the brokered portion of these market segments is the reverse of the trend in the overall market: the share of spot transactions rose sharply as part of the rise of automated brokerage systems (which, as yet, broker only spot transactions). The interbank volume in Japan was 36.4% in spot and 63.6% in forwards and swaps. In Tokyo, the (smaller) volume of customer transactions was 28.7% in spot and 71.3% in forwards and swaps. In London, forward transactions rose to 59% of total transactions in 1995 compared with 41% in spot.

Customer composition
The most striking aspect of the foreign exchange market, after its total volume, has long been the low percentage of trades made on behalf of ultimate customers. Ultimate customers are those, like exporters or issuers of international bonds, who wish to sell foreign exchange or those, like importers or international investors, who wish to buy foreign exchange. A much-cited figure of 5% of transactions made with non-financial customers and 95% with other dealers comes from earlier surveys. In the 1992 survey, the figure had increased to 12%.[6]

Still, this figure says that each dollar of foreign exchange that is cashed in by a customer is passed around about eight times among dealers, like a "hot potato", until it finds someone willing to hold it. One interpretation is that these traders are buying and selling based on frequently changing and differently perceived news regarding monetary fundamentals or other information relevant for determining the value of the currency. The alternative is that for some reason it is cheaper for each dealer to pass the foreign exchange on to the next dealer who he or she happens to encounter and who is marginally more willing to hold the currency, than it is, for example, to auction it off in order to try to find the one trader who most wants to hold it.[7]

According to the 1995 surveys, the percentage of New York trading with non-financial customers had grown another three percentage points since 1992, to 17% from 14%. The percentage of trading volume with financial customers was 27% (figure 2.4). The percentage of Tokyo trading volume with all customers (financial and non-financial, that is, all non-banks) was 26.5%, having *fallen* slightly, from 26.8% in 1992 and 30.3% in 1989. In London, the share with financial customers continued a steady upward trend, to 18%, and the share with non-financial customers was fairly steady at 7%. The three markets together imply an

Figure 2.4 Counter-party distribution, 1995

(billions of US dollars per day)

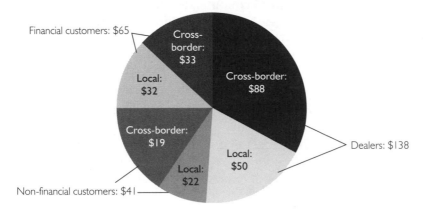

Source: Federal Reserve Bank of New York (1995).

aggregate customer-to-transaction ratio of 0.306. The London and New York statistics imply a ratio for non-financial customers of 0.18. (The Bank of Japan does not offer this breakdown.)

The US survey reports that the volume of trade grew most rapidly with financial customers (100% growth) compared with non-financial customers (78% growth) and interdealer trading (22% growth) (Federal Reserve Bank of New York 1995, p. 9). It seems likely that the rapid growth in trade with financial customers reflects in large part the increased participation of hedge funds, corporate treasurers and other institutions, for example, the universally-cited George Soros.[8] The 1993 IMF *Capital Markets Report* described the growing importance of such players in the market. The corporate treasurers, in fact, are reported to be more important than the Soroses. It is likely that such customers would respond more to an increase in transaction costs, such as a Tobin tax, than would traditional customers, like importers and exporters. This is worth keeping in mind when we discuss the likely effect of the tax on the volume of transactions.

Academic findings on how well the market works

Everyone describes floating exchange rates as highly volatile. But volatile compared to what? They are more volatile than they were expected to be before the 1973 move to floating rates, more volatile than the prices of goods and services and more volatile than apparent monetary fundamentals. This is not the same, however, as saying that they are excessively volatile. Even if foreign exchange markets are functioning properly, fundamental economic determinants, such as monetary policy, should produce a lot of variability in the exchange rate. Dornbusch's famous overshooting theory of exchange rate determination, for example, predicts that a relatively small increase in the money supply will cause a relatively large increase in the price of foreign exchange. (The foreign currency will appreciate so much that it is generally perceived as "overvalued", in the sense that it is expected to depreciate gradually in the future—at a speed that is just sufficient to compensate investors for the fact that domestic assets pay a lower interest rate.) The important questions are whether volatility is higher than necessary and what the harmful effects might be.

Evidence of adverse effects from short-term volatility

The concern about exchange rate volatility has always been about possible adverse effects on trade and investment. Here, the academic attack has been muted, large swings or "misalignments" receiving more concern from academic economists. Most studies have concluded that short-term volatility has little effect on trade.[9] But the belief in an adverse effect has nevertheless been a major motivation behind attempts to link European currencies, through the ERM and now through the European Monetary Union (EMU).

A study of bilateral trade shows statistically significant effects of bilateral volatility in the 1960s and 1970s (Frankel and Wei 1995). When estimated by ordinary least squares (OLS), the effect on trade of adopting fixed exchange rates worldwide in 1980 was large: +22%. We must immediately add three major qualifications, however. First, the estimated effect disappears in the 1980s. Quite possibly, the spreading use of futures, options and other instruments means that firms learned in the 1980s how to hedge currency risk effectively. Second, there is certainly a simultaneity problem in the OLS estimates: one cannot tell from the correlation whether stabilizing bilateral exchange rate variability promotes bilateral trade, or strong trade links lead to the decision to stabilize exchange rates with respect to particular trade partners. An allowance for this simultaneity produces an estimated volatility effect that, while significant up to 1980, is far smaller in magnitude. Third, the observed exchange rate variability could be inevitable real risk, which would pop up elsewhere if suppressed in the foreign exchange market. There is evidence relevant to this last point.

If volatility were suppressed in the foreign exchange market, would it show up elsewhere?

Econometric research has failed to explain most exchange rate movements by fundamentals, especially on a short-term basis.[10] Logically, this failure leaves two possible explanations: unobservable fundamentals or bubbles (defined as exchange rate movements not based on fundamentals). In the first case, we would still be subject to the standard presumption of neoclassical economics that if volatility were somehow suppressed in the foreign exchange market, it would simply show up elsewhere. Imagine, for example, that the fundamental origin of the appreciation of the dollar in the first half of the 1980s was an increase in worldwide demand for US goods and therefore an increase in demand for US currency to buy those goods (a real appreciation). An attempt on the part of the US monetary authorities to suppress the appreciation would consist of purchases of foreign currencies, putting more dollars in the hands of the public. This increase in the US money supply would have been inflationary. The increase in US relative prices (the real appreciation) would have occurred anyway, but it would simply have taken the undesirable form of inflation.

Evidence from fixed versus floating regimes

Can we judge that exchange rate movements are due to unobservable fundamentals, rather than bubbles? Arguing against the unobservable fundamentals explanation is the pattern whereby nominal and real exchange rate variability has increased whenever there has been a shift from a fixed to a floating regime.[11] Furthermore, there is no reduction in variability of fundamentals to keep the exchange rate in line when moving from floating rate regimes to fixed rate regimes (see, for example, Flood and Rose 1995). This seems to leave speculative bubbles as the remaining explanation for much of the short-term variation in exchange rates. If this conclusion is correct, it would likely follow that exchange rates are unnecessarily volatile.

Are forecasters biased and markets inefficient?

There is a widely documented bias in expectations as reflected, for example, in the forward exchange market. The forward discount actually points the wrong way as a predictor of the exchange rate. The bias is usually interpreted simply as an exchange risk premium, but there is some evidence against this view.[12] It is possible that the bias is evidence of market inefficiency.

Is speculation destabilizing?

There is also evidence in survey data of extrapolation on the part of market participants in forecasts at short horizons—under three months. If traders act based on such extrapolative expectations, they will create bandwagons: an upward blip will generate expectations of future appreciation, leading to buy orders, and thereby contributing to the upward trend. Unless the survey data are misleading us, there seems to be evidence of destabilizing speculation.[13]

But at longer horizons—three months to one year—forecasts seem to fit the patterns of adaptive, regressive or distributed lag expectations better. All three mechanisms of expectations formation, if acted upon by traders, would lead to stabilizing speculation (Frankel and Froot 1987a, b).

The key results (from Frankel 1993, p.324) from the survey studies show that the estimated extrapolative parameter is relatively high at the one week horizon: a 1% appreciation in a given week generates on average an expectation of 0.13% further appreciation over the coming week (table 2.1). The extrapolative parameter is lower at the four-week horizon. It changes sign at the three-month horizon: a 1% appreciation generates an expectation of 0.08% *depreciation* over the coming three months. The tendency to expect a reversal continues to get stronger with longer horizons. The 1% appreciation generates an expectation of 0.33% depreciation over the coming 12 months.

Which horizon dominates foreign currency trading? The horizon at which most trading takes place is actually shorter than one day. Traders at most banks take large positions for a few hours, but limit their overnight and weekend positions sharply or close them out altogether (Fieleke 1981). This does not necessarily mean that the determination of the market price is dominated by short horizons. If traders are fully rational, even though they trade at short horizons, their expectation of how much a currency will be worth one period from now will be tied down by their rational forecast of how much it will be worth one year from now. The question is whether this tying of the short-term to the long-term is in fact operative. The survey data results summarized in table 2.1 seem to suggest that short-term expectations are not formed by looking far into the future. Given the high level of volatility, the one-hour share of a rationally expected year-long return to fundamentals equilibrium is a very minor factor in traders' calculation on each trade.[14]

Overshooting the overshooting equilibrium

The effects of exogenous changes in monetary policy are apparently not instantaneous, as they should be in theory, but are drawn out over time (Eichenbaum and Evans 1995). This could be an example of how speculative bubbles get started.

A number of researchers have deviated from the rational expectations paradigm to sketch what might be called theories of endogenous speculative bubbles. They typically start from the proposition that market participants' forecasts are drawn from competing views, including both technical analysis and economic fundamentals. From there, they attempt to build models of exchange rate determination.[15] In such models, changes in the weights assigned by the market to competing models can themselves alter asset demands and give rise to changes in the exchange rate. DeGrauwe and Dewachter (1990) show that the interaction of chartists and fundamentalists can give rise to an exchange rate process characterized by chaos: a process that is essentially unpredictable, despite the fact that the underlying model is deterministic. Krugman and Miller (1993) show the role of stop-loss order traders.

If it takes a year, for example, for the full effects of a monetary tightening to be felt in the exchange rate, then during most of that year, those who forecast by extrapolating (the technical analysts or chartists) have had a good track record. Observing this, traders switch from fun-

Table 2.1 Do forecasters extrapolate? OLS regressions of expected future rate of depreciation against most recent actual depreciation

	Survey data source				
	MMS international		Economist financial report		
Sample period	Oct. 1984–Jan.1988		June 1981–Aug. 1988		
Term of forecast	1-week	4-week	3-month	6-month	12-month
Estimate of extrapolative parameter	0.13	0.08	−0.08	−0.17	−0.33
Standard error (GMM)	0.03	0.05	0.03	0.03	0.06
± statistic	4.32[a]	1.60	−2.98[a]	−4.98[a]	−5.59[a]

a. Significant at 99 percent confidence level.
Source: Frankel and Froot (1990).

damentalist forecasting techniques to technical analysis, thereby increasing the demand for the appreciating currency and prolonging the appreciation, even after the fundamentals may have turned around (as they had for the dollar by July 1984 and probably had for the yen by February 1994). This is what I mean by overshooting the overshooting equilibrium. It is capable of explaining some of the other puzzling findings, such as the tendency of the currency to move up in the future when the forward discount or interest differential points down. In the aftermath of an increase in the interest rate differential, the currency appreciates over the subsequent year rather than appreciating instantaneously and then depreciating gradually, as it should according to the efficient-markets overshooting theory.

What is the case for a Tobin tax in the foreign exchange market?

An interesting aspect of the proposal to tax international financial transactions is that it has three distinct justifications. Many proponents emphasize one or two of them to the exclusion of the others. The motivations are: reforming the international monetary system, shifting resources away from the financial sector (particularly away from speculators) and raising revenue for new projects. International economists think of the proposal as motivated by a desire to reform international currency markets, especially a desire to reduce exchange rate volatility. Those countries that have already tried securities transactions taxes—levied on trading in stocks and bonds, not foreign exchange transactions—have been motivated primarily by a desire to scoop up what is popularly seen as excessive compensation accruing to financial traders.[16] Surprisingly, reducing market volatility is mentioned seldomly. Finally, many proponents of a Tobin tax, particularly those who have revived the idea in the 1990s, are motivated by a desire to fund worthy international ventures. D'Orville and Najman (1995), for example, explicitly recommend against relying on the first or second justifications. They present the Tobin tax as one of the more promising on a list of possible ways of financing needed international projects. The financial sector is not deliberately targeted beyond the observation that taxing international activities has more legitimacy for such purposes than taxing domestic activities.

Might a Tobin tax reduce speculative activity?

The question for economists is: How could a Tobin tax discourage undesirable destabilizing speculation without at the same time discouraging desirable investment? As a number of authors have demonstrated, the Tobin tax would penalize short-term transactions far more than long-term transactions.[17] Suppose the rate of return at home is i% a year. The required rate of return abroad (including tax evasion and exchange gains), i^*, depends on the Tobin tax, t, and on the duration of the investment, y, measured as the number of years, or fraction of years, for which a foreign position is held.

As a first example, consider a round trip investment. Those seeking to invest abroad must pay the tax twice, once when the foreign asset is bought and again when it is sold. For returns to be equalized on domestic investments and foreign investments, we must have:

$$(1 + i^*y)(1 - t) - t = 1 + iy.$$

Solving for the required rate of return abroad,

$$i^* = \frac{iy + 2t}{y(1 - t)}$$

$$= \frac{i + \frac{2t}{y}}{1 - t}$$

As a second example, assume that only the interest earnings are brought back, and the principal is left in foreign currency. Those seeking to invest abroad must still pay the tax twice, once when the foreign asset is bought and again when the interest earnings are repatriated. For returns to be equalized on domestic investments and foreign investments, we must have:

$$i^*y(1 - t) - t = iy.$$

Solving for the required rate of return abroad,

$$i^* = \frac{iy + t}{y(1 - t)}$$

$$= \frac{i + \frac{t}{y}}{1 - t}$$

It is apparent that the Tobin tax penalizes short-term investments more the shorter the horizon. For example, with a home interest rate of 10%, a 1% tax and a 12-month investment horizon, the foreign yield would have to be at least 11% (=.11/.99) to attract the investor. If the horizon were one month (1/12 of a year), the foreign yield would have to rise to 22% a year to remain attractive. If the horizon were only one week (1/52 of a year), the foreign yield would have to be 62% a year!

How discouraging short-term speculation might reduce volatility

Appendix C to this paper presents a model that constitutes an attempt, albeit a very simple one, to appraise in a macroeconomic model the claim that the Tobin tax would reduce exchange rate volatility. The point is often made that there is no way of discouraging destabilizing speculation without at the same time discouraging international capital flows that are desirable for many other reasons (stabilizing speculation, risk-sharing, intertemporal consumption-smoothing and so on). But it is in fact possible to put a positive interpretation on the Tobin tax.[18]

We have seen in the previous section that a small tax in proportion to the size of the foreign exchange purchase will not be much of a deterrent to anyone contemplating the purchase of a foreign security for longer-term investing. But it will discourage the spot trader, who is now accustomed to buying foreign exchange with the intention of selling it a few hours later. Let us apply the more modest tax rate of 0.001% to the previous example. With a 12-month investment horizon, the foreign yield would have to be at least 10.1% to compete with a 10.0% interest rate at home. If the horizon were as short as one day, as it is for most traders, the foreign yield would have to rise to 46.5% to remain attractive. At such short horizons, all but the boldest speculators would be driven out pretty quickly.

Frankel and Froot (1987a, b, 1990) reported that "technical analysis" became increasingly prevalent in the exchange rate forecasting business during the first half of the 1980s. Similarly, Taylor and Allen (1992) conducted a questionnaire survey on the use of technical analysis in the London foreign exchange in 1988. At least 90% of respondents reported placing some weight on technical analysis, with the proportion rising steadily with the shortness of the horizon. These short-horizon technical analysts bear a striking resemblance to the infamous destabilizing speculators of classical financial mythology. Most of the rules of technical analysis seem to fit into the category of destabilizing behaviour, such as the "momentum" models that call for buying when the current price exceeds the price that held, for example, five days earlier.

If the destabilizing speculators in the model of Appendix C are indeed the short-term forecasters that the expectations survey data in table 2.1 suggest, and the stabilizing speculators are the long-term investors, then the tax may reduce the variance of the exchange rate. In terms of the model in the Appendix, it will reduce f_s without having much effect on f_i. The turnover tax in this light is crucially different from other capital controls, such as the taxes on international interest earnings that were levied before 1973 by the United States to discourage capital outflow or by Germany to discourage capital inflow. Such taxes reduced the rate of return to long-term investing just as much as the rate of return to short-term speculation (perhaps more, if one considers that capital gains were taxed at a lower rate than interest earnings).

Might a Tobin tax restore some independence to national monetary policies?

A corollary of the statement that a Tobin tax might reduce the volatility of exchange rates for any given movements in economic fundamentals is the proposition that it might allow larger movements in fundamentals for any given exchange rate path. In other words, for countries seeking to maintain exchange rate stability, it might restore some measure of monetary policy independence. The question could be broken into three parts. To what extent is independence desirable? How much independence has been lost? And would a small Tobin tax help restore independence?

Clearly, for countries that seek to stabilize their exchange rates, such as the European countries that have been members of the ERM and are putative candidates for EMU, a lot of independence has been lost. For many of them, some measure of independence is desirable. Hence the conflict that forced Italy and the United Kingdom out of the ERM in 1992. This is the famous "impossible trinity": a country can have any two of the attributes of financial openness, currency stability and monetary independence, but it cannot have all three. The key question then becomes whether a sacrifice of financial integration as minor as a small Tobin tax would be sufficient to restore the other two legs of the trinity. I am sceptical. The speculators who successfully pushed against the limits of the ERM in September 1992 and August 1993 were seeking (successfully, as it turned out) returns well in excess of the 47% annual rate that a small Tobin tax would counteract. The same is true of the large inflows and outflows such as those Mexico underwent, respectively, in 1990–93 and 1994. Monetary independence will continue to be a privilege of those willing to live with large movements in their exchange rates.

Proceeds from the tax

Clearly, a major motivation for the tax is the large amount of revenue that it would generate. This, in turn, raises concerns over how the tax revenue would be spent and whether the Tobin tax is the least-distortionary means of raising revenue for those purposes.

Revenue projections
Some wishful estimates of the amount of revenue that could be raised have simply multiplied the proposed tax rate times the volume of foreign exchange trading reported in the 1992 BIS survey, obtaining numbers as high as $10 billion a day for a worldwide 1% tax (or even $3,650 billion a year, if the figure is incorrectly annualized by multiplying by 365 days). Tobin himself has suggested a figure of $1,500 billion a year to be raised from a worldwide tax of 0.5%.[19]

D'Orville and Najman (1995) estimate the amount of revenue that could be raised by a tax on foreign exchange transactions, as of 1992, at about $140.1 billion for a tax of 0.25%, or $56.32 billion for a 0.1 % tax.[20] The authors—who are otherwise careful—have made a major mistake in calculating these amounts. They have assumed, incorrectly, that only the portion of transactions carried out through foreign exchange brokers would be subject to the tax—about one-third of the total.[21] The mistake probably arose from assuming that the term "brokers" applies to all foreign exchange dealers or traders. In reality, the other two-thirds of transactions are handled directly by foreign exchange dealers at private banks, who would be subject to a Tobin tax every bit as much as brokers. (Dealers are defined as market-makers, who are willing to both buy and sell all the time.[22] Again, brokers are those who match buy and sell orders without taking a position themselves. If a tax were applied to them and not to other dealers, the only effect would most likely be to eliminate brokers, without raising any revenue.) Indeed, given the increasing use of automated dealer systems in interdealer trading, one might argue that a tax would be more easily applied to this segment of trading than to the transactions that pass through brokers.

Thus the proper basis should have been something close to the full $880 billion of daily turnover from the 1992 survey, multiplied by 240 trading days, which equals $211 trillion a year. While this basis is triple that used by d'Orville and Najman, an offsetting correction arises from the allowance for reduction in trading volume in response to the tax. They reduce volume by 20%, leaving the tax base at 80% of its pre-tax level, which they regard as conservative. That their reduction is invariant with respect to the size of the tax—the same 20% for a charge of 1% as for a charge of 0.05%—suggests that something is wrong. A more standard assumption for the responsiveness of the supply of a service, in this case foreign exchange trading, in response to a tax would be a constant elasticity. A typical transaction cost for foreign exchange might be 0.1%. (This is a generous estimate, applicable to a trade between a bank and a corporate customer. The actual number is likely to be much smaller for interdealer trading, which is the majority of trading currently.) So, a charge of 0.1% would constitute at least a doubling of the current transaction cost. If such a tax reduces trading volume by 20%, then the elasticity is about 0.32.[23] If this same elasticity held for a tax of 1.0%, so that the transaction cost were going up by a factor of 10 instead of by a factor of 2, then the drop in trading volume would be about five times as large as that suggested by the two authors, and the downward effect on tax revenue would be proportionate.

Of course, the 20% figure is arbitrary, as would be a decision to associate it with the 0.1% tax rather than a higher tax. Another consideration must be factored in. Most authors realize that any attempt to impose a non-negligible tax in one country alone, or even in all major industrialized countries, would drive much of the foreign exchange trading offshore. For that reason, the assumption is made that the tax would be imposed by "all" countries. The 20% reduction in volume is meant to capture diversion to non-cooperating offshore centres and evasion, for example, transactions conducted among corporate affiliates, made in the street or disguised as derivative contracts, as well as a reduction in actual trading volume. But there is reason to think that actual trading volume would decline by more than this amount.

The decline in trading volume could be greater, particularly if the decentralized dealer system were to collapse as a result of the tax and give way to a centralized structure. As noted earlier, the foreign exchange market is decentralized—each dollar of foreign exchange that is cashed in by an exporter or other customer is passed around many times among dealers, like a hot potato, until it finds someone willing to hold it for more than just a few hours. One can debate whether this structure is efficient. But it probably would not have evolved if transaction costs were not as razor-thin as they are. Indeed, the fall in transaction costs must be one major reason for the oft-noted increase in trading volume (by 50 times in the United States between 1977 and 1995).[24] It is possible that the imposition of a Tobin tax, especially one as large as 0.5% or 1.0%, as has often been proposed, would alter the structure of the market in a fundamental way. It might become more like other major financial markets, in which a sale or purchase by a customer generates only one or two transactions, rather than five or eight. This would be the case particularly if such a tax triggered a transition to a new trading structure equilibrium, with the decentralized dealer network currency replaced by a system in which foreign currency was traded on a centralized exchange in the manner of the NYSE. If the ratio of transactions to customer orders had fallen from eight to two, for example, the 1992 base would have fallen from $211 trillion a year to $53 trillion. A 1% tax would have raised "only" $530 billion a year. That is still a lot of money.

The most recent estimate of worldwide volume conducted in April 1995 is $1,230 billion per day and $295.2 trillion a year (240 trading days). The New York and London figures show that about 18% of trades involve non-financial customers. If the ratio of total trades to trades with non-financial customers was to fall from 5:1 to 2:1, that would be a 60% reduction in annual trading volume, from $295.2 trillion to $118.1 trillion. A 1% tax would thus raise $1.181 trillion.

All of the foregoing calculations assume no change in the volume of customer transactions. In reality, the volume of orders from customers would change if the cost to them changed. I see no reason for a decline in orders from exporters and importers.[25] It seems reasonable to leave the transactions of non-financial customers alone, although one should be aware that even that segment of trading is far larger than the exports and imports that show up in the balance of payments.[26]

Many of the customer transactions are financial in nature. The hedge funds and other institutional investors would presumably trade less if the cost of trading went up. Campbell and Froot (1994) review several authors' estimates of the sensitivity of securities trading volume in Sweden and the United Kingdom with respect to changes in transactions taxes. The estimates vary from 0.85 to 1.7. These effects include the migration of trading offshore, which would be less relevant for a Tobin tax that was adopted in all countries.

The estimate of the revenue effect can be refined a bit. An elasticity of 0.32 for transactions initiated by financial customers might not be a bad guess. As already noted, such an elasticity would imply that a doubling of transaction costs to financial customers would reduce their trading volume by 20%. As financial customers account for 41% of total customer transactions in New York and London combined, the implication is that customers (in the aggregate) would decide to make transactions 8% less frequently [0.08 = 0.41 x 0.20]—from the currently estimated worldwide total of $376 billion a day [= 0.306 x $1,230] to $346 billion a day [= 0.92 x 376]. This drop would exacerbate the fall in total trading volume suggested above.

If the dealer-intermediated system disappeared altogether, would the total trading volume fall to $346 billion? No, it would fall to *half* this level, or $173 billion a day, because each trade would involve two customers transacting directly with each other, where it now involves only one.[27] The 0.1% tax, if it were big enough to change the structure of trading in this way, would then raise only $42 billion in yearly revenue [= 0.001 x 240 days x 173]. Admittedly, this outcome is unlikely. A tax as low as 0.1% would not be sufficient to collapse the structure of trading and eliminate dealer-intermediation from the system. If we assume that the customer-to-transaction ratio rises only from the current 0.31 to 0.5, the new transactions volume would be $693 billion a day [= 346/0.5], and revenue would be $166 billion a year [= 0.001 x 240 days x 693].

What if a higher tax rate of 1% were enough to eliminate dealer intermediation? As in the earlier calculation based on an elasticity of 0.32 (footnote 23), let us guess that increasing transaction costs by a factor of 10 would reduce financial customer transactions by half. Then, total customer desire to trade would fall by 20% [= 0.41 x 0.5] to $301 billion a day [= 0.8 x 376]; total two-party transactions to half that, or $151 billion a day; and yearly revenue to $361 billion.[28] All of these estimates must be regarded as both preliminary and exceedingly rough.

Uses for the tax revenue
In evaluating the proposal, much depends on how the funds are actually spent. Many items on the agenda, such as those laid out by d'Orville and Najman (1995) and Mendez (1995b), strike an outsider as among the most useful contributions to world welfare that the public sector could make—if they could be carried out with a reasonable level of international consensus and administrative efficiency. Concerns arise over whether such international undertakings can in fact be carried out this effectively.

Public opinion in many countries, particularly the United States, is opposed to even current levels of international cooperation, let alone to the massive increases in spending and activity envisioned in such an agenda. To assert that the needed political consensus currently exists is wishful thinking.[29] Popular conceptions envision large do-nothing bureaucracies whose major function is to provide sinecures for favoured nationals from member countries. Much of the harsh opinion is based on ignorance, ranging from the mild to the extreme.[30]

One can take some encouragement from public opinion polls that have been carefully conducted by Kull (1995) of the Center for the Study of Policy Attitudes. They find greater numbers of people in the United States prepared to allocate resources to worthy international causes than is generally assumed. It would probably be necessary for countries to be able to agree on reformed institutional mechanisms to ensure that the money was well-spent, such as agreeing to choose staff based more on merit and less on national quotas. It would probably also be necessary to start out on a smaller scale than the proposed list of projects, many of which cost $10–$100 billion each and higher. Relatively more modest projects, such as disaster relief, peacekeeping operations and nuclear safety related to the former Soviet Union, strike me as being the highest priorities. Using a new tax to fund successful activities of this sort might gradually earn increased public support for UN activities. This is less likely to happen if idealists push for immediate, massive funding of international initiatives that many people do not yet see the need for. These, at least, are the reactions of one who is not an expert in this area.[31]

Alternative ways of raising tax revenue
Perhaps the most effective way of arguing against those concerned with the distortions that a Tobin tax would create is to determine whether there are alternative methods of raising $166 billion that would be less distortionary. Such mainstays of public finance as taxing incomes or international trade are probably far more distortionary. It is difficult to see, for example, what damage a Tobin tax could do to the foreign exchange market that would be commensurate to the damage to international trade from tariffs that raised the same amount of revenue.

What is the case against a Tobin tax?

The arguments against the Tobin tax fall into two categories: distortions of economic activity and difficulties of enforceability. They are addressed by several other papers in this volume. If they were not at least mentioned here, however, the paper would be incomplete, and perhaps misleading.

Distortions and inefficiencies

Any tax tends to distort the economic activities to which it is applied. Those who call a tax of 1% or 2% modest and thus expect no consequent shifts in private sector behaviour are engaging in wishful thinking. Given the razor-thin margins in modern financial markets, a transaction cost of 1%, or even substantially less, can have major effects on the location, nature and volume of trading. Fortunately, as we have demonstrated, the effect of a 0.1% tax on investments with moderately long-term horizons would be small, while the effect on very short-term transactions would be large.

Even assuming that a 0.1% tax would be a material disincentive to only short-term transactions and that these transactions are the only ones that one wishes to discourage, there are still other ways that the allocation of resources could be distorted. The loss of liquidity might lead to larger spreads to customers. Investors who hold assets like US Treasury securities, even with long-term horizons, do so in part because of their liquidity: the market in Treasury securities is sufficiently liquid that investors can count on being able to sell quickly and on getting close to the market price. If the volume of foreign exchange trading were to fall substantially in response to a Tobin tax, the reduced liquidity could impair cross-border investments at every horizon. This problem is more likely to be serious for small, thinly traded currencies.

As noted when discussing the possible effects on trading volume, a Tobin tax could change the structure of the market in a fundamental way. This issue has hardly been addressed by others.

There is no obvious reason why foreign exchange markets should be organized as decentralized dealer-driven markets, while many markets in equities and commodities are centralized and customer-driven. If anything, there may be a presumption that decentralized markets are more suited to assets with lower volume trading and more asymmetric information; this would explain the tendency for small stocks to list on the NASDAQ, which is an over-the-counter market, and larger stocks to list on the centralized NYSE.[32] Major currencies would seem to resemble large stocks more than small stocks.

As we have seen, there is a trend towards automated systems for trading foreign exchange, particularly within the class of brokered transactions. So far, customers are completely excluded from participating. Let us, however, engage in a bit of finance fantasy. It is possible that at some point in the future, one of the automated brokerage systems would allow customers to participate. (Currently, the systems are too dependent on dealers for business to offend them by breaking the no-customer rule.) If so, a centralized customer-driven market could expand at the expense of the decentralized dealer-driven market. It is conceivable that a 1% Tobin tax would accelerate this trend, because the number of transactions per customer order is much greater under the current system. The provision of liquidity by customers, for example, through limit order books, would substitute for the current inter-dealer mechanism of risk-sharing.

Such a change in market structure would be momentous. It is not guaranteed that the change would be for the worse. It is difficult to say whether the new system would be more efficient than the current one. If the switch were to happen on its own, the presumption would be that the centralized system was more efficient. On the other hand, it is surely significant that all foreign exchange markets around the world have evolved as decentralized systems and that none has made the jump to a centralized system. If the switch were to occur as the result of a substantial Tobin tax, it would be hard to know ex ante whether the switch would lead to a gain or loss in efficiency. Ex post, one might judge by seeing whether the transaction costs to customers went up or down. I am not brave enough to want to tamper with Mother Nature in this way.

Mendez (1994, 1995a,b) is confident of the superior efficiency of a centralized electronic system to match customers' buy and sell orders, considers it a natural monopoly and proposes that the UN or other international organizations set one up. He asserts that costs to customers would go down. He is so confident of the efficiency gains that he believes that huge sums of revenue could be raised, in the manner of the Tobin tax, apparently without even attempting to ban legally untaxed foreign exchange trading of the conventional sort. The question that has not been answered satisfactorily is why, if the centralized system would be so efficient and profitable, someone hasn't already started one somewhere.

Enforceability

Enforceability is a big problem. The issue is considered at length by Garber (1996) and Kenen (1996), and so shall be considered only very briefly here.[33]

If any of the proponents of a Tobin tax once thought that it could be enacted in the United States alone, they have probably been convinced otherwise by now. It is clear that the foreign exchange markets would move elsewhere in response, even to a tax as small 0.1%. In this regard, it is worth noting that the magnitude of dollar–deutsche mark trading in London *already* exceeds the amount traded in New York ($102 billion a day versus $73 billion a day, according to the 1995 surveys). The same holds if the tax were applied to a set of the largest markets. If the tax were limited to the G-7, the markets would move to Singapore and Luxembourg. If it were limited to the OECD plus Hong Kong and Singapore, the markets would move to the Cayman Islands and the Isle of Man.

For the policy to achieve any of its goals, it would have to be the outcome of an international agreement that was virtually universal. (It could withstand a few "outlaw" states like North Korea and Iraq, since they are already so cut off from international financial business.) Achieving international agreement for such a tax is the greatest practical difficulty to its enactment. It is not the place of academic observers to prejudge political practicality, however; if we don't try to judge innovative new proposals on their merits, nobody will.

Enforcement could even be a problem if all countries were to sign an agreement. As it is, foreign exchange is already traded on street corners in many countries of the world, in markets that are various shades of gray and black. For small tax rates and large transactions, street corners are less of a problem.

Some have suggested that the automated systems that are growing in use, in brokering as well as in direct interdealer trading, could make collection easier. If the problem of international agreement could be solved, there is no reason to think that enforcement would be more difficult for financial transaction taxes as compared to, say, income taxes.

Conclusion

I am by no means ready to endorse the Tobin tax, especially one on the order of 1% or 2%. Doubts over enforceability, even by themselves, are too great. Some proponents of the tax have not thought through carefully enough the implications for the magnitude, location and microstructure of the foreign exchange market.[34]

Proponents should realize that most economists would oppose such a tax. Their opposition cannot be dismissed quite as easily as the self-interested opposition of the banks, even though the language will often sound similar. The economists' basic points must be acknowledged:

- There is a presumption that decisions made collectively by the private sector in competitive markets, such as where to set the market price for foreign exchange or even how to organize the market itself, have sound reasons behind them.
- Economic behaviour responds endogenously to taxes.
- There is no reason to think that the public sector will necessarily spend resources more efficiently than the private sector.

On the other hand, economists are wrong to be content at stopping at such reflexive reactions as these. The arguments on the positive side are easily summed up:

- There is evidence that the foreign exchange market does not currently operate in the optimal way that the theoretical ideal would have us believe.
- Contrary to standard claims, there is at least some reason to believe that a Tobin tax might affect destabilizing short-term speculation more than stabilizing long-term speculation.
- Subject to the hugely important condition of worldwide enforcement, the Tobin tax could raise a lot of revenue.
- Subject to the equally important condition that public finance was handled more responsibly than is often the case in national politics, let alone international politics, worthwhile projects could be financed at the cost of substantially lower economic distortions than would be the case with (for example) tariffs.

The difficulty of meeting these last two conditions is the primary reason why I am not yet ready to sign on. Nevertheless, the proposal is worthy of more serious study than economists have hitherto given it.

Appendix A: Three proposals for sand in the wheels and how they differ

	Chile's deposit requirement on inflows	Eichengreen-Wyplosz deposit requirement proposal	Tobin tax proposal
Motive	Prevent over-indebtedness	Protect balance of payments	Reduce volatility of exchange rates (and raise revenue)
Tax applied to:	Capital inflows	Capital outflows (and inflows)	All foreign exchange transactions, including trade
Paid immediately by:	Foreign investors	Banks	All traders (mostly banks)
Paid immediately to:	Central bank (foreign currency earnings)	Central bank (seignorage only)	Tax authority (domestic revenue)
Relationship of tax amount to interest rate:	Rises with foreign interest rate	Rises with domestic interest rate	Invariant to interest rate
Relationship to maturity:	Tax falls at 3 mos. (or 12 mos.)	Falls with maturity? But does not apply to intraday trading	Fixed amount. In percent per year terms, falls continuously with maturity.
Where imposed:	One country (facing inflows)	One country (facing outflows)	Must be worldwide
Probable level of tax rate:	Moderate	High (to discourage speculative attacks)	Low (to avoid distortions and substitution)

Appendix B: Transactions taxes around the world

Country	Tax Size	Description	Notes: Changes since 1991
Australia	0.3%	Transactions tax	Additional stamp tax removed in 1991
Austria	0.15% 0.06% 0.04%–0.09%	Transfer tax Arrangement fee Courtage fee	May be avoided by trading off exchange May be avoided by trading off exchange
Belgium	0.17% 0.025%	Stamp tax on buys and sells Stock market fee	No tax ex country; maximum of 10,000 Belgian francs No tax ex country; maximum of 2,500 Belgian francs
Canada		No taxes	
Denmark		No taxes for non-residents	
Finland	0.5%	Transactions tax	Waived if parties foreign; eliminated in 1992
France	0.15%	Trading tax	Tax on trades greater than 1 million francs; rate is doubled on smaller transactions; may be avoided by trading ex country
Germany	0.125% 0.06%	Boersenumsatzsteuer Courtage tax (official broker fee)	Residents only May be avoided by trading ex country
Hong Kong	0.25% 0.006% 0.05%	Stamp duty Special levy Exchange levy	 May be avoided by trading off market May be avoided by trading off market
Italy	0.05%	Stamp duty tax	May be avoided by trading ex country
Japan	0.30%	Sales tax	May be avoided by trading ex country
Malaysia	0.05% 0.3%	Clearing fee Transfer stamp duty on purchases and sales	Maximum $100; may by avoided by trading off exchange Eliminated in 1992
Netherlands		No taxes	
New Zealand	0.0057% plus per trade fee	Transaction levy	May be avoided by trading off exchange; eliminated in 1992
Norway		No taxes	
Singapore	0.1% 0.05% 0.2%	Contract stamp duty Clearing fee Transfer stamp duty	May be avoided by trading off exchange Maximum $100; may be avoided by trading off exchange Purchase only; eliminated in 1992
Sweden	0.5%	Turnover tax	May be avoided by trading ex country; eliminated in 1991
Switzerland	0.0005% 0.01% 0.075%	Exchange fee State tax Stamp tax	May be avoided by trading ex country May be avoided by trading ex country May be avoided by trading ex country
United States	0.0033%	SEC fee	
United Kingdom	2 pounds 0.5%	Levy Stamp duty tax	On trades over £5,000 On purchases only

Source: UBS Phillips and Drew, as reported by Cambell and Froot (1994).

Appendix C: A model in which a reduction in short-term speculation is stabilizing

Assume that the spot exchange rate, s in log form, is determined by the ratio of the supply of domestic assets (relative to foreign assets), m in log form, to the relative demand for domestic assets, d in log form:

$$s = m - d + u,$$

where u is an unknown error term. Assume that a fraction w of partici-pants[35] in the foreign exchange market are long-term investors and a frac-tion $1 - w$ are short-term speculators. Then demand can be decomposed:

$$d = w\,d_i + (1 - w)\,d_s$$

Assume that the investors expect the exchange rate to regress towards its long-run equilibrium value, as in the Dornbusch over-shooting model, at rate θ, and that the speculators expect it to diverge, as along a speculative bubble path, at rate δ:

$$\text{exp depr}_i = -\theta\,(s - \bar{s})$$

$$\text{exp depr}_s = +\delta\,(s - \bar{s})$$

Assume further that f_i and f_s represent the elasticity of each group's demand for foreign assets with respect to their expectations. The f para-meters can be interpreted as the degree of international capital mobil-ity, or substitutability. Then, total demand for domestic assets is given by:

$$d = wf_i\theta(s - \bar{s}) - (1 - w)f_s\delta(s - \bar{s})$$

Solving for the spot rate gives:

$$s = \frac{\{m + [-(1 - w)f_s\delta + (w)f_i\theta]\bar{s} + u\}}{\{1 - (1 - w)f_s\delta + (w)f_i\theta\}}$$

Thus the variability of the spot rate is given by:

$$\text{Var}(s) = \frac{\text{Var}(m + u)}{[1 + wf_i\theta - (1 - w)f_s\delta]^2}$$

For a given variance of money supplies, m, and other determinants, u, the investors, i, act to reduce the variance of the exchange rate, and the speculators, s, to increase it. The position of McKinnon (1976) could be interpreted as worrying that volatility is too high because f_i, the responsiveness of investors to their expectations, is too low, and the position of Tobin could be interpreted as worrying that volatility is too high because f_s, the responsiveness of speculators to their expectations, is too high. The overall argument could also be stated more simply: high volatility stems from a low w, the number of investors relative to speculators. This fits in with concerns of some observers about excessively short horizons in financial markets. A Tobin tax could be expected to lower f_s or to raise w. Either way, by decreasing the role of destabilizing speculation, the tax would, in this model, result in a lower variance of the exchange rate.

Notes

1. See, for example, Obstfeld (1994) and Flood and Garber (1991).

2. See, for example, Tobin (1992) and Eichengreen, Tobin and Wyplosz (1995). It should be noted, however, that the Tobin tax differs in a number of important ways from other sand in the wheels taxes or controls on international capital flows, such as the proposal of Eichengreen and Wyplosz (1996), or the reserve requirements on capital inflows that have been adopted by Chile in the 1990s (see, for example, Agosin and Ffrench-Davis 1996). Appendix A sketches out the differences in the three proposals.

3. See Frankel and Froot (1990); Hsieh and Kleidon (1994); and Jorion (1994). Judging by options prices, implied volatility in April was double the level of December 1994 to February 1995.

4. A set of Reuters 2000–1 data is analysed by Lyons (1994, 1995a, 1995b). A set of Reuters 2000–2 data is analysed by Goodhart, Ito and Payne (1996). See the comment by Lyons, 1995b.

5. The New York survey (Federal Reserve Bank of New York 1995) covered 130 foreign exchange dealers active in the United States (see its Annex I). The average deal size was $15 million per trade (p.11), though most spot trades were smaller.

6. In London, "the proportion of business with non-financial customers and other financial institutions has risen to 23% of daily turnover." (Bank of England 1992, p.408.)

7. The hot potato interpretation is supported empirically in a study of the actual second-by-second behaviour of an individual trader. See Lyons (1995a, b).

8. Hedge funds manage portfolios for a small number of relatively large individual investors. They deal heavily in derivatives, but the implication of the name is the reverse of the truth: they speculate rather than hedge.

9. The evidence has been reviewed by Goldstein (1995).

10. See, for example, Meese and Rogoff (1983) and Campbell and Clarida (1987). A recent survey of the empirical literature on exchange rate determination is Frankel and Rose (1995).

11. The example of Ireland is a particularly convincing demonstration. See Mussa (1990).

12. See, for example, Froot and Frankel (1989) and other chapters in Frankel (1993). Engel (1996) has recently surveyed the subject.

13. See Frankel and Froot (1987b, 1990); Froot and Ito (1989); Ito (1994).

14. The short horizon of most foreign exchange trading is documented in many places, including in Frankel (1993).

15. Relevant studies include Goodhart (1988), Frankel and Froot (1987a, b, 1990), Cutler, Poterba and Summers (1991), De Long and others (1990) and Goldberg and Frydman (1993).

16. Campbell and Froot (1994) relate the experience in Sweden and the United Kingdom. Turnover taxes have also been used in recent years in Germany, Switzerland, Japan and a majority of OECD countries. Even the United States has a nominal Securities and Exchange Commission (SEC) fee ($0.01 assessed on sales per $300 of value; Hakkio 1994, p.19). The tax rates for many countries are reported in Appendix B, borrowed from Campbell and Froot. Appendix A offers a systematic comparison between the Tobin tax and selected national measures.

17. This version is drawn from Dornbusch and Frankel (1988).

18. This line of argument was developed in Frankel (1988, pp. 177–88).

19. Others have adopted this figure or have associated simple multiples of it with corresponding multiples of the 0.5% tax. (UNDP 1994, pp. 7, 69, as cited in d'Orville and Najman 1995, p.34).

20. D'Orville and Najman propose applying a uniform 0.1% tax on government securities, Eurobonds and derivatives, as well as on foreign exchange, for a total estimated revenue of $120 billion, plus an unestimated amount for a similar tax on corporate stocks and bonds.

21. "Some two-thirds of the turnover was generated by central banks and other actors (for example, governments and official international organizations) which would be tax-exempt" (p.31). "As brokers handled, on average, 33% of the turnover . . . their 1992 turnover was some US$ 70.4 trillion. In the absence of regular data, this adjusted figure should serve as the basis for developing recommendations as to the level of a transaction charge and calculating its notional yield" (p.32). In reality, the official share of transactions, whether liable to tax or not, is much smaller than two-thirds. A gross upper bound on the share of official authorities was 1.3% in April 1989 (the figure also includes turnover in exchange-traded options and futures) and 8.6% in April 1992 (this figure includes transactions with other non-reporting financial institutions) (BIS 1993, p.12). The "basis" that the authors have in mind should be the entire $880 billion of daily turnover in April 1992 ($211 trillion annualized), not just one-third of that. Of course, the basis then has to be reduced to reflect the response to a tax.

22. Market participants themselves often apply the term "traders" to dealers. We will stick with the latter term in order to avoid confusion with traders, like George Soros, who are financial customers.

23. $\log(0.8)/\log(2.0) = -0.322$.

24. The average bid-ask spread in deutsche marks in New York was twice as large in 1971, at 0.11%, as in the late 1980s, according to Froot (1990).

25. If the cost of hedging foreign exchange risk is considered a material disincentive to importers and exporters, then a 1% tax would also have a negative effect on trade. On the other hand, if it succeeded in reducing exchange rate risk, there might be an offsetting positive effect. For the speculative financial customers, a decrease in volatility might, if anything, have a negative effect on trading activity rather than a positive effect.

26. Dollar trading is roughly 200 times the sum of the gross credits and debits in the US balance of payments under trade, investment income and capital flows. The role of the dollar in other countries explains some of this difference, but still leaves a large ratio. Total foreign exchange trading is approximately 100 times total world trade in goods and services.

27. In other words, the total number of transactions per customer transactions would fall by a factor of about six. We are assuming here that there is no change in the frequency with which a vehicle currency (usually the dollar) is used. If the vehicle currency system were to disappear and minor currencies were exchanged directly, the number of transactions would fall by almost an additional factor of two.

28. If the transaction-to-customer ratio fell only modestly, from three to two (instead of falling to one-half), the volume would be $602 billion a day, and yearly revenue would be $1.445 trillion [= 0.01 x 240 x 602].

29. Walker (1993) takes encouragement from the fact that the European Union (EU) is already collecting taxes from its members: "The principal of supranational taxes for supranational purposes has been established." But it is a very long way from claiming sufficient political consensus in the EU for federal public finance to claiming that such an international consensus exists more broadly.

30. Typical of mild ignorance is the tendency to blame UN military inaction in the face of crises on the institution itself, instead of on the failure of its most important members to agree on the proper course of action (and to contribute their share of the costs). Typical of more extreme ignorance is the belief that the UN possesses armed forces of its own, and even that these may have operated inside the United States.

31. We saw in the revenue estimates that a tax on the order of 1% raises more revenue than a tax on the order of 0.1%, notwithstanding the large decline in trading volume that is likely to occur. A proposal phrased so as to raise hundreds of billions of dollars of revenue is unlikely to be adopted, however. In this light, a strategy of backing a more modest proposal for a tax of 0.1% may actually carry a higher expected revenue pay-off than would a strategy of backing a tax of 1.0%.

32. There is a sizable literature on such microstructure questions for equity markets (including, for example, the theoretical contributions of Madhavan

1992 and Glosten 1994). Unfortunately, the conclusions that emerge from this literature are unclear. Moreover, the corresponding microstructure literature for the case of foreign exchange markets has barely gotten started.

33. Most studies of financial transactions taxes in general, such as Campbell and Froot (1994), Hakkio (1994), Schwert and Seguin (1993) and Shome and Stotsky (1995), conclude that enforcement is a serious problem, even in the domestic context. Some, notably Summers (1987) and Summers and Summers (1990), are much more optimistic.

34. Though other proponents *have* thought these issues through carefully.

35. To be more precise, we should define d to be the fraction of world wealth allocated to domestic assets, and define w and $1 - w$ to be the shares of wealth held by the two classes of market participants. Then s would be given by $m - \log [d/(1 - d)] + u$.

References

Agosin, Manuel and Ffrench-Davis, Ricardo. 1996. "Managing Capital Flows in Latin America." This volume.

Bank of England. 1986. "The Market in Foreign Exchange in London." Press notice. August.

———. 1992. "The Foreign Exchange Market in London." *Bank of England Quarterly Bulletin* 32(4):408–17.

———. 1995. "The Foreign Exchange Market in London." Press notice. September 19.

BIS (Bank for International Settlements). 1990. "Central Bank Survey of Foreign Exchange Market Activity." Basle. April.

———. 1993. "Central Bank Survey of Foreign Exchange Market Activity in April 1992." Basle. March.

———. 1995a. "Central Bank Survey of Foreign Exchange Market Activity in April 1995: Preliminary Global Findings." Basle. October 24.

———. 1995b. "Central Bank Survey of Derivatives Market Activity." Press communique. Basle. December 18.

Bank of Japan. 1995. "Tokyo Foreign Exchange Market Turnover Survey (April 1995)." Tokyo. September 19.

Campbell, John Y. and Richard Clarida. 1987. "The Dollar and Real Interest Rates." *Carnegie-Rochester Conference on Public Policy* 27(August):109-39.

Campbell, John Y. and Kenneth Froot. 1994. "International Experiences with Securities Transaction Taxes." In Jeffrey Frankel, ed., *The Internationalization of Equity Markets*. Chicago: University of Chicago Press.

Cutler, David, James Poterba and Lawrence Summers. 1991. "Speculative Dynamics." *Review of Economics Studies* 58(May):529–46.

DeGrauwe, Paul and Hans Dewachter. 1990. "A Chaotic Monetary Model of The Exchange Rate." CEPR Discussion Paper 466. London.

De Long, J. Bradford, Andrei Shleifer, Lawrence Summers and Robert Waldmann. 1990. "Noise Trader Risk in Financial Markets." *Journal of Political Economy* 98(4):703–38.

Dornbusch, Rudiger and Jeffrey Frankel. 1988. "The Flexible Exchange Rate System: Experience and Alternatives." In Silvio Borner, ed., *International Finance and Trade*. London: International Economics Association in association with Macmillan Press.

Eichenbaum, Martin and Charles Evans. 1995. "Some Empirical Evidence on the Effects of Monetary Policy Shocks on Exchange Rates." *Quarterly Journal of Economics* 110(4):975–1110.

Eichengreen, Barry, James Tobin and Charles Wyplosz. 1995. "Two Cases for Sand in the Wheels of International Finance." *Economic Journal* 105(January):162–72.

Eichengreen, Barry and Charles Wyplosz. 1996. "Taxing International Financial Transactions to Enhance the Operation of the International Monetary System." This volume.

Engel, Charles. 1996. "The Forward Discount Anomaly and the Risk Premium: Recent Evidence." NBER Working Paper 5312. Cambridge, Mass. Forthcoming, *Journal of Empirical Finance*.

Federal Reserve Bank of New York. 1983. "Treasury and Federal Reserve Foreign Exchange Operations." Press release. September 7.

———. 1989. "Summary of Results of US Foreign Exchange Market Survey Conducted in April 1989." Press release. September 13.

———. 1992. "Summary of Results of the US Foreign Exchange Market Turnover Survey Conducted in April 1992." Press release. September 19.

———. 1995. "April 1995 Central Bank Survey of Foreign Exchange Market Activity." September 19.

Fieleke, Norman. 1981. "Foreign-Currency Positioning by U.S. Firms: Some New Evidence." *Review of Economics and Statistics* 63(1):35–42.

Flood, Robert A. and Peter Garber. 1991. "The Linkage between Speculative Attack and Target Zone Models of Exchange Rates." *Quarterly Journal of Economics* 106(2):1367–72.

Flood, Robert and Andrew Rose. 1995. "Fixing Exchange Rates." *Journal of Monetary Economics* 36(1):3–37.

Frankel Jeffrey. 1988. "International Capital Mobility and Exchange Rate Volatility." In Norman Fieleke, ed., *International Payments Imbalances in the 1980's*. Boston: Federal Reserve Bank of Boston.

————. 1993. *On Exchange Rates.* Cambridge, Mass.: MIT Press.

Frankel, Jeffrey and Kenneth Froot. 1987a. "Short-Term and Long-Term Expectations of the Yen/Dollar Exchange Rate: Evidence from Survey Data." *Journal of the Japanese and International Economies* 1(3):249–74.

————. 1987b. "Using Survey Data to Test Standard Propositions Regarding Exchange Rate Expectations." *American Economic Review* 77(1):133–53.

————. 1990. "Chartists, Fundamentalists, and the Demand for Dollars." In Anthony Courakis and Mark Taylor, eds., *Private Behavior and Government Policy in Interdependent Economies.* Oxford: Clarendon Press.

Frankel Jeffrey and Andrew Rose. 1995. "A Survey of Empirical Research on Nominal Exchange Rates." In Gene Grossman and Kenneth Rogoff, eds. *Handbook of International Economics.* Amsterdam: North-Holland.

Frankel, Jeffrey and Shang-Jin Wei. 1995. "Regionalization of World Trade and Currencies: Economics and Politics." Paper presented at the NBER conference. Woodstock, Vermont, October 19–21. Forthcoming in Jeffrey Frankel, ed., *The Regionalization of the World Economy.* Chicago: University of Chicago Press.

Friedman, Milton. 1953. "The Case for Flexible Exchange Rates." In *Essays in Positive Economics.* Chicago: University of Chicago Press.

Froot, Kenneth. 1990. "Multinational Corporations, Exchange Rates, and Direct Investment." In W. Branson, Jacob Frenkel and Morris Goldstein, eds., *International Policy Coordination and Exchange Rate Fluctuations.* Chicago: University of Chicago Press.

Froot, Kenneth and Jeffrey Frankel. 1989. "Forward Discount Bias: Is it an Exchange Risk Premium?" *Quarterly Journal of Economics* 104(1):139–61.

Froot, Kenneth A. and Takatoshi Ito. 1989. "On the Consistency of Short-Run and Long-Run Exchange Rate Expectations." *Journal of International Money and Finance* 8(4):487–510.

Garber, Peter. 1996. "Issues of Enforcement and Evasion in a Tax on Foreign Exchange Transactions." This volume.

Glosten, Lawrence. 1994. "Is the Electronic Open Limit Order Book Inevitable?" *Journal of Finance* 49(4):1127–61.

Goldberg, Michael and Roman Frydman. Forthcoming. "Theories Consistent Expectations and Exchange Rate Dynamics." In Helmut Frisch and Andreas Worgoter, eds., *Open-Economy Macroeconomics.* London: Macmillan.

Goldstein, Morris. 1995. *The Exchange Rate System and the IMF: A Modest Agenda.* Policy Analyses in International Economics No. 39. Washington, D.C.: Institute for International Economics.

Goldstein, Morris, David Folkerts-Landau, Peter Garber, Liliana Rojas-Suarez and Michael Spencer. 1993. *International Capital Markets: Part I. Exchange Rate Management and International Capital Flows.* World Economic and Financial

Surveys. Washington, D.C.: International Monetary Fund.

Goodhart, Charles. 1988. "The Foreign Exchange Market: A Random Walk with a Dragging Anchor." *Economica* 55(220):437–60.

Goodhart, Charles, Takatoshi Ito and R. Payne. 1996. "One Day in June, 1993: A Study of the Working of Reuters 2000–2 Electronic Foreign Exchange System." In Jeffrey Frankel, Giampaolo Galli and Alberto Giovannini, eds., *The Microstructure of Foreign Exchange Markets*. Chicago: University of Chicago Press.

Hakkio, Craig. 1994. "Should We Throw Sand in the Gears of Financial Markets?" *Federal Reserve Bank of Kansas City Economic Review* 79(2):17–31.

Hsieh, David and Allan Kleidon. 1996. "Bid-Ask Spreads in Foreign Exchange Markets: Implications for Models of Asymmetric Information." In Jeffrey Frankel, Giampaolo Galli and Alberto Giovannini, eds., *The Microstructure of Foreign Exchange Markets*. Chicago: University of Chicago Press.

Hubbard, R. Glenn. 1993. "Securities Transactions Taxes: Tax Design, Revenue, and Policy Considerations." *Tax Notes*. November 22, pp.985–1000.

Ito, Takatoshi. 1994. "Short-Run and Long-Run Expectations of the Yen/Dollar Exchange Rate." *Journal of the Japanese and International Economies* 8(2):119–43.

Jorion, Philippe. 1996. "Risk and Turnover in the Foreign Exchange Market." In Jeffrey Frankel, Giampaolo Galli and Alberto Giovannini, eds., *The Microstructure of Foreign Exchange Markets*. Chicago: University of Chicago Press.

Kenen, Peter. 1996. "The Feasibility of Taxing Foreign Exchange Transactions." This volume.

Krugman, Paul and Marcus Miller. 1993. "Why Have a Target Zone?" *Carnegie-Rochester Conference Series on Public Policy* 38(8):279–314.

Kull, Steven. 1995. "Americans and Foreign Aid: A Study of American Public Attitudes." Program on International Policy Attitudes, Washington, D.C., January 23.

Lyons, Richard. 1993. "Tests of Microstructural Hypotheses in the Foreign Exchange Market." *Journal of Financial Economics* 39(October):321–51.

Lyons, Richard. 1991. "Information Intermediation in the Microstructure of the Foreign Exchange Market." NBER Working Paper 3889. Cambridge, Mass.

———. 1995a. "Is Profit Taking Rational? A Foreign Exchange Dealer's Response." NBER Summer Institute, July 14.

———. 1995b. "Tests of Microstructural Hypotheses in the Foreign Exchange Market." *Journal of Financial Economics* 39(October):321–51.

———. 1996a. "Comment on 'One Day in June, 1993: A Study of the Working of Reuters 2000–2 Electronic Foreign Exchange System'." In Jeffrey Frankel, Giampaolo Galli and Alberto Giovannini, eds., *The Microstructure of Foreign Exchange Markets*. Chicago: University of Chicago Press.

———. 1996b. "Foreign Exchange Volume: Sound and Fury Signifying Nothing?" In Jeffrey Frankel, Giampaolo Galli and Alberto Giovannini, eds., *The Microstructure of Foreign Exchange Markets.* Chicago: University of Chicago Press.

Madhavan, Ananth. 1992. "Trading Mechanisms in Securities Markets." *Journal of Finance* 47(2):607–612.

McKinnon, Ronald. 1976. "Floating Exchange Rates 1973–74: The Emperor's New Clothes." In K. Brunner and A. Meltzer, eds., *Journal of Monetary Economics* 3(2):79–114.

Meese, Richard and Kenneth Rogoff. 1983. "Empirical Exchange Rate Models of the Seventies." *Journal of International Economics* 14(1–2):3–24.

Mendez, Ruben. 1994. "Harnessing the Global Foreign Currency Market: Proposal for A Foreign Currency Exchange (FXE)." In Commission on Global Governace 1995. *Issues in Global Governance* (companion volume to the Commission's report, *Our Global Neighborhood*). London and The Hague: Kluwer Law International.

———. 1995a. "Harnessing the Global Currency Market for the Global Common Good." *Choices.* (March):16–17.

———. 1995b. "Paying for Peace and Development." *Foreign Policy* 100(September):19–31.

Mussa, Michael. 1990. "Exchange Rates in Theory and in Reality." Essays in International Finance 179. Department of Economics. Princeton University.

D'Orville, Hans and Dragoljub Najman. 1995. *Towards a New Multilateralism: Funding Global Priorities.* New York: United Nations.

Obstfeld, Maurice. 1994. "The Logic of Currency Crises." *Cahiers Economiques et Monétaires.* Paris: Banque de France. Abridged version in Barry Eichengreen, Jeffry Frieden and Jurgen von Hagen, eds. 1995. *Monetary and Fiscal Policy in an Integrated Europe.* New York and Heidelberg: Springer-Verlag Press.

Schwert, G. William and Paul Seguin. 1993. "Securities Transactions Taxes: An Overview of Costs, Benefits and Unresolved Questions." *Financial Analysts Journal* 46(September-October):27–35.

Shome, Parthasarathi and Janet Stotsky. 1995. "Financial Transactions Taxes." IMF Working Paper 95–77. Washington, D.C.

Summers, Lawrence. 1987. "A Few Good Taxes." *The New Republic.* November 30, pp.14–15.

Summers, Lawrence and Victoria Summers. 1990. "The Case for a Securities Transactions Excise Tax." *Tax Notes.* August 13, pp.879–84.

Taylor, Mark and Helen Allen. 1992. "The Use of Technical Analysis in the Foreign Exchange Market." *Journal of International Money and Finance* 11(3):304–14.

Tobin, James. 1978. "A Proposal for International Monetary Reform." *Eastern Economic Journal* 4 (July-October):153–59.

———. 1992. "Tax the Speculators." *Financial Times*. December 22.

Walker, Martin. 1993. "Paying for Peace." *International Economic Insights* (September-October):25–6.

Williamson, John. 1985. *The Exchange Rate System*. Policy Analyses in International Economics 5. Washington, D.C.: Institute for International Economics.

3

The Tobin Tax:
Good Theory, Weak Evidence,
Questionable Policy

Michael P. Dooley

The papers prepared for this volume focus on the important elements of the debate over transactions taxes for foreign exchange and international capital markets. The value added of this paper lies in its drawing out the implications for policy. The case for transactions taxes rests on a sequence of conditions being met, each of which is necessary to support government intervention in these markets. The evidence reviewed below suggests that the joint probability that these conditions are met is very low. It follows that an initiative to distort international capital markets with such taxes would be a bad policy choice.

The necessary conditions for a tax on all foreign exchange transactions or cross-border capital account transactions to be welfare-improving include:
- An existing distortion in international capital markets must be identified.
- The intervention must be effective in discouraging welfare-reducing private behaviour.
- The intervention must not discourage welfare-enhancing private behaviour.
- The intervention must not be avoided entirely.
- The intervention must not be used by governments to increase distortions in other markets.

My reading of the evidence suggests that none of these conditions is satisfied with a probability of more than 50%. Moreover, the odds favouring two or three of the links are much smaller than 50%. Since each of these conditions seems independent of the others, and since the tax must pass all tests to meet its objectives, the odds that a transactions tax will not be good public policy is at least 32:1. This "accounting" is of course arbitrary. Some observers would raise the odds on some conditions and lower the odds on others. Suppose, for example, that a generous interpretation of the evidence reduces the odds to 8:1. The policy choice still seems poor.

I argue below that the weakest link is the assumption that a tax on transactions will fall differentially on speculators who base their positions on price dynamics as compared to speculators who base their positions on fundamentals. In the context of foreign exchange markets, international economists have generally accepted the proposition that international transactions initiated by direct investors are based on fundamentals and have longer holding periods compared with other speculators. In contrast, "hot" portfolio investment is thought to be motivated by price dynamics and held for short time periods. The presumption that hot short-term capital flows are based on different behaviour than long-term and direct investment is the basis for the balance of payments reporting system for capital flows and has frequently been the basis for controls over short-term capital flows.

There is no way to directly measure subjective-time discount rates for various classes of investors. But it is possible to measure holding periods. Recent empirical work reported in Claessens, Dooley and Warner (1995) suggests that holding periods of direct investors and international holders of long-term capital (as defined in balance of payments statistics) are in fact not longer, more persistent or more predictable over time compared with investors in short-term capital. In particular, I argue below that direct investors are likely to be the first out of a country or a currency when market sentiment turns against the country for good or bad reasons.

The fact that types of capital flows do not have predictable holding periods may not be important for the effectiveness of transactions taxes. Some advocates of the tax would probably be comfortable with the possibility that the tax might fall disproportionately on direct investment or other types of capital flows often assumed to be welfare enhancing. Others, however, might view this possibility as an important objection to the tax. Our point is simply that a transactions tax designed to discourage short holding periods would have no predictable effect on the composition of capital flows.

The plan of the paper is as follows. In the next section we review the theoretical arguments that suggest that distortions exist and can be identified. The following section deals with the issue of whether or not a transactions tax is likely to limit undesirable capital flows or transactions. We will then explore the possibility that transactions taxes that discourage destabilizing speculation also discourage stabilizing speculation. The chapter will conclude with sections on the problem of enforcement and on the political economy of capital controls.

Market failures: Theory and evidence

That both savers and borrowers reap private benefits from access to international capital markets is a basic conclusion of welfare economics. Free movement allocates capital to its most productive uses across countries and allows residents of different countries to engage in welfare-improving intertemporal consumption smoothing. In a competitive model with perfect foresight and complete markets, the welfare benefit from intertemporal trade is identical to the welfare benefit from international trade in goods and services. This general conclusion is not sensitive to the exchange rate regime (Helpman 1981).

Although this general result imposes considerable discipline on the search for optimal limits on capital mobility, economic theory also suggests that exceptions to this general rule are possible in cases in which pre-existing distortions violate the assumptions necessary to support a "first-best" competitive equilibrium. The basic idea is quite simple. If the economy is assumed to suffer from one distortion, it is possible to improve welfare through the judicious introduction of another distortion.

Pathological speculation

Many of the disagreements about the desirability of capital flows can be traced to different assumptions concerning the efficiency of private intertemporal decisions. While most economists argue that markets work well in the static allocation of resources, there is a strong tradition of mistrusting "speculative" behaviour as being contrary to the collective interests of the community. This mistrust has led to proposals for throwing sand in the wheels of international capital movements.

Tobin (1978) proposed such a tax, and the arguments are updated in Summers and Summers (1989) and Eichengreen, Tobin and Wyplosz (1995). The basic idea is that adjustment in international goods and labour markets is slow and restricted and "when some markets adjust imperfectly, welfare can be enhanced by intervening in the adjustment of others" (Eichengreen, Tobin and Wyplosz 1995, p.164). An important aspect of the argument that distinguishes this intervention from other capital control programmes is that a turnover tax is designed to slow the adjustment speed of capital flows and the exchange rate, but not to distort the stock of net flows or the level of the exchange rate over the long run.

This class of models posits the existence of private investors who are motivated by rumours, noise trading, band wagons, bubbles and so forth. In a way, these are the most straightforward arguments in favour of transactions taxes—capital flows themselves are the source of the disturbance to the competitive equilibrium. It follows that controlling these kinds of capital flows restores a first-best competitive equilibrium. The difficulty, of course, is to discriminate in the capital control programme between stabilizing and destabilizing capital flows.

Van Wijnbergen (1985) draws out a more explicit link between variability of government policies and less-than-optimal domestic investment. Unnecessary variance causes underinvestment because investors will value the option of waiting until the uncertainty is resolved. Tornell (1990) develops a model in which the increased variance resulting from private capital transactions results in less-than-optimal real investment because investors value the option to wait for more settled times before making irreversible real investments in a country. Finally, Aizenman and Marion (1993) provide some evidence that uncertainty has a measurable negative effect on capital formation.

Pathological speculation: Empirical evidence

There is substantial evidence that foreign exchange markets do not behave as predicted by simple models of efficient markets. A large body of empirical work indicates that forward premiums are systematically biased and in fact "predict" changes in spot exchange rates that are in the opposite direction to those actually observed. Moreover, the bias seems to be economically meaningful in that simple trading rules that account for transaction costs and interest rate differentials have consistently yielded profits that appear to be quite large relative to the risks involved (Dooley and Shafer 1982). In addition, several characteristics of the distribution of exchange rate changes, for example the fact that rates seem to be more volatile when trading is open, suggest that "private information" has some influence on exchange rates. The private information may be about fundamentals or bubbles, but this evidence suggests that more than fundamentals may be at work (Ito, Lyons and Melvin, 1996).

Meese (1986) provides interesting data-based evidence rejecting the joint hypothesis that exchange rates are determined by a simple monetary model, and no bubbles. However, Flood, Mathieson and Rose (1991) suggest that the evidence for bubbles is quite weak.

There is little agreement concerning the likely source of these departures from the simple efficient markets model. Speculation based on observing and reacting to price data is an obvious possibility. But since a joint hypothesis is always tested, several other possibilities are equally likely. First, assets denominated in different currencies might not be perfect substitutes. Second, government intervention in foreign exchange markets might be the source of speculation, unrelated to fundamentals. Finally, because floating exchange rates are a relatively new and evolving regime, it is likely that the fundamentals are themselves evolving over time. This makes it difficult to identify an adequate model with the short time series available. The fundamentals typically included in econometric models explain none of the out-of-sample behaviour of exchange rates. Given such weak models of the economic determinants of exchange rates, it is very difficult to interpret deviations from these models as driven by speculation or by fundamental factors that are omitted or poorly measured.

Another bit of evidence in favour of the view that price dynamics dominate exchange rate determination can be found in surveys of traders' expectations of exchange rates. Frankel (1996) points out that surveys of investors' expectations suggest that short horizon forecasts are dominated by "technical models", which reflect the idea that speculators watch other speculators rather than fundamentals. This is an interesting direct test of the behaviour of some speculators, but it does not indicate that such behaviour dominates exchange rate determination.

Domestic credit market distortions

A distortion that has recently been emphasized as a rationale for capital controls in emerging financial markets arises from government insurance of the liabilities of domestic financial intermediaries. Dooley (1994, 1996) discusses the possible role of capital controls in offsetting government insurance. The most obvious example of a domestic credit market distortion is deposit insurance for banks. But even in the absence of formal insurance, governments frequently intervene to protect creditors of institutions that are believed to be too large to fail. The usual reason for such intervention is to prevent "contagion" of doubts about the solvency of large institutions from generating runs on solvent institutions and associated general declines in asset values.

The well-known problem with this policy is that it encourages financial institutions to reach for risk. The argument is simply that profits from favourable outcomes are paid out to owners of the institution, while losses are shared with the government. The usual prudential regulations designed to limit the government's exposure to loss include requirements that the institution maintain adequate capital—that is, that current accounting profits are not immediately paid to equity holders—and various restrictions on the nature and concentration of assets held.

There is nothing unique about international capital flows in this context, except that new types of assets, and therefore new types of risks, are opened to insured intermediaries when they are given access to international capital transactions. Mathieson and Rojas-Suarez (1993) argue that opening markets can generate important efficiency gains but that "potential official credit risks arising from the institutional failures that can be created by the mispricing of risk or widespread fraud provide a strong case for improving the domestic system of prudential supervision" (pp. 343–4). Dooley (1995a) argues that commercial banks in the United States acquired claims on individual developing countries in the 1970s that exceeded the concentration ratios that were enforced for domestic lending. The problem was that regulators did not enforce country lending limits, a decision that was justified by the erroneous view that loans to many entities within a country constituted a diversified portfolio. Kane (1995) argues that the unwillingness of authorities to force a write-down of debt following the 1982 debt crisis validated the assumption that the government would provide "free" equity to insured institutions in the event of a bad outcome for their investments. Finally, Dooley (1996) develops the argument that the combination of a strong guarantee of a fixed exchange rate and the domestic currency value of banks' liabilities will generate capital inflows roughly equal to the expected net worth of the government. Such inflows are clearly unrelated to fundamentals.

Corbo, de Melo and Tybout (1986) cite the stabilization in Chile as an example of a case in which a weak banking system generated inefficient capital inflows. Akerlof and Romer (1993) argue that exchange risk provides a vehicle for banks to exploit government insurance in developing countries. Using Chile during 1979–81 as a possible example, they argue that the expectation that the peso might be devalued led domestic firms and domestic banks to enter into dollar-denominated loans at interest rates that did not fully reflect the risk that the firms would be unable to repay the dollar liability in the event of a devaluation of the currency.

Domestic credit market distortions: Empirical evidence

Frankel and Rose (1996) present evidence that successful speculative attacks are less likely to occur in countries with a relatively high share of direct investment inflows. One interpretation of this evidence is that in countries where foreign investors bypass domestic financial markets, particularly banks, foreign savings are more likely to be transformed into productive capital. This tends to support the view that imperfections in domestic financial markets would justify measures that discourage portfolio capital flows. But it is equally possible that some other feature of direct investment, for example transfer of technology, accounts for these results.

Multiple equilibria

Not all arguments for government intervention in international capital markets are based on second-best considerations. A different exception to the general rule that government constraints on capital mobility are welfare-reducing arises in cases in which stable, multiple equilibria are predicted. The turmoil in the European exchange rate mechanism (ERM) that emerged in 1992 and the more recent breakdown of a fixed exchange rate regime in Mexico have generated a resurgence of interest in models of "self-fulfilling" speculative attacks. It has long been recognized that changes in the policy regime that are expected to prevail following a successful attack can generate a successful speculative attack even if the government follows policies preceding the attack that are consistent with no change in the regime. If multiple equilibria can possibly arise, it follows that the first-best equilibrium might be attained or maintained through government intervention in capital markets.

This is a much more recent contribution to the debate concerning transactions taxes. In reviewing these arguments, it is important to clarify the special circumstances under which such theoretical arguments are valid. A self-fulfilling attack is one in which the change in the exchange rate regime generates a "fundamental" change in the optimal path for policy. For example, if the private sector expects a more expansionary monetary policy following a successful attack, it is possible that such expectations could generate the collapse of a system that is otherwise fully viable. A stringent condition for such a model holds that the expected change in policy following a successful attack is optimal, given the change in the economic environment generated by the attack.

The lesson from these models is that the exchange rate regime is secondary to the monetary policy the government is expected to pursue, not just in the short run, but over the indefinite future. If the speculative attack is interpreted by the private sector as a signal that the government will also abandon monetary restraint in the future, then by the usual arguments, speculation in financial markets will result in capital movements today in anticipation of this, perhaps distant, event. It seems to follow that capital controls might significantly slow the onset of the attack. Moreover, an optimistic assessment of the potential role of capital controls might be that the conditions that generate the multiple equilibria will change. For example, the government might find a way to recommit to not altering its behaviour following an attack.

It is ironic that the first clear statement of these issues (in Flood and Garber 1984) was heavily conditioned by the warning that an announced commitment to a regime—in this model a commodity "standard" rather than an exchange rate "standard"—was unlikely to alter the private sector's expectations about monetary policy over the long run.

> Behind the sequential transitions from one monetary regime to another . . . must lie a political economy that we have ignored. Such political economic forces determine the complete dynamic panorama of the monetary process. . . A commodity system can be interpreted as a discipline imposing rule only if the commodity standard's permanence is somehow guaranteed. As there is no means to ensure such performance, the notion of a commodity standard as a stabilizing rule is a chimera. (p. 105)

Flood and Garber (1984) and Obstfeld (1986) show that if governments are assumed to follow more expansionary monetary policies following a successful speculative attack on the fixed exchange rate regime, policy regimes that are otherwise viable could collapse because of self-fulfilling private expectations. Obstfeld (1994) refines the argument by specifying the political economy that might account for the government's behaviour before and after an attack. The analysis sets out a rational government that seeks to maximize a plausible objective function. Since the government's objectives are the same in any exchange rate regime, it follows that policy setting under different regimes must reflect changes in the economic environment rather than arbitrary assumptions concerning the government's behaviour.

For example, one model developed by Obstfeld assumes that the government values price stability and the ability to offset negative output shocks. A sudden shift in expectations concerning the government's preferences for high levels of employment can trigger an attack on a regime that would be viable under different expectations. These models are interesting because the government's decision to abandon the peg is fully consistent with an objective function that is the same under both regimes. The only thing that changes over time is private expectations concerning the viability of the regime.

Eichengreen and Wyplosz (1993) argue that the benefits of membership in a European Economic Union made it rational for governments to pursue conservative monetary policies. An important condition for membership was the maintenance of a stable exchange rate for two years preceding membership. Thus a successful attack made membership in the first round impossible and perhaps implied that future membership would be more costly to attain. Once this opportunity was removed by a successful speculative attack on the currency, it was then rational for the authorities to relax monetary policy. Thus the speculative attack generated the subsequent government behaviour that validated the attack.

Multiple equilibria: Empirical evidence

Eichengreen, Rose, and Wyplosz (1995) offer empirical evidence that the fundamentals behaved differently in the months leading up to the ERM crisis compared with a sample of crises in other fixed exchange rate regimes. In particular, they argue that the ERM crisis was not preceded by excessive money growth, growth in domestic assets, fiscal deficits or a number of other variables usually associated with inconsistent policies.

A weakness in their interpretation of the evidence, which the authors acknowledge, is that a variety of factors might rationally lead to an expected change in the government's behaviour but leave no evidence leading up to the attack. In particular, they consider, but are not persuaded by, the possibility that rising unemployment associated with tight monetary policy in Germany might have generated expectations that monetary policy in other countries would be eased in the future as the political cost of unemployment accumulated.

Would transactions taxes reduce undesirable capital flows?

The idea that transactions taxes would prevent the emergence of destabilizing speculation, as defined by one of the three arguments presented in the previous section, is nicely summarized by Eichengreen, Tobin and Wyplosz (1995):

> The hope that transactions taxes will diminish excess volatility depends on the likelihood that Keynes's speculators have shorter time horizons and holding periods than market participants engaged in long-term foreign investment and otherwise oriented towards fundamentals. If so, it is speculators who are the more deterred by the tax (p. 165).

Once the speculators are taxed out of the foreign exchange business, fundamental traders will emerge as the dominant market force.

Transaction costs and pathological speculation

It is impossible to directly examine the effects of transaction costs on observed exchange rate variability. There is clear evidence that transaction costs, as measured by bid-ask spreads in foreign exchange, are positively related to the volatility of spot exchange rates. Moreover, adjusting for volatility, there has been no apparent trend in transaction costs for foreign exchange under floating rates (Glassman 1987). It would be foolish to argue that the increases in transaction costs caused the increase in volatility of exchange rates.

In other speculative markets, however, it is possible to evaluate the effects of independent changes in transaction costs. Roll (1989) studied equity markets in 32 countries from 1978–89 and found no relationship between volatility of prices and transaction costs. A reasonable interpretation of this evidence is that while transaction costs discourage short holding periods, it is not clear that short holding periods are associated with desirable (fundamental) or undesirable (speculative) investment objectives. Housing and land markets are characterized by high transaction costs but seem no less volatile than markets with low transaction costs.

In foreign exchange markets, the evidence from filter rules discussed above can be interpreted as evidence that private speculation is dominated by speculation based on price dynamics. But this does not imply that a transactions tax would discourage such speculation. The problem is that even though such trading rules are based on short horizon forecasts, profitable trading rules do not, in fact, call for frequent transactions. In general, noise traders following a filter rule hold their positions for fairly long time periods. It is not clear that higher transaction costs would tend to discourage these speculators compared with those betting on fundamentals.

The assumption that speculation, or investment, based on fundamentals is associated with long holding periods is also suspect. The image of direct investment as factories that are difficult to move from country to country or a long-term bond that is held to maturity seems to provide the intuition behind the association between motives and holding periods.

In fact, direct investors are not constrained by the nature of their assets in quickly responding to changes in market conditions. Since factories are clearly difficult to move and since returns to physical assets depend on economic and political conditions in the host country, direct investors can and do hedge this exposure. The most obvious hedge is borrowing from local credit markets. If a direct investor must exit a country quickly, she simply leaves the factory and the local bank loan behind. Moreover, because equity markets index trading and derivatives in these indices have developed, it is now possible in most emerging markets to hedge risks common to equity positions in that country without credit market transactions. Direct investors might take the academic literature as an insult to their intelligence in that they are assumed to passively accept the risks associated with exploiting the advantages of production in different countries. Direct investment may be special for many reasons—an example is technology transfer—but direct investors are not passive investors that ignore the market and focus on long-run fundamentals. To the contrary, they are often the better informed and more enthusiastic participants in capital markets.

Claessens, Dooley and Warner (1995) examine the volatility of different types of capital flows for a sample of industrial and developing countries. Their interpretation of the data is that the labels assigned to various types of capital flows are of no value in predicting their time series behaviour. Direct investment is no more persistent over time than is short-term capital. Perhaps more important, knowledge of the composition of capital flows is useless in predicting the time series behaviour of net capital flows.

Experimental data reported by King and others (1990) are interpreted by the authors as showing that transaction costs had no effect on the likelihood that bubbles would be generated in experimental settings in which such bubbles were common.

Transactions taxes and multiple equilibria

The role of capital controls in preventing self-fulfilling speculative attacks is also far from obvious. It is possible that effective transactions taxes would prevent the demise of a "good" regime that suffered a spontaneous change in private expectations. An extended life for the good equilibrium, made possible in this case by taxes on capital flows, would presumably be desirable. This assumption is reinforced if it is assumed that the ultimate destination for the regime is a credible common currency, since the control programme would then be temporary.

Nevertheless, the contrary argument is equally plausible. If the private sector knows that the system is protected by controls, they would be less impressed by observed stability. Lane and Rojas-Suarez (1992), for example, argue that the use of controls has ambiguous implications for credibility of a monetary policy regime.

The role of capital controls is also problematic, because self-fulfilling attacks can go in the opposite direction. For example, a spontaneous decline in private inflationary expectations could set in motion a sequence of falling interest rates and fiscal deficits that generate a good equilibrium. It is informative that there seem to be few examples of changes in private expectations generating self-fulfilling virtuous responses by governments. Countries that start from a bad equilibrium should shun capital controls, because they would delay adjustment to the new, more optimistic private expectations.

A number of papers have exploited the idea that controls themselves might be powerful signals of a government's future policies. Dellas and Stockman (1993) show that a speculative attack might be generated by the expectation that capital controls will be introduced. If the government can commit to not introduce controls, the fixed rate regime is sustainable. In this model, a regime that is otherwise viable becomes vulnerable to expectations that controls will be imposed in response to the attack. This increases interest rates before the attack and generates the conditions for a self-fulfilling devaluation.

Labán and Larraín (1993) argue that removing controls on capital outflows generates capital inflows because controls on outflows make investment irreversible. Thus by altering expectations concerning the terms on which investments can be reversed, the decontrol of capital flows helps to generate welfare-increasing capital inflows.

Bartolini and Drazen (1994) develop the idea that controls themselves are a signal that affects private sector expectations of the government's future treatment of investors. In their model, the removal of controls signals to investors that the government is less likely to tax foreign capital income or reimpose controls once the capital inflow is in place.

Finally, Obstfeld (1986) shows that with capital mobility capital controls can generate multiple equilibria where none exist. In this model, multiple equilibria are a feature of a maximizing model with effective capital controls. Residents of the controlled economy maximize the utility of real money holdings and consumption over time subject to their balance sheet constraint. Owing to effective capital controls, residents can accumulate real money balances only through current account surpluses, which have as a mirror image increases in the central bank's net foreign assets. Because the net foreign asset position of the central bank earns the world interest rate, a current account surplus generates an increase in the expected permanent income of residents. An unstable equilibrium occurs if the increase in real money balances and the associated increase in expected income are not more than matched by an increase in current consumption. If not, the current account surplus increases, and money balances and income continue to rise until a stable equilibrium is reached. This is not an argument for or against capital controls. It only demonstrates that when the domestic interest rate is distorted through a capital control programme, the usual assumptions that generate convergence to a unique steady-state equilibrium are not sufficient.

This literature presents a genuine problem for the policy implications of capital controls. On the one hand, an effective capital control programme might buy enough time for the government to move the fundamentals to a region where self-fulfilling speculative attacks are less likely. The implication seems to be that controls might be a temporary measure to buy time for a virtuous government to establish its reputation. On the other hand, it is easy to show that the fact that controls might be introduced in the future can generate attacks where none would be observed otherwise.

Would a transactions tax suppress stabilizing speculation?

Would a transactions tax that discourages destabilizing speculation generate benefits that outweigh the costs? Proponents of the tax generally agree that transactions for trade in goods and services and stabilizing capital flows would also have to be taxed, thereby reducing the value of temporal and intertemporal international trade.

Comparisons of costs and benefits are difficult, but a recent paper by Kupiec (1995) makes a point that is very damaging to the case for transactions taxes. His argument is that even in a model in which the presence of destabilizing noise trading is assumed, the general equilibrium welfare effects of a transactions tax are likely to be negative. The model first shows that noise trading generates a more volatile path for market prices of a security traded between generations in order to smooth consumption. A transactions tax clearly reduces this volatility, bringing prices closer to the optimal path. But the model also takes into account the fact that the transactions tax necessarily reduces the market price of the assets by the present value of expected transactions taxes. For a range of plausible tax rates, the model suggests that the reduction in price volatility is dominated by a reduction in the price of the traded asset, so that the volatility of holding-period yields is increased by the transactions tax. In almost any utility framework, volatility of returns is a better measure of welfare effects compared with price volatility.

The problem with less formal commentary on the costs of transactions taxes is that the small size of proposed taxes is thought to make the welfare costs small. But the present value of a string of expected future taxes is not small, and small taxes also generate small reductions in volatility. This result is model dependent. But it springs from a framework that appears to be consistent with the pattern of distortions that proponents of the transactions tax have in mind.

Could a transactions tax be enforced?

Proponents of a transactions tax agree that such a tax would have to be universal. One very large computer on one small island could clear most of the foreign exchange transactions currently undertaken. What is perhaps less obvious is that a tax high enough to discourage speculation would also provide a very large incentive for tax competition. Moreover, there are enough potential entrants to make continuous bribes or threats to discourage entry into the tax haven business impractical. Existing centres for foreign exchange trading— New York and London come to mind—are unlikely to be enthusiastic about such a tax.

A tax on all transactions involving foreign exchange

Much more problematic is the fact that speculators need not buy or sell spot foreign exchange in order to take a speculative position in a currency. If there are noise traders out there, they probably are unfamiliar with spot positions. If derivative positions are not taxed, and it is worth recalling that forward exchange and swap transactions were common derivative positions before we knew they were derivatives, there will be very little tax collected—and that collected would be from tourists and traders in goods and services. But if derivatives are taxed, we will need a very large police force to keep up with the new institutions and forms of such transactions. Garber and Taylor (1995) discuss examples of the inventiveness of derivative traders.

The only effective rule would be that any financial contract that alters the economic exposure of the transactor to exchange rates is taxed according to the spot exchange equivalent of that transaction. Right away there will be an argument about what this cash equivalent is. Suppose I offer a "runway" contract that pays off as long as the spot rate stays within a stated interval but is worthless if the spot rate moves outside that interval. There are a set of equivalent spot transactions, but it would be very difficult to design a tax that did not move all transactions from the spot market to the derivative market or the reverse.

It is clear that the existing pattern of foreign exchange and derivative trading would be dramatically altered by a transactions tax, but it is probably impossible to predict how the equilibrium will be affected. The interbank market, which now accounts for much of the volume, would probably be much reduced. And this alone would call into question the effect of the tax on efficient trades that spread risk among market participants.

Perhaps more important, effective tax regimes are, for the most part, self-enforcing. The private sector must believe at some level that the tax is fair and necessary. My guess is that the financial sector would consider efforts to avoid a transactions tax as little short of their moral and patriotic duty. Advocates of the tax sometimes argue that a few heavy fines will ensure compliance but neglect the problem that enforcement depends on widespread acceptance of the tax's fairness and necessity.

A tax on residents of one country

Traditional capital controls on transactions that involve residents of one country might be sufficient to limit multiple equilibria or to discourage private capital inflows to emerging markets. Dornbusch (1996) argues that a transactions tax on net or gross cross-border capital flows would not share the apparently fatal requirement that it be universal. In fact, such a tax is equivalent to a large number of capital controls currently in place in both industrial and developing countries. Experience suggests that such taxes can be effective if the incentives for avoidance are limited.

Empirical work on the "effectiveness" of capital controls has suffered from the lack of a widely accepted definition of what constitutes an effective control programme. At one end of the spectrum, evidence of effectiveness has been defined as the ability to detect over extended time periods different average behaviour of selected economic variables for countries with and without capital control programmes. At the other end, effectiveness has been defined as the ability to maintain an inconsistent macroeconomic policy regime forever.

For this reason, observers have examined the same or similar data sets and reached very different qualitative conclusions concerning the effectiveness of controls. Those who see controls as a short-term device to allow the government time to react and adjust other policy tools generally argue that controls can be effective. Those who study the collapse of regimes and observe that these events are often preceded by the imposition of controls argue that controls are not effective.

The reading here of the extensive empirical literature for industrial and developing countries is that it generally supports the conclusion that governments can drive a small wedge between domestic and international yields on similar short-term financial instruments for extended time periods. This conclusion is similar to those of recent surveys by Epstein and Schor (1992) and Obstfeld (1995). Thus capital control programmes have had measurable effects on economic variables. Control programmes have also generated large yield differentials for a few weeks or months, but these seem to diminish over time as the private sector invests in techniques to avoid the controls.

Perhaps the most direct evidence for the effects of a control programme in the very limited sense described above is the spread between the commercial and financial spot exchange rates in dual exchange rate systems. Gros (1988) reports the spread for the Belgian franc over 1979–87 and the Mexican peso during 1982–86. His interpretation of both these data sets is that the authorities were able to sustain a sizable differential for about one year before the private sector found ways to avoid the controls.

Cairncross (1973) provides data for the UK investment currency market in 1961–72. These data indicate that the control system was effective in that the investment currency premium remained in excess of 20% for several years and at times reached nearly 50%. Nevertheless, Cairncross finds little evidence that the intended restriction on private capital outflows was effective.

For currencies with extensive offshore markets for bank deposits, another simple and informative test of the effects of controls is a comparison of returns on domestic bank deposits and similar deposits offered by offshore branches of the same or similar banks. An early attempt to measure the effectiveness of controls using this data is reported in Dooley and Isard (1980). This paper presents a model in which onshore and offshore interest rates on bank deposits denominated in the same currency are related to the extensive capital control programme introduced by the German government over 1970–74 and to the risk that such controls might be intensified. A problem for tests of the effectiveness of control programmes is that they are complicated legal programmes that are difficult to quantify. In this paper, the controls are quantified according to a qualitative evaluation of the size of penalties or taxes on individual types of transactions, as well as the extensiveness of the controls in terms of the types of transactions subject to control. The data suggest that the authorities managed to generate a four percentage point differential for a brief time, during which virtually all private capital inflows were prohibited.

In this respect, the controls had clearly measurable effects. Nevertheless, a speculative attack on the currency generated a very large— by 1970s standards—increase in Germany's international reserves, and the fixed exchange rate was abandoned. As the models reviewed above suggest, the control programme does appear to have slowed down the demise of the system but could not preserve the par value system.

Gros (1987) reports spreads between Euro- and domestic deposits for Italy and France from 1979–86. He interprets these differentials, that were for short time periods as high as 20–24 percentage points, as consistent with his model that predicts that controls are temporarily effective in restraining large changes in investors' positions. That is, during times of turbulence in the ERM, private speculators were not able to adjust their open positions costlessly. Nevertheless, over longer horizons, the interest differentials rapidly returned to very low levels.

Similar evidence for five industrial countries from 1982–92 is reported in Obstfeld (1994). He concludes that for industrial countries, the links between onshore and offshore markets are very close but that "the data also show that actual or prospective government interventions remain a significant factor in times of turbulence" (p. 217). These data decisively reject the view that capital controls are always ineffective. But they also suggest that either the governments involved quickly removed the incentives for speculation, through policy changes, or that speculators simply retreated to await another attack.

Browne and McNelis (1990) provide a careful study of the imposition of controls over capital flows in Ireland from 1979–86. Forward exchange rates are available in this data set, and the study is unusual in that it considers a number of domestic and international interest rates. The relative importance of domestic monetary conditions and the yield on similar UK instruments are compared before and after the imposition of controls in December 1978.

Their results suggest that there was a jump in the importance of domestic monetary factors in determining some interest rates in Ireland immediately after controls were imposed. However, as with the other studies, the effects of monetary conditions were short-lived—on average only about six months. The usual story emerges—the central bank gained some independence for a short time.

The evidence also suggests that interest rates in domestic financial markets that are poorly integrated with other domestic markets are much more sensitive to domestic money shocks than are bank deposit markets. For example, Browne and McNelis (1990) find that changes in domestic monetary conditions had no impact on yields on bank deposits. Yet, they find significant influence for domestic conditions on rates of return in relatively non-competitive domestic loan and mortgage markets.

Fieleke (1994) compares short-term Euro interest rates to similar domestic interest rates for Spain, Ireland and Portugal during the 1992 ERM crisis. In each case, the authorities enforced controls on capital outflows as part of a defence of the exchange rate arrangement. Although the controls did result in measurable deviations between onshore and offshore interest rates, in the end, they did not prevent a change in the exchange rate.

Fieleke also points out that the ERM members that did not use controls, Norway and Sweden, experienced much larger fluctuations in domestic interest rates in trying to maintain their exchange rate targets. He concludes that, "It may be that Spain and Portugal did acquire some temporary insulation" (p. 34).

Eichengreen, Rose and Wyplosz (1995) challenge this interpretation of the ERM experience. They make the point that focusing on actual devaluations biases the sample towards episodes in which capital control programmes have failed. To overcome this, they examine the behaviour of a number of economic variables during crisis and non-crisis periods to see if there are systematic differences in the experience of countries with controls compared with countries without controls. This, they argue, is a more useful measure of the effectiveness of controls. During crisis periods, countries with controls experienced higher inflation, higher rates of money growth and higher growth of domestic assets. Controls did not seem to affect the loss of reserves, interest rate differentials or fiscal imbalances. During non-crisis periods, controls affected all the macroeconomic variables tested except reserves.

Their conclusion is consistent with the literature surveyed above.

Controls do not allow countries which pursue policies inconsistent with a peg to keep their exchange rate unchanged forever. They do not prevent attacks, nor do they permit countries to avoid reserve losses or interest rate increases when attacks occur. Controls merely render expansionary monetary policies viable for a longer period by attenuating the link between crises and exchange rate regime collapse (p. 8).

Would governments remain virtuous after the tax is in place?

The literature has generally not focused on the question of whether or not observed capital control programmes actually mitigate the effects of well-defined distortions. Recent empirical work has attempted to relate countries' use of capital market restrictions to a variety of structural characteristics of the economy. This literature views policy regimes as endogenous responses to institutional and political features of the economy. Alesina, Grilli and Milesi-Ferretti (1994) test the relevance of a number of rationalizations for the use of capital controls outlined above by looking for common characteristics of OECD countries. Their reading of the theoretical literature suggests that the use of controls should be related to the exchange rate regime, to the desire to tax capital income and to the desire to tax money balances. They find that highly managed exchange rate regimes seem to be associated with the use of controls.

Preferences for taxing capital income and money balances are, in turn, related to a variety of attributes of the political system. For example, inflation might result from weak governments that cannot enforce other types of taxes or strong governments that decide to tax capital income. Governments with independent central banks might resist both inflation and controls designed to preserve the inflationary tax base. Their findings suggest that countries with strong governments and dependent central banks are likely to use controls, presumably to generate revenue from inflation and to reduce real debt service.

They also test the impact of controls on other macroeconomic variables. Controlling for political stability, they find that controls have a negative effect on the stock of government debt. This is consistent with models discussed above that suggest that revenue from inflation is enhanced by controls and that domestic real interest rates kept below the world rate might limit debt service costs. The structure of the economy also seems to be an important determinant of the use of controls. The data also suggest that, controlling for initial income levels and political stability, controls do not seem to influence growth rates.

Grilli and Milesi-Ferretti (1995) find similar results for a sample of 61 developing and industrial countries. In particular, over an extended time period, countries with controls seem to experience high rates of inflation, relatively high shares of government revenue from seignorage and relatively low real interest rates. These recent results suggest that fiscal considerations are the most important determinants of the use of capital controls and that the controls, or some factor highly correlated with the use of controls, have measurable effects on government revenues.

It is interesting to speculate about how governments would use this new form of taxation. If existing capital controls are used to protect revenues that arise from financial repression, why would an international application of the same tax be used differently? Proponents of such taxes assume that the proceeds would be devoted to international good works. This begs the question of why more traditional taxes are not now employed in these pursuits. It seems extraordinarily unlikely that the governments would find it optimal to devote all the proceeds of a new revenue to a single policy objective, especially one chosen by an international organization.

Before we arm governments with another distortion and charge them to "go forth and do good", we should carefully examine the historical record of what governments have actually gone forth and done. The record is not encouraging.

References

Aizenman, Joshua and Nancy P. Marion. 1993. "Macroeconomic Uncertainty and Private Investment." *Economic Letters* 41(2): 207–10.

Akerlof, George A. and Paul M. Romer. 1993. "Looting: The Economic Underworld of Bankruptcy for Profit." *Brookings Papers on Economic Activity* 2:1–60; 70–74.

Alesina, Alberto, Vittorio Grilli and Gian Maria Milesi-Ferretti. 1994. "The Political Economy of Capital Controls." In Leonardo Leiderman and Assaf Razin, eds., *Capital Mobility: The Impact on Consumption, Investment, and Growth*. Cambridge, U.K./New York: Cambridge University Press.

Bartolini, Leonardo and Allan Drazen. 1994. "Capital Account Liberalization as a Signal." IMF Working Paper 9. Washington, D.C.

Browne, Francis X. and Paul D. McNelis. 1990. "Exchange Controls and Interest Rate Determination with Traded and Non-Traded Assets: The Irish-United Kingdom Experience." *Journal of International Money and Finance* 9(1):41–59.

Cairncross, Alec. 1973. *Control of Long-Term International Capital Movements*. Washington, D.C.: The Brookings Institution.

Claessens, Stijn, Michael Dooley and Andrew Warner. 1995. "Portfolio Capital Flows: Hot or Cool?" *World Bank Economic Review* 9(1):153–74.

Corbo, Vittorio, Jaime de Melo and James Tybout. 1986. "What Went Wrong with Recent Reforms in the Southern Cone?" *Economic Development and Cultural Change* 34(April):607–40.

Dellas, Harris and Allan Stockman. 1993. "Self-Fulfilling Expectations, Speculative Attack, and Capital Controls." *Journal of Money, Credit and Banking* 25(4):721–30.

Dooley, Michael P. 1994. "Are Recent Capital Inflows to Developing Countries a Vote For or Against Economic Policy Reforms?" Working Paper 295. Department of Economics. University of California, Santa Cruz.

———. 1995a. "A Survey of Academic Literature on Controls Over International Capital Transactions." NBER Working Paper 5352. Cambridge, Mass.

———. 1995b. "A Retrospective on the Debt Crisis." In Peter Kenen, ed., *Understanding Interdependence: The Macroeconomics of the Open Economy*. Princeton: Princeton University Press.

———. Forthcoming. "Capital Controls and Emerging Markets." *Journal of International Finance and Economics*.

Dooley, Michael P. and Peter Isard. 1980. "Capital Controls, Political Risk, and Deviations from Interest-Rate Parity." *Journal of Political Economy*. 88(2):370–84.

Dooley, Michael P. and Jeffrey R. Shafer. 1982. "Analysis of Short-Run Exchange Rate Behavior: March 1973 to November 1981." In David Bigman and Teizo Taya, eds., *Exchange Rate and Trade Instability: Causes and Consequences.* Ballinger.

Dornbusch, Rudiger. 1996. "Crossborder Payments Taxes and Alternative Capital Account Regimes." Department of Economics. Massachusetts Institute of Technology. Processed.

Eichengreen, Barry, Andrew K. Rose and Charles Wyplosz. 1995. "Speculative Attacks on Pegged Exchange Rates: An Empirical Exploration with Special Reference to the European Monetary System." In Matthew Canzoneri, Paul Masson and Vittorio Grilli, eds., *Transatlantic Economic Issues.* Cambridge, U.K.: Cambridge University Press.

Eichengreen, Barry, James Tobin and Charles Wyplosz. 1995. "Two Cases for Sand in the Wheels of International Finance." *Economic Journal* 105 (January):162–72.

Eichengreen, Barry and Charles Wyplosz. 1993. "The Unstable EMS." *Brookings Papers on Economic Activity* 1:51–143.

Epstein, Gerald A. and Juliet B. Schor. 1992. "Structural Determinants and Economic Effects of Capital Controls in OECD Countries." In Tariq Banuri and Juliet Schor, eds., *Financial Openness and National Autonomy: Opportunities Constraints.* Oxford: Clarendon Press.

Fieleke, Norman S. 1994. "International Capital Transactions: Should They Be Restricted?" *New England Economic Review* (March/April):27–39.

Flood, Robert P., and Peter M. Garber. 1984. "Gold Monetization and Gold Discipline." *Journal of Political Economy* 92(1):90–107.

Flood, Robert P., Donald Mathieson and Andrew K. Rose. 1991. "An Empirical Exploration of Exchange-Rate Target Zones." *Carnegie-Rochester Conference Series on Public Policy* 35 (Autumn):7–65.

Frankel, Jeffrey A. 1996. "How Well Do Foreign Exchange Markets Function? Might a Tobin Tax Help?" This volume.

Frankel, Jeffrey A. and Andrew Rose. 1996. "Currency Crashes in Emerging Markets: An Empirical Treatment." Board of Governors of the Federal Reserve System, IFDP 534. Washington, D.C.

Garber, Peter M. and Mark P. Taylor. 1995. "Sand in the Wheels of Foreign Exchange Markets: A Skeptical Note." *Economic Journal* 105 (January):173–80.

Glassman, Debra. 1987. "Exchange Rate Risk and Transactions Costs: Evidence from Bid-Ask Spreads." *Journal of International Money and Finance* 6(4):479–90.

Grilli, Vittorio and Gian Maria Milesi-Ferretti. 1995. "Economic Effects and Structural Determinants of Capital Controls." IMF Working Paper 95–31. Washington, D.C.

Gros, Daniel. 1987. "The Effectiveness of Capital Controls: Implications for Monetary Autonomy in the Presence of Incomplete Market Separation." *IMF Staff Papers* 34(4): 621–42.

———. 1988. "Dual Exchange Rates in the Presence of Incomplete Market Separation: Long-Run Effectiveness and Policy Implications." *IMF Staff Papers* 35(3):437–60.

Helpman, Elhanan. 1981. "An Exploration in the Theory of Exchange Rate Regimes." *Journal of Political Economy* 89(5):865–90.

Ito, Takatoshi, Richard K. Lyons and Michael T. Melvin. 1996. "Is There Private Information in the FX Market? The Tokyo Experiment." Mimeo. January.

Kane, Edward J. 1995. *The Gathering Crisis in Federal Deposit Insurance.* Cambridge, Mass.: MIT Press.

King, Ronald R., Vernon L. Smith, Arlington W. Williams and Mark Van Boening. 1992. "The Robustness of Bubbles and Crashes in Experimental Stock Markets." In Ilya Prigogine, Richard Day and Ping Chen, eds., *Nonlinear Dynamics and Evolutionary Economics.* Oxford: Oxford University Press.

Kupiec, Paul H. 1995. "Noise Traders, Excess Volatility, and a Securities Transaction Tax." Board of Governors of the Federal Reserve System, Finance and Economics Discussion Series 95–26. Washington, D.C.

Labán, Raul and Felipe Larraín. 1993. "Can a Liberalization of Capital Outflows Increase Net Capital Inflows?" Working Paper 155. Instituto de Economia, Pontificia Universidad Católica de Chile.

Lane, Timothy and Liliana Rojas-Suarez. 1992. "Credibility, Capital Controls, and the EMS." *Journal of International Economics* 32(May):321–37.

Mathieson, Donald J. and Liliana Rojas-Suarez. 1993. "Liberalization of the Capital Account, Experiences and Issues." IMF Occasional Paper 103. Washington, D.C.

Meese, Richard. 1986. "Testing for Bubbles in Exchange Markets: A Case of Sparkling Rates?" *Journal of Political Economy* 94(April):345–72.

Obstfeld, Maurice. 1986. "Rational and Self-Fulfilling Balance-of-Payments Crises." *American Economic Review* 6(1):72–81.

———. 1994. "The Logic of Currency Crises." NBER Working Paper 4640. Cambridge, Mass.

———. 1995. "International Capital Mobility in the 1990s." In Peter Kenen, ed., *Understanding Interdependence: The Macroeconomics of the Open Economy.* Princeton: Princeton University Press.

Roll, Richard. 1989. "Price Volatility, International Market Links, and Their Implications for Regulatory Policies." *Journal of Financial Services Research* 3(2–3):211–46.

Summers, Lawrence and Victoria P. Summers. 1989, "When Financial Markets Work Too Well: A Cautious Case for a Securities Transactions Tax." *Journal of Financial Services Research* 3(2–3):163–88.

Tobin, James. 1978. "A Proposal for International Monetary Reform." *Eastern Economic Journal* 4(July-October):153–9.

Tornell, Aaron.1990. "Real vs. Financial Investment, Can Tobin Taxes Eliminate the Irreversibility Distortion?" *Journal of Development Economics* 32(2):419–44.

van Wijnbergen, Sweder. 1985. "Trade Reform, Aggregate Investment and Capital Flight." *Economic Letters* 19(4):369–72.

Technical Feasibility
and Implementation

4

The Feasibility of Taxing
Foreign Exchange Transactions

Peter B. Kenen

This chapter focuses on the feasibility of imposing a tax on foreign exchange transactions. It is not concerned with the effects of the tax on exchange rate volatility or with the tax's revenue-raising potential, although the problems that it concentrates on relate to the revenue-raising issue. The feasibility of such a tax cannot be assessed without asking whether the tax can be evaded or avoided, which is another way of asking what will happen to the tax base.

Rather than explore these issues abstractly, the chapter will outline and discuss a specific plan. The plan seeks to minimize tax evasion by requiring banks and other dealers in the foreign exchange market to pay an ad valorem tax on all of their transactions—transactions with other banks and dealers, other financial institutions and commercial customers. There are two types of tax avoidance that the plan will address: the substitution of tax-free for taxable transactions and the migration of transactions to tax-free jurisdictions. It counters the risk of substitution by applying the tax to swap, forward and futures contracts, as well as to spot transactions. (Options pose special problems, which are discussed below.) And it counters the risk of migration by

This chapter reflects extensive discussions with market participants and experts at official institutions, as well as the comments of colleagues. But these individuals bear no responsibility for the views expressed, nor does UNDP.

applying the tax at a penalty rate to transactions with banks and other parties residing in tax-free jurisdictions.

The paper will argue, however, that these arrangements cannot be perfectly effective and that their effectiveness could wear off gradually. The viability of such a tax can be preserved only by keeping the tax rate low to discourage substitution and migration. Hence, the tax rate used in this paper is 5 basis points (that is, 0.05%), a rate lower than that used in most other papers. Still, such a low tax applied in the manner described below could have raised as much as $100 billion in 1992.[1]

The chapter begins by reviewing certain key characteristics of the foreign exchange market. It then develops the tax plan by focusing first on spot transactions. Subsequent sections study the risks of substitution and migration. There is then a brief digression on the issue of tax incidence, which argues that much of the tax burden may be borne by banks' customers, because they will confront an increase in spreads. Finally, the chapter asks how a tax on foreign exchange transactions might be administered internationally.

Describing the foreign exchange market

The foreign exchange market has two parts, a "wholesale" market and a "retail" market. In the wholesale market, often called the interbank market, dealers quote prices (exchange rates) for various currencies and stand ready to strike deals at those prices. Most of the dealers are banks, but not all banks are dealers.[2] Spreads in the wholesale market are well below 10 basis points for the major currencies—which says that the tax rate proposed in this paper is not all that small.[3] In the retail market, banks and other dealers meet their customers' needs; their customers include other financial institutions, such as pension and mutual funds, and non-financial firms engaged in foreign trade and investment.

Both markets engage in spot transactions, which are settled in fewer than three days; in outright forward transactions, which are settled in three or more days; and in swap transactions, which pair a spot transaction with an offsetting forward transaction (or pair two forward contracts with different maturities), both transactions being made with the same counter-party.

There are also active markets for foreign exchange futures and options, although they are smaller than spot and forward markets (and smaller than futures and options markets for other financial instruments).[4] Unlike spot and forward contracts, however, futures and options are not typically settled by actually delivering the currencies involved. A futures contract to deliver yen for dollars will normally be settled in a single currency, with one party paying the other the difference between the exchange rate implicit in the contract and the rate prevailing when the settlement is made.[5]

Surveys compiled by the Bank for International Settlements (BIS) cover the volume of trading in spot, forward and other foreign exchange contracts in 26 countries. They show that spot and swap transactions dominate and that the volume of transactions between dealers is much larger than the volume of transactions between dealers and others, except for outright forwards (table 4.1). Another such survey was conducted in the spring of 1995, but comprehensive results were not available when this paper was written. They may show significant changes in the relative sizes of national markets and in the importance of various instruments.

A transaction in the wholesale market involves three distinct steps, which may occur in different locations:

- A deal is struck between two dealers. Each dealer then regards the other as its legal counter-party. The two dealers may be located in the same market (such as in London) or in different markets (such as in London and Tokyo). Those locations are described hereafter

Table 4.1 Average daily turnover in foreign exchange markets, April 1992
(billions of US dollars, net of local and cross-border double counting)

Category	Total
Spot	393.7
With other dealers	282.0
With other financial institutions	47.4
With customers	62.0
Outright forward	58.5
With other dealers	20.6
With other financial institutions	10.0
With customers	27.9
Swap	324.3
With other dealers	237.6
With other financial institutions	39.2
With customers	47.0
Futures	9.5
Options	37.6
Exchange-traded	5.3
Over-the-counter	31.0
Total	832.0

Note: Detail may not sum to total because some respondents did not provide the necessary data.
Source: BIS (1993, tables V and 1-A). These figures have been slightly readjusted in later estimates.

as *dealing sites*. Each dealer will, of course, record the quantities of currencies to be exchanged, the place at which each dealer will book the deal and the manner in which the deal will be settled.[6]

- Each dealer will then book the deal at an office of his or her bank. These *booking sites* need not be the same as the dealing sites; a bank may prefer to book all of its transactions at its head office in order to keep close track of its global exposure in each currency.
- When a transaction is due to be settled, bank balances are transferred between the parties. When a New York bank trades dollars for yen with another New York bank, the dollars are transferred between the banks on the books of the New York Federal Reserve Bank, and the yen are transferred between the two banks' correspondent accounts at Japanese banks in Tokyo.[7] (If they keep those accounts at different banks in Tokyo, the settlement between the Japanese banks will involve a transfer on the books of the Bank of Japan.) It should be noted that a foreign exchange transaction typically involves two settlement sites, because it involves two currencies.

Although foreign exchange transactions are typically settled in the manner just described, a tax on foreign exchange transactions could not be levied at the settlement sites.[8] Too many transactions are netted before they are settled—a process known as novation—and there will be additional netting later unless the relevant payment systems use gross real-time settlements. Furthermore, it is not presently possible to segregate the subset of interbank transfers that arise from foreign exchange trading. When a US bank buys Japanese securities from another US bank for itself or for a customer and pays with yen, the transfers on the books of Japanese banks are just like those resulting from a foreign exchange transaction.

For different reasons, transactions should be taxed at dealing sites rather than at booking sites. If a tax were levied at a booking site, banks could avoid the tax merely by putting computers in tax-free jurisdictions and using them to book all of their transactions; they would not have to move their dealing rooms and dealers.[9]

How transactions might be taxed

Under the plan outlined in this section, all banks and all other foreign exchange dealers would pay a tax on all of their foreign exchange transactions—those with other banks and dealers (described simply as "banks" below) and those with their customers. The tax would be assessed at the dealing site, using the paper trail generated at that site. Banks that do not keep such records at their dealing sites but forward them directly to their booking sites, would have to duplicate them at their dealing sites and be ready to produce them for regular audits. Governments collecting the transactions tax would keep part of the tax revenue for domestic use and make the rest available for international use.

There are, however, two ways to collect the tax—on a national basis or on a market basis. In the first case, the head office of each bank would collect and consolidate the necessary data on all of the bank's transactions—those conducted at every dealing site—and pay the corresponding tax to the bank's home country, which is the country where the bank has its headquarters. In the second case, the tax due on transactions at each dealing site would be paid to the host country, which is the country where the dealing site is located.

If the tax were levied on a national basis, banks could not avoid it by moving their dealing sites to tax-free locations—to countries whose governments did not collect the tax. That is the main advantage of the national approach. But there are four disadvantages. First, the national approach would impose an extra burden on the banks themselves: the need to consolidate the necessary data.[10] Second, a government that wanted to provide a tax-free dealing site could adopt or invoke legislation to confer confidentiality on individual foreign exchange transactions. The local offices of foreign banks might then be prevented from sending data to their head offices. Third, the national approach would tilt the playing field in favour of banks whose home countries refused to impose the tax. Those banks would enjoy a competitive advantage in all foreign exchange markets, not only in their own home markets. Finally, the national approach might be disadvantageous to a country such as the United Kingdom, which has the largest foreign exchange market (table 4.2). Total transactions by foreign banks in London appear to be larger than total transactions by British banks at all other dealing sites. Hence, Britain would collect less tax revenue under the national approach than under the market approach, and it might refuse to impose any tax if the national approach were adopted. If Britain refused to cooperate, moreover, much tax revenue would be lost to the world—the global transactions of British banks are very large, even though they are smaller than those of foreign banks in London. If Britain refused to cooperate, moreover, the previous objection would

Table 4.2 Average daily turnover in the fifteen largest foreign exchange markets, April 1992
(billions of US dollars, net of local double counting)

Market	Total	In own currency
United Kingdom	300.2	71.8
United States	192.5	170.7
Japan	126.1	93.2
Singapore	75.9	2.4
Switzerland	68.1	31.6
Hong Kong	60.9	8.8
Germany	56.5	47.1
France	35.5	17.4
Australia	29.8	12.4
Denmark	27.6	4.5
Canada	22.5	14.7
Sweden	21.5	10.9
Netherlands	20.1	9.5
Belgium	15.9	4.0
Italy	15.5	12.9

Note: Some countries listed have more than one market; the figures shown here are totals for all markets.
Source: BIS (1993, tables 2-A and 2-D).

take on more importance because British banks would have a competitive advantage in all foreign exchange markets.[11]

If the tax were levied on a market basis, the risk of migration would grow, because banks could avoid the tax completely by establishing dealing sites in tax-free locations. But governments would have less of an incentive to offer such tax havens. A country can benefit indirectly by luring foreign banks to its foreign exchange market: jobs are created, buildings are erected and property values will rise. But it cannot confer a competitive advantage on its own banks simply by refusing to impose the tax. Moreover, for a country like Singapore, which has a large local market, the revenues accruing from the tax may exceed those obtainable from trying to attract additional tax-free business.[12] For all these reasons, the plan laid out below uses a market-based tax.

How, then, would the plan work? Banks would be required to collect the tax on all of their foreign exchange transactions, apart from transactions exempted explicitly for reasons discussed below. The 5 basis point tax would be payable in full whenever a bank engaged in a spot transaction with any retail customer. It could be added explicitly to the sum payable by the customer or could be paid by the bank itself and then added to its spread. The ultimate incidence of the tax would not be affected by the way it was paid.

The same tax would be levied on wholesale transactions, but each party would pay half the tax (2.5 basis points). Otherwise, those transactions would be taxed twice as heavily as retail transactions. Each party to a particular deal would have to know whether its counter-party was a "tax collector" at its own dealing site. If not, the first party would have to assess and pay the full 5 basis point tax on that particular deal (or, as proposed below, the higher penalty tax payable on transactions with tax-free dealing sites). Therefore, each bank would have to maintain an up-to-date list of the tax-collecting banks at every dealing site. But governments could periodically issue such lists, which could be stored in the banks' computers for use in coding transactions and computing tax payments.

There is an obvious gap in this plan. Retail transactions between non-banks would escape taxation unless they could be monitored and the parties made to pay the tax. (As in the case of wholesale transactions, it would be necessary to split the tax in order to avoid double taxation.) Although these transactions are relatively small, individually and in the aggregate, compared with those involving banks, it may be important to tax them. Otherwise, non-banks would deal increasingly with each other rather than with banks, and the tax base would shrink sharply. Some financial institutions that operate now in the interbank market might even exit from that market rather than incur the tax and cost of collecting it, and they would then meet their own foreign exchange needs by dealing directly with other financial institutions and with non-financial firms.[13]

The nuisance value of the tax could be easily minimized by exempting all transactions smaller than $1 million. It might then pay to break up large transactions into small pieces, but that can be costly. It would hardly pay to break a $50 million transaction into 51 small pieces simply to avoid a 5 basis point tax.

Should there be other exemptions? If the countries of the European Union (EU) reach the final stage of monetary union and replace their national currencies with one EU currency, there will be no more trading in national currencies, and this will greatly reduce the size of the global tax base. Even earlier, however, when the EU countries lock their exchange rates irrevocably, their national currencies will be exchangeable at par in over-the-counter transactions through banks, not through the foreign exchange market (see Kenen 1995). Therefore, those transactions should not be taxed.[14] For similar reasons, Spahn (1995) suggests an exemption for currency boards. (Several authors suggest exemptions for other official transactions, including official intervention in the foreign exchange market, but do not explain why these should be granted.)

It has sometimes been suggested that developing countries be relieved of any obligation to tax transactions in their own markets or, more narrowly, those transactions involving their countries' own currencies. (A broader exemption for all transactions would allow developing countries to become tax havens and shrink the global tax base.) An infant-industry argument is sometimes made for this sort of exemption, but if the tax is imposed on a market basis and thus collected from every domestic and foreign bank trading in a particular market, domestic banks cannot benefit uniquely from a tax exemption. The case for such an exemption must be based instead on the fact that markets are thin in developing countries, so that spreads are wide, and a tax would make them wider.[15]

There is, however, a more compelling case for this sort of exemption, and it applies in principle to a larger group of countries, not just developing countries. Although there has been rapid growth in the volume of direct bilateral trading between several pairs of currencies, many other pairs must be exchanged by using a vehicle currency. Someone wanting to sell Mexican pesos for Indian rupees must first sell pesos for dollars and then sell dollars for rupees. These transactions would be taxed twice under the plan proposed here.

Unfortunately, there is no neat solution to this problem. Double taxation can be avoided by exempting all sales or purchases of currencies that have to be traded through a vehicle currency (but not exempting both sales and purchases).[16] But most sales of pesos for dollars are not made to buy third currencies; they are made to purchase goods from the United States. Furthermore, some currencies are traded directly, but not for every other currency. Even now, some EU currencies are not traded bilaterally with all others—only with the mark and the pound. Therefore, an exemption for the currencies from developing countries would be too broad in that it would cover too many transactions, but not broad enough in that it would not meet the vehicle currency needs of industrial countries. As a second-best solution, it may be most sensible to exempt all transactions in developing countries' currencies and to count on double taxation of vehicle currency trading to foster direct bilateral trading in all important pairs of currencies from industrial countries. The number of such pairs will fall, of course, if a large number of EU countries move to monetary union.[17]

Countering avoidance by substitution

Two forms of substitution are considered here—substitution into existing instruments and substitution into newly created instruments designed expressly to avoid the tax on transactions in existing instruments.

Clearly, a tax on spot transactions could be avoided easily by using short-dated forward transactions. A three-day forward contract is indeed a very close substitute for a two-day spot contract. A firm needing a currency on Friday would only have to buy it forward on Tuesday, rather than buy it spot on Wednesday. Therefore, a tax on spot transactions must also be levied on forward transactions.[18]

What, then, should be done about swap transactions? A swap transaction combines a spot with an offsetting forward. Should it be treated as two separate transactions and thus taxed twice or treated as a single transaction and thus taxed only once? Because swap transactions are used mainly by banks for covered interest arbitrage and for managing their foreign currency positions, the volume of swap transactions may be extremely sensitive to a small cost increase, and the double taxation of swaps could greatly reduce tax revenue. It may therefore be most sensible to treat a swap as a single transaction and tax it only once.[19]

If forward contracts are taxed, futures contracts should perhaps be taxed, although the two are not perfect substitutes. (If futures contracts were always settled by delivering the currencies involved, not by net settlement in a single currency, they would be very close substitutes for forward contracts, and it might then be necessary to tax them.) If futures are taxed, however, when should the tax be levied? As a purchase and subsequent sale of a futures contract can serve the same purpose as a spot purchase and subsequent sale, a futures contract should probably be taxed when written and taxed again whenever it was traded. The standard 5 basis point tax should be levied on the notional value of the contract and would be collected by the futures exchange on which it was traded.[20]

If forwards and futures are taxed, should options be taxed too? This is a difficult question. In fact, comments made on previous versions of this paper dealt mainly with this question—and did not agree on the answer.

Because an option may never be exercised, it should not be taxed on its notional value at the standard 5 basis point rate, as was proposed above for a futures contract.[21] Furthermore, a tax on a "plain vanilla" currency option would merely inspire the "rocket scientists" to design synthetic currency options and more complex contracts.[22] If options are not taxed, however, they will start to crowd out forwards and futures, especially if the writers of options begin to require actual deliveries of currencies. There will then be a large adverse effect on the tax base, along with another worrisome effect: those who would normally use forwards and futures to hedge their foreign currency positions, but started to use options instead, would expose themselves to the additional risks of dealing in complex derivative instruments. Furthermore, it would be hard to justify a tax on futures if options were not taxed. The two are fairly close substitutes, and strong objections are raised whenever someone proposes a change in the trading regime for futures or options without proposing an equivalent change in the other regime.

But the case for taxing futures and options may not be strong if they are not written to require actual deliveries of currency and if the tax on foreign exchange transactions is aimed mainly at raising revenue, not curbing speculation. Consider a firm that will need a fixed number of yen three months from now. By buying yen in the forward market, it can hedge against an appreciation of the yen and obtain the yen just when it needs them. By buying a futures contract or a call option, it can hedge against an appreciation of the yen but may not actually obtain the yen; it will have to buy them on the spot market. Suppose that the firm would use the forward market if forwards, futures and options were taxed equivalently (or not taxed at all). A tax on forward transactions alone might then cause the firm to buy a futures contract or a call option, which would reduce the volume of forward transactions. Three months later, however, the firm would have to buy yen in the spot market, which would increase the volume of spot transactions. Hence, the total tax base would not be affected by taxing forwards without taxing futures or options: there would be a decrease in the volume of forward transactions, but it would be offset by an increase in the volume of spot transactions.[23]

Unfortunately, this reasoning does not apply to a firm that wants to profit from an expected appreciation of the yen but will not actually need the yen. If it substitutes futures or options for forwards when forwards are taxed, there will be a net reduction in the volume of taxable transactions. Therefore, the strength of the case for taxing futures and options depends on the motives of those who presently use the forward market, and the question cannot be resolved abstractly. If hedgers dominate speculators, an exemption for futures and options will not greatly reduce the combined volume of spot and forward transactions, and the adverse effect on the tax base will not be large. If speculators dominate hedgers, however, the opposite will be true, and the adverse effect on the tax base could be quite large.

What types of new instruments could be devised to avoid a tax on existing instruments? One possibility was mentioned earlier—the design of complex options to replace simple currency options—and another, more disturbing possibility is raised by Garber and Taylor (1995). If a spot transaction is defined for tax purposes as an exchange of bank deposits in different currencies, then "gross trading in these claims will be effectively eliminated in favour of T-bill swaps in currencies with liquid (same-day) T-bill markets. The swapped T-bills will be immediately sold for deposits" (p. 179). But consider the costs and risks of this swap. There are four extra transactions, each with its own cost, because both parties must buy Treasury bills, swap them and then sell them. If the transactions cannot be perfectly synchronized, moreover, both parties will be exposed to the risk of an interest rate change in one or both of the countries involved.[24] That interest rate risk could be hedged—the two banks could agree to repurchase the Treasury bills at the prices prevailing just before the swap. In that case, however, governments could readily rule that the swap was designed expressly for tax avoidance and could thus treat it as a taxable transaction. More strenuous efforts might be made to disguise it, but they would add new costs or risks, or, as Garber and Taylor note, call for the use of derivative instruments having less and less liquid markets. All this to avoid a fairly low tax on a simple, low-risk transaction in the spot foreign exchange market!

Countering avoidance by migration

When assessing the risk of migration to tax-free dealing sites, we must consider two possibilities—migration to existing dealing sites and migration to newly established sites. The reason becomes clear when we look at the case of a new dealing site.

To move to a new dealing site, a bank must invest in a trading room and persuade some of its traders to move to the new site. Trading rooms are very expensive. Dealers have other options (no pun intended). At some point, however, a bank must decide whether to renovate an old facility or equip a new one, and if it opts for a new one, it must decide where to put it. That is the time when the bank may decide to move to a tax-free trading site. But if it is the first to move to a particular site, it will have to do all its trading with other dealing sites. Therefore, it can be deterred from moving to such a site by a punitive tax imposed on all transactions with that site. Instead of paying a 2.5 basis point tax on wholesale transactions with banks at that site, banks at other dealing sites might be required to pay a 500 basis point tax (that is, 5%).[25]

If the punitive tax rate is properly chosen, the problem will be solved. No one will want to be the first mover. If the tax rate is not high enough, it will become even less effective thereafter. Once the first mover has moved, any other bank that moves to the new dealing site can trade with the first bank, the third can trade with the first and second and so on—with each such move diluting the deterrent effect of the punitive tax.

This story explains why a punitive tax is less likely to prevent migration to an established dealing site—which explains, in turn, why any transactions tax would have to be applied and enforced at all major dealing sites. All of the G-7 countries (Canada, France, Germany, Italy, Japan, the United Kingdom and the United States) were included in the 1992 list of countries with the largest foreign exchange markets, but they accounted for only five of the ten largest markets (table 4.2). The others were in Singapore, Switzerland, Hong Kong, Australia and Denmark. The ordering may be slightly different now, but the basic point is clear. The risk of migration to established dealing sites is certain to occur if the transactions tax is not adopted and levied uniformly by the European Union, the United States, Japan, Singapore, Switzerland, Hong Kong, Australia, Canada and, perhaps, some other countries.[26]

Digressing on tax incidence and spreads

A tax on foreign exchange transactions will make them more costly, but the ultimate effects on volume and spreads are far from clear.[27] If transactions in the wholesale market are made chiefly to profit from small exchange rate changes, a small increase in the cost of trading can be expected to cause a significant reduction in volume. In that case, however, it may not have much effect on spreads in the wholesale or retail market, apart from the direct effect of the tax itself. But much of the activity in the wholesale market appears to reflect the efforts of market-makers to avoid large fluctuations in their net positions. This is the "hot potato" story of foreign exchange trading told by dealers themselves. A large order by a single customer will trigger a chain of transactions between dealers, as each dealer passes on to others part of the requisite change in the net position that they must accept collectively.[28] According to this interpretation, a small increase in the cost of trading should not lead to a large reduction in volume. Insofar as it does reduce volume, however, it will widen spreads; market-makers will require compensation for bearing the increase in risk caused by the fall in volume.[29]

It is sometimes said that a tax on wholesale trading will widen the retail spread by the amount of the tax. If that were true, of course, the 5 basis point tax discussed in this paper would widen the retail spread by 10 basis points (because it would be levied twice—on both wholesale trading and retail trading). But this calculation assumes implicitly that there is a one-to-one correspondence between markets—that each retail trade produces a single wholesale trade—which is not the case. The hot potato story says that each retail trade will lead to a sequence of wholesale trades, and even if that is not literally true, there is still reason to believe that the tax will widen retail spreads by more than 10 basis points.

If the retail demand for spot foreign exchange were completely inelastic, the whole increase in the cost of wholesale trading would be borne by the retail trade—and the numbers in table 4.1 can be used to show what would happen. In April 1992, the volume of wholesale trading in the spot, forward and swap markets averaged $540 billion a day, so a 5 basis point tax would have raised the total cost of that trading by $270 million a day. But the volume of retail trading averaged only $233 billion a day, including transactions with financial and commercial customers, so the requisite increase in the retail spread would have been about 12 basis points before adding the tax on retail trade, or 17 basis points after adding the tax. This figure is bigger than the mere sum of the two taxes, but it may not be large enough to depress foreign trade or long-term foreign investment.

Implementing and administering a transactions tax

It would be difficult and inappropriate for a small group of countries to impose a tax on foreign exchange trading, even if those countries accounted for all of the large foreign exchange markets. There must be an agreement to impose the tax; an agreement to accept and apply uniform rules and procedures, including procedures for amending the initial rules in the light of subsequent experience; and an agreement on making decisions about the use of tax revenue.[30] When agreeing to impose the tax initially, moreover, governments must also agree to impose a punitive tax on transactions within tax-free trading sites, although this will surely antagonize other governments. These decisions will affect many governments, including all of those that have any interest whatsoever in the disposition of the tax revenue. Hence, the decisions will not command the respect of those governments unless they are adopted collectively.

Under the plan discussed in this paper, governments cannot refuse to impose the tax without exposing themselves to punitive taxation. (Developing countries must therefore impose it, even if they do not have to tax transactions involving their own currencies.) But 150 governments cannot be expected to negotiate the details. Hence, they would have to establish an international agency to perform three tasks—draft a tax code, interpret and amend the code thereafter and collect the portion of the tax revenue that is earmarked for international purposes. The agency might also be invited to make recommendations regarding the ultimate uses of the revenue, but the final decisions would have to be made by the governments themselves.

Some authors have suggested that an existing institution might be asked to take on this responsibility. The International Monetary Fund is mentioned most often.[31] But most of the existing institutions will want to claim some of the tax revenue—even the IMF, which may want to fund or replenish special concessional facilities, such as the Enhanced Structural Adjustment Facility (ESAF). Therefore, it may be best to create a new institution—one with no other task. Major policy decisions would have to be made by the entire membership (the governments that had agreed to impose the tax), including decisions regarding the disposition of the tax revenue, but unanimity should not be required. More technical matters could be decided by a smaller body. Weighted majority voting might have to be used for making both sorts of decisions. The countries with large foreign exchange markets would probably insist on it.

We cannot be optimistic about the prospects for early agreement on the taxing of foreign exchange transactions; some key countries would probably oppose it, even if it enjoyed widespread support in the international community. Nor can we be sure that such a tax would be the most appropriate way to raise additional revenue for international purposes. But the plan discussed in this paper suggests that such a tax would be technically feasible.

Notes

1.   This estimate assumes that a 5 basis point tax would not have caused any reduction in the volume of transactions. Hence, the tax is applied to the $880

billion daily turnover recorded in April 1992 (the turnover shown in table 4.1 plus an allowance for trading in markets not covered by the table) multiplied by 240 trading days. For estimates using other rates, from 10 to 100 basis points, and various assumptions about the effects on volume, see Felix (1995) and Spahn (1995). Using preliminary data from the 1995 survey, Frankel (1996) concludes that the daily turnover is now in the neighbourhood of $1,300 billion, which would raise the revenue estimate to about $150 billion.

2. For the principal participants in US foreign exchange markets at the time of the survey (summarized in table 4.1), see Federal Reserve Bank of New York (1995), which lists participants in the 1995 survey of foreign exchange turnover (the successor to the survey summarized in table 4.1). Non-bank dealers are more prominent in futures and options markets than in spot and forward markets. The structure and functioning of the foreign exchange market are described more fully in Frankel (1996).

3. On the size and variability of wholesale spreads, see, for example, Goldstein and others (1993, p.59).

4. Futures contracts differ from forward contracts in that forwards are customized—the quantities of currencies and maturities are chosen to meet buyers' needs—and they are not traded after being written. Futures contracts, by contrast, are standardized in order to facilitate subsequent trading. Hence, a traded option can thus be regarded as the counterpart of a futures contract, and an over-the-counter option can be regarded as the counterpart of a forward contract.

5. Futures traders typically close out their positions by buying an offsetting futures contract before maturity—which is why there are net settlements rather than actual deliveries of currencies. If a contract is held to maturity, however, there can and will be an actual exchange of currencies.

6. It is thus difficult to understand why the Commission on Global Governance (1995) is concerned about the adequacy of the paper trail produced by foreign exchange transactions. For a detailed description of that paper trail, see Lyons (1994).

7. Individual transactions may not be settled on the books of the Federal Reserve Bank, they may clear through CHIPS, the payment system maintained by the New York Clearing House Association. But the banks involved will settle their net positions by transfers on the books of the Federal Reserve Bank.

8. This is the approach proposed by Spahn (1995), and other authors seem to have the same approach in mind.

9. But they might have to allocate some of their capital to the tax-free booking site to meet the requirements of other banks and dealers, which could reduce rates of return.

10. It would also impose an extra burden on the home countries' tax auditors, who would have to make sure that large multinational banks reported and paid the tax for all of their foreign dealing sites.

11. Singapore has a very large foreign exchange market, but foreign banks account for most of the transactions there, and Singapore's banks are not big players in other countries' markets. If Singapore refused to impose the tax, little tax revenue would be lost. But if it refused to participate in a market-based tax plan, the revenue loss would be huge and could get larger over time, as additional trading would migrate to Singapore.

12. But this fine calculation will not be decisive. No country with a large foreign exchange market will agree to impose the tax unless it is convinced that the tax plan will protect it from the emergence of new foreign exchange markets in countries that refuse to impose the tax. One such safeguard—a penalty tax on transactions with dealers in tax-free locations—is discussed below.

13. This possibility is mentioned by Frankel (1996), who goes much further. The dealer-intermediated system might disappear, which would greatly reduce the volume of transactions and thus reduce the tax base. (Note that a practical problem would complicate any attempt to tax transactions between non-banks. Should each party pay half the tax, as with transactions between banks, or should each party be liable for the whole tax, for want of any way to prove that the other party is paying it too?)

14. The same point is made by Felix (1995) and Spahn (1995).

15. Tobin (1994) suggests a different way to favour developing countries: they would have to collect the tax on all transactions in their markets but would be allowed to retain most of the tax revenue.

16. A similar suggestion has been made by Kelly (1993).

17. There is, of course, a risk that traders may start to avoid the tax by using the currency of a developing country as a vehicle for transactions between the currencies of industrial countries—by using dollars to buy pesos and pesos to buy marks in order to avoid the tax on a sale of dollars for marks. That method will not be profitable, however, if the tax rate does not exceed the spread on the purchase or sale of a developing country's currency.

18. Felix (1995) takes the opposite view but does not say why. Eichengreen and Wyplosz (1996) also take that view, but give a reason. If a firm buys deutsche marks forward rather than spot, the dealer selling the deutsche marks forward will have a short position and will have to cover it by buying deutsche marks spot. Hence, a substitution of forward for spot transactions will not really reduce the volume of spot transactions, and there is thus no need to tax forward transactions. But this reasoning is flawed. Suppose that the firm had bought deutsche marks spot. Once again, the dealer selling the deutsche marks will be short deutsche marks and must therefore buy them. In other words, any deutsche

marks purchase by the firm, whether spot or forward, will cause the dealer to buy deutsche marks spot to cover the dealer's position. If the firm buys deutsche marks forward, however, because forward contracts are not taxed, there is a net fall in the volume of taxable retail trading. So, forward transactions must be taxed to discourage substitution. Eichengreen and Wyplosz make the same argument with respect to options, and the same answer applies.

19. Nevertheless, this would produce a minor anomaly, because synthetic swaps would be taxed twice as heavily as ordinary swaps. (A synthetic swap combines a spot transaction with one counter-party and a forward transaction with a different counter-party. It is used instead of an ordinary swap when the combination of spot and forward rates obtainable through a synthetic swap is more attractive than the rate obtainable through an ordinary swap.)

20. An earlier draft of this paper suggested that futures contracts be taxed only once, when they are written, which is how forward contracts would be taxed. But the analogy is misleading because forward contracts are not traded—thus there is no other way to tax them. If forward contracts were traded, it would make sense to tax them each time they were traded. Forwards and futures would not be penalized relative to spot transactions, as each successive buyer of the contract benefits equally from holding it.

21. Stiglitz (1989) notes that buying a call option and writing a put option are jointly equivalent to holding the underlying asset outright. If the price of the asset rises, the call can be exercised (which amounts to selling the asset at a profit). If the price of the asset falls, the put may be exercised (which amounts to selling the asset at a loss). Therefore, Stiglitz suggests that each option should be taxed at half the rate applied to the underlying asset (here, spot foreign exchange). But the formal equivalence holds only for a strike price that equals the market price of the asset itself when the call is purchased and the put is written, and only when anticipated prices are distributed symmetrically around that market price. For more on the problems of taxing options, see Summers and Summers (1989).

22. There is a practical problem as well. Because over-the-counter options are not written exclusively by foreign exchange dealers, but by other financial institutions and, indeed, by non-financial firms, it would be difficult to collect a tax, even at the time when options are written—and virtually impossible to collect it if and when options are exercised.

23. There is another way to look at this outcome: taxes on spot and forward transactions have offsetting effects on this firm, because the tax on forward transactions gives it an incentive to substitute futures or options for forwards, but the tax on spot transactions makes substitution more expensive.

24. Garber (1996) acknowledges this point, as well as some other objections, but believes that markets will adapt to facilitate transactions of this sort.

25. The same suggestion has been made by Spahn (1995). One reader has pointed out, however, that punitive taxation could have political side effects. Suppose that the Chinese government tries to attract foreign exchange trading to Shanghai—or the Russian government tries to attract it to St. Petersburg—and a punitive tax is imposed on transactions with those sites. Would the tax not be viewed as an attempt to stifle the development of the Chinese or Russian financial system?

26. The inclusion of the whole European Union would add four of the next five largest markets—those of Luxembourg, Spain, Finland and Ireland—if the ordering has not changed since 1992. (Mention of Hong Kong in the text, however, raises a question resembling the one in the previous note: Would China agree to impose a tax on trading in Hong Kong after 1997?)

27. It is even harder to forecast the impact on short-term exchange rate volatility. Eichengreen, Tobin and Wyplosz (1995) believe that volatility will fall but concede that their forecast depends on the supposition that noise traders, whose trading presumably raises volatility, have shorter horizons and holding periods than traders whose strategies are based on a sound reading of the fundamentals. Stiglitz (1989) takes the same view but hedges his own bet. If a 5 basis point tax made it unattractive to buy or sell an asset unless its price deviated by more than 5 basis points from its "true" value, there might be more volatility, but only within the 5 basis point range. Working with equity prices, Jones and Seguin (1995) have shown that a reduction in transaction costs (commissions) is associated with a reduction in price volatility, which appears to say that the increase in transaction costs resulting from a tax on foreign-exchange transactions would raise exchange rate volatility.

28. Lyons (1994) models this process formally and provides empirical support for his model.

29. This point is made repeatedly in the literature. See, for example, Kelly (1993), d'Orville and Najman (1995) and Spahn (1995). Furthermore, Black (1991) finds that spreads vary inversely with volume in the foreign exchange market. Stiglitz (1989) argues that the increase in spreads should be quite small. But he assumes that dealers will accept short-term fluctuations in their net positions, and this assumption is not strictly consistent with the hot potato story.

30. These issues are stressed by Folkerts-Landau and Ito (1995), who also note that it has been very difficult for governments to agree on other fiscal matters.

31. Tobin (1994) goes even further in suggesting that a government refusing to impose the tax should not be allowed to draw on IMF resources.

References

BIS (Bank for International Settlements). 1993. "Central Bank Survey of Foreign Exchange Market Activity in April 1992." Basle. March.

Black, Stanley W. 1991. "Transactions Costs and Vehicle Currencies." *Journal of International Money and Finance* 10(4):512–26.

Commission on Global Governance. 1995. *Our Global Neighborhood.* Oxford: Oxford University Press.

D'Orville, Hans and Dragoljub Najman. 1995. *Towards a New Multilateralism: Funding Global Priorities.* New York: United Nations.

Eichengreen, Barry, James Tobin and Charles Wyplosz. 1996. "Two Cases for Sand in the Wheels of International Finance." *Economic Journal* 105(January):162–72.

Eichengreen, Barry and Charles Wyplosz. 1995. "Taxing International Financial Transactions to Enhance the Operation of the International Monetary System." This volume.

Federal Reserve Bank of New York. 1995. "April 1995 Survey of Foreign Exchange Market Activity in the United States." New York.

Felix, David. 1995. "The Tobin Tax Proposal: Background, Issues and Prospects." *Futures* 27(2):195–213.

Folkerts-Landau, David and Takatoshi Ito. 1995. *International Capital Markets: Developments, Prospects and Policy Issues.* Washington, D.C.: International Monetary Fund.

Frankel, Jeffrey. 1996. "How Well Do Foreign Exchange Markets Function: Might a Tobin Tax Help?" This volume.

Garber, Peter. 1996. "Issues of Enforcement and Evasion in a Tax on Foreign Exchange Transactions." This volume.

Garber, Peter and Mark P. Taylor. 1995. "Sand in the Wheels of Foreign Exchange Markets: A Skeptical Note." *Economic Journal* 105(January):173–80.

Goldstein, Morris, David Folkerts-Landau, Peter Garber, Liliana Rojas-Suarez and Michael Spencer. 1993. *International Capital Markets: Part I. Exchange Rate Management and International Capital Flows.* Washington, D.C.: International Monetary Fund.

Jones, Charles M., and Paul J. Seguin. 1995. "Transactions Costs and Price Volatility: Evidence from Commission Deregulation." Financial Research Center Memorandum 151. Department of Economics. Princeton University.

Kelly, Ruth. 1993. *Taxing the Speculator: The Route to Forex Stability.* Fabian Society Discussion Paper 15. London.

Kenen, Peter B. 1995. *Economic and Monetary Union in Europe: Moving Beyond Maastricht.* Cambridge, U.K.: Cambridge University Press.

Lyons, Richard K. 1994. "Foreign Exchange Volume: Sound and Fury Signifying Nothing?" In Jeffrey Frankel, Giampaolo Galli and Alberto Giovanni, eds., *The Microstructure of Foreign Exchange Markets*. Chicago: University of Chicago Press.

Spahn, Paul Bernd. 1995. "International Financial Flows and Transaction Taxes: Survey and Options." IMF Fiscal Affairs Working Paper 60. Washington, D.C.

Stiglitz, Joseph E. 1989. "Using Tax Policy To Curb Speculative Short-Term Trading." *Journal of Financial Services Research* 3(2–3):101–15.

Summers, Lawrence H. and Victoria P. Summers. 1989. "When Financial Markets Work Too Well: A Cautious Case for a Securities Transactions Tax." *Journal of Financial Services Research* 3(2–3):163–88.

Tobin, James. 1994. "A Currency Transactions Tax: Why and How." Università La Sapienza, Rome.

5

Issues of Enforcement and Evasion in a Tax on Foreign Exchange Transactions

Peter M. Garber

In this chapter, I study, qualitatively, how the volume of foreign exchange transactions reacts to the imposition of a transactions tax. Here, I assume that most countries agree to implement a tax on foreign exchange operations but that the coverage may or may not be comprehensive.[1] First, I consider the situation that will arise if a country with a large financial centre does not impose the tax. Then, I analyse the situation in which only countries with smaller financial centres do not impose the tax, and there is no enforcement mechanism that penalizes them for not cooperating. Finally, I consider a situation in which all countries uniformly accept the tax and the tax can be readily imposed on those transactions that are conventionally considered foreign exchange operations—spot, futures and forward foreign exchange trades, and "plain vanilla" currency swaps and options—but not readily imposed on those transactions that are not traditionally considered foreign exchange. Because activity will move from the taxed set of transactions to the untaxed, I consider a range of products that may serve as untaxed substitutes.

To address these issues, I discuss whether foreign exchange currency transactions are controllable across country borders, particularly when they assume non-traditional forms. I also consider the methods of tax evasion and the relation between trading in spot markets and futures or forward markets. I conclude that—even aside from the problematic issues of political feasibility—it is unlikely that the tax could be readily enforced or that it could generate large amounts of revenue unless it is applied to a wide range of financial products. Several issues should be addressed in future research, particularly those concerning the feasibility of foreign exchange operations moving offshore, out of reach of the tax, or into new products outside of traditional definitions of foreign exchange.

Potential transactions tax revenue

The recent literature on taxing foreign exchange transactions has been spurred by the high volatility in exchange rates experienced during the European exchange rate mechanism (ERM) crisis and by movements among the major bloc currencies—the yen, the deutsche mark and the US dollar. Such movements have been considered destabilizing, caused in part by speculative activities that have generated large trading volumes. Some economists have proposed a tax on either transactions or position-taking in foreign exchange to control these large volumes and reduce volatility. Such taxes are known generally under the rubric of the "Tobin tax".[2]

Recent academic proponents of the tax are looking to reduce volatility and volume and are not directly concerned with the amount of revenue that could be raised. Nevertheless, the large volume of transactions—totalling more than $1 trillion a day—is largely untaxed; and such a large gross flow has naturally attracted attention as a potential tax base. Perhaps because their international character has associated them more closely with development compared with other rich tax bases, such as the general flow of financial transactions or income, taxes on foreign exchange transactions have come to be regarded as a potential revenue source for providing aid to developing countries.

To determine whether foreign exchange transactions would provide a solid tax base, we must calculate the elasticity of the volume of transactions with respect to the widened bid-ask spread that a transactions tax will generate. According to the standard principle of public finance, we should tax the inelastic markets and leave the elastic markets relatively unburdened. Inelastic markets provide revenue and do not create large distortions when they are taxed. Elastic markets, however, do not provide a solid revenue base, and large-scale reallocations may materialize if they are taxed.

Typically, it is easier to tax real activities based on capital in place, because the capital is frozen, creating inelasticity at least in the short run. Financial transactions, on the other hand, are much more difficult to tax in the absence of thorough-going regulations—themselves a major cause of resource misallocation. Financial transactions can be undertaken and booked in any location. And, for security, they depend on financial capital, which is not firmly locked in place.[3] This places a limit on the magnitude of the tax rate.

Of course, revenues earned from securities transactions that are locked in place can be very high. For example, in Japan, transfer taxes on sales by securities companies are 1 basis point for bonds, 6 basis points for convertible bonds, and 12 basis points for stock. For other sellers, the taxes are 3, 16 and 30 basis points, respectively. For stock futures on organized exchanges, the tax is 1 basis point. These taxes raised a peak of about 4.2% of government general account revenue in 1988—about 2.1 trillion yen (Tax Administration Agency 1994). Almost all of this revenue came from trading in equities during the height of speculative trading on the stock market. The collapse of the bubble economy and the shift in speculative trading to the much-less-taxed futures exchange in Osaka, and then offshore to Singapore, led to a dramatic decline in tax revenue—to 0.96% of general account revenues in 1993 (about 500 billion yen). Of this amount, more than half came from trading in equities.

Markets for foreign exchange products

The foreign exchange market is the largest financial market in the world, with average daily turnover in the three largest financial centres—London, New York and Tokyo—estimated at about $620 billion in April 1992.[4] The market for spot delivery generated slightly less than half the total volume in 1992. Foreign exchange swaps accounted for 39% of market turnover. Forward sales, options and futures contributed 7%, 5% and 1% of turnover, respectively. Eighty-four percent of transactions were interdealer trades among financial institutions and other foreign exchange dealers, in which dealers sought to balance their positions.[5]

The over-the-counter markets in derivative products are concentrated in a small number of large banks and securities firms in the major financial centres. For example, bank holding companies with more than $10 billion in assets hold between 98% and 100% of all over-the-counter derivative positions taken by US banks.[6]

Foreign exchange derivatives are important components of foreign exchange markets, particularly the over-the-counter markets. The notional principal of outstanding, exchange-traded foreign exchange derivatives at the end of 1992 was $105 billion. In contrast, there were $860 billion in currency swaps and $5.5 trillion in foreign exchange forwards and over-the-counter options outstanding. The over-the-counter market dominates trading in currency options, accounting for 85% of turnover in April 1992. Two-thirds of the notional principal of banks' options transactions involved dealers as counter-parties. The foreign exchange market across the spectrum of products is therefore a bank market whose location depends on the location of bank capital.

Maturities of forward contracts are mainly short-term: 64% of contracts mature within seven days, and only 1% have a maturity of longer than one year. Because a transactions tax imposed at a uniform rate across maturities falls more heavily on short maturity instruments with a large normal turnover than on longer maturity trades, these data show clearly that the bulk of the market will be strongly affected by such a tax.[7]

Because of the presence of intricate hedging techniques, transaction volumes across the various foreign exchange products are closely related. A foreign exchange transaction between a bank and an end-user will generate four times as many interdealer transactions (by value), as banks pass the market risk through the banking system until another end-user is found who is willing to take the opposite position.

For example, if a bank enters a one-month forward contract with a customer to sell pounds for dollars, it will immediately hedge the currency risk by selling dollars for pounds in the spot foreign exchange market. And it will hedge the maturity risk by entering a currency swap to deliver pounds for dollars spot and dollars for pounds for one-month settlement. Thus, one transaction with a final customer generates two more of equal value in which the bank perfectly hedges its market risk. This initial round, however, generates additional transactions, as the dealer banks that entered the spot and swap contracts hedge their newly acquired market risks with further interdealer transactions. These transactions come to an end only when the world banking system finds another end-user or bank willing to take on the risk.

To hedge the risks acquired from their over-the-counter options transactions with other dealers, banks typically construct a dynamic hedge by purchasing or selling currency in the spot market to close the currency exposure. They simultaneously enter into a swap contract to shift the exposure so that it coincides with the maturity date of the option (Walmsley 1992). The foreign exchange position is then adjusted as exchange rates move to maintain the hedge. Reported volume totals are therefore deceptive—they are not the sum of the values of independent transactions. A given percentage tax on spot, futures, swap or option transactions will have a differential impact across products, depending on which require more trading for hedging operations.

Feasibility of a Tobin tax

It is a well-known feature of financial markets that attempts at regulation and taxation are frequently thwarted, because market participants formulate sophisticated ways of avoiding the tax. I therefore investigate what the likely actions of market participants will be in attempting to evade taxes on foreign exchange transactions imposed either by a subset of countries or in an internationally consistent fashion that includes the dominant financial centres.[8]

A non-universal tax on gross foreign exchange transactions

I assume that a tax is levied on all foreign exchange transactions, including spot transactions and deliveries on futures contracts and options, amounting to a fixed percentage of the amount of the contract.[9] I first consider the implications of imposing such a measure when at least one major financial centre does not participate. For example, suppose that the authorities in all financial centres but London impose a transactions tax of 10 basis points of the domestic currency value equivalent on all foreign exchange transactions—spot, forward and derivative.[10] A foreign exchange transaction is defined as an agreement specifying delivery by one party of bank deposits denominated in one currency against the delivery by a counter-party of bank deposits denominated in a different currency.[11]

As market participants try to avoid the tax, its implementation will immediately push foreign exchange transactions out of the taxed centres to London. The transactions will be booked there and undertaken from abroad through subsidiaries. In turn, the subsidiaries will be funded with credit from parent companies in the taxed jurisdiction, and they will lend the foreign exchange obtained in a credit operation to the parent. If regulators are able to impose the tax on domestically owned bank subsidiaries abroad, the banks chartered in the taxed centres will be cut out of the foreign exchange business.

Suppose that on a normal day, the foreign exchange market involving the currencies of the taxed centres clears without central bank intervention. All foreign exchange transactions will be booked in London on the books of banks located outside the taxed jurisdictions. The role of banks in the taxed jurisdictions will be to provide cross-border credit to the untaxed banks.[12] Gross values and volumes of foreign exchange trading are then unaffected, and no one pays the tax.

On days that these central banks intervene or some other official entity engages in a foreign exchange operation, however, some banks must engage in an explicit foreign exchange transaction with a counter-party in the taxed jurisdiction and pay the 10 basis point tax. In this operation, the central bank in the taxed jurisdiction effectively pays out the market exchange rate for its currency to its counter-party and takes back 10 basis points of the value of the transaction for the tax. Counter-parties will then deal with central banks in the taxed jurisdictions only if foreign exchange rates are marked up by 10 basis points—and these central banks will then bear the full burden of the tax. Hence, a transactions tax policy that is not fully binding internationally is equivalent to nothing more than a depreciation of the central banks' intervention point. Imposed unilaterally, a transactions tax is almost completely ineffective.

This is especially likely given that regulatory authorities in major industrial countries are eager to move business to their financial centres and have acted to remove or reduce impediments to such business. The French, for example, have reduced or limited transactions taxes and invested heavily in their clearing and settlement operations. Regulators have pinpointed several factors as contributing to the location of financial business, such as communication and transportation infrastructure, the quality of the labour force and the availability of entertainment. UK authorities, in particular, are anxious to keep London attractive for overseas institutions, and they regularly consult with the financial institutions to pinpoint methods to reduce costs of operations. Indeed, many companies have contingency plans to relocate financial businesses if costs rise excessively. Such costs now take the form of regulatory burdens, such as regulatory capital. Corporate taxes are also important in determining the location of financial centres. London is generally regarded in Europe as being less expensive in social security charges and value added tax (VAT) rates, so it is preferred for labour-intensive activities—thus, foreign exchange operations locate in London more than in other centres. A high VAT in other countries pushes activity into Euromarket operations. Note that such taxes, though key to determining the location of business, are relatively low in relation to the overall volume in the foreign exchange market. Suppose, for example, that a VAT of 15% is charged on the wages paid to traders in London. Assuming that there are 2,000 such traders with annual incomes of $250,000, the tax bill is $75 million. On an annual volume of $116 trillion in foreign exchange transactions in London, this amounts to a charge of 6/1000 of a basis point. Even taxes of this magnitude make authorities edgy about the mobility of their financial business. Thus, this amount is about the maximum that one might reasonably exact in imposing a transactions tax rather than the amount from the relatively immense 10 basis point tax discussed above.

A comprehensive system

Now, suppose that all major financial centres cooperate with the implementation of a tax on foreign exchange transactions. Cooperation would make the tax more difficult to circumvent; thus, it would generate more revenue. Of interest in this context is the nature of the substitute to foreign exchange activity that would arise in the major financial centres. I will assume that the reach of the major country supervisors is comprehensive—all elements in a bank's corporate structure, including offshore subsidiaries, are within the web of national regulations. In addition, non-banks with active Treasuries must be subject to the tax. I also assume that all industrial countries—notably those with the largest financial centres—impose a tax uniformly on foreign exchange transactions, but that some minor centres do not impose the tax.

Some transactions and balance sheet bookings would shift to the minor offshore centres—here, Singapore will represent those centres—but the magnitude of the shift would depend on how much bank capital can move to the offshore centres in support of such business. As an upper bound, the limits against capital of the 100 largest European banks might permit them to take a net position of $250 billion in all currencies. Doubling this amount to account for similar positions for US and Japanese dealing banks would imply a maximum world banking system position of $500 billion in all currencies. But this figure is an overstatement—even during the ERM crisis, the large dealing banks took nowhere near this net position. Suppose, for example, that the maximum net foreign exchange position was $250 billion, which is still an overly large amount. During the ERM crisis, New York banks found it an acceptable risk to allow customers to leverage up to tenfold on collateral in forward contracts. Thus, a capital fund of $25 billion should provide an adequate settlement guarantee for all foreign exchange position-taking and trading that might occur on Singapore bank balance sheets.

Foreign investors putting this amount of capital into Singapore banks might magnify sovereign risk—that is, the risk of expropriation— but only a few small centres could readily absorb this capital with small sovereign risk. Thus, a minor financial centre could quickly take over much of the existing explicit foreign exchange market and undermine industrial countries cooperation. In addition, funds that engage in foreign exchange operations, many of which are already located in minor financial centres, would move their capital to these centres. To avoid this problem, controls would have to be placed on cross-border transactions and credit given to addresses in such centres. These controls might take the form of taxes or quantity limits or even the total prohibition of access of financial institutions in the minor centres to payments mechanisms or correspondent services in the taxed jurisdictions.

Suppose, however, that minor financial centres do not chisel the system. The transactions tax would now fall on overall foreign exchange volume, not just on visits to the foreign exchange windows of the central banks. There is no incentive for foreign exchange transactions to move offshore. Gross volume would then be affected internationally, but the overall effect would depend on how a foreign exchange transaction is defined in the tax regulations.

If a foreign exchange transaction is defined as an exchange of one bank deposit for another in a different currency, gross trading in these claims might be effectively eliminated in favour of Treasury bill swaps in currencies with liquid (same-day) Treasury bill markets.[13] The swapped Treasury bills can be immediately sold for deposits.[14] If the foreign exchange market shifts to this form, no tax will be paid, and position-taking will not be directly affected.[15]

If an outright exchange of Treasury bills becomes taxable in the transactions tax regime, the market could shift to a transaction in which one party borrows a dollar Treasury bill for a short sale and collateralizes it with a sterling Treasury bill—effectively a substitute for a currency swap. Alternatively, the two parties can provide credit to each other in the two currencies collateralized by the claim that each has on the other. The increased use and legal recognition of netting arrangements makes this easy to do without additional credit risks. Especially between major dealers, buying and selling would balance to zero-out net positions. Similarly, other bank products might be mobilized to circumvent a tax on explicit foreign exchange transactions. For example, a pair of interest rate swaps in the two currencies—priced to assure a desired cash delivery of each currency in two days—might be independently arranged between two counter-parties.

If supervisors and tax authorities have the sophistication and legal clout to see through these subterfuges and begin taxing them, other methods can be employed. For example, certain combinations of stock market baskets and index options are equivalent to cash according to options pricing theory. Such combinations in one country can be swapped for similar combinations in another country—this is equivalent to a foreign exchange transaction.[16]

Again, to control this operation, the tax would have to be extended beyond straight foreign exchange to transactions in an ever-widening ring of securities and derivatives markets. Indeed, gross cross-border credit would also have to be subject to the tax. Note, however, that as they move away from bank deposits, such subterfuges deal in markets that are becoming less and less liquid, and that, currently, are not perfect substitutes for foreign exchange. A point may be reached, therefore, when extending the tax to transactions in additional securities markets will cause explicit foreign exchange transactions to reemerge, although on a reduced scale. This point will be reached when the liquidity premium on the less liquid asset equals the transactions tax.

It is difficult to predict where this point will be. Just as the reach of the tax will have to be dynamic, so will the nature of liquidity in different markets. If it is a useful device for avoiding the tax, the market for a given financial product or group of products will attract trading volume. Even if they are illiquid in an untaxed environment, such markets can become quite liquid under a transactions tax regime. On which market instrument the trading flock will land is unclear—indeed, some exotic, low-volume product in the current environment may become the substitute for spot foreign exchange once a tax is imposed. Moreover, even the dynamic contest between regulation and innovation will be one-sided; the extension of the tax to additional instruments will, by nature, be more time consuming than the near-instantaneous introduction of tax-avoiding products.

Issues for further research

The conclusions reached in this paper depend on assumptions about the extent to which foreign exchange transactions can avoid the tax, either by moving to untaxed jurisdictions or by assuming untaxed forms. Several of these avenues require further research to determine if they do, in fact, represent large potential escape hatches for foreign exchange operations:

- The extent to which minor offshore centres can channel the bulk of foreign exchange trading through their markets depends on the ability to relocate the bank capital that backs foreign exchange trades and positions in the major centres. Are there legal or political constraints—for example, risk of expropriation—that block sufficient capital from moving to these centres? How much capital movement would be required?
- If foreign exchange trading migrates to an untaxed centre—whether major or minor—to what extent can credit to that centre from banks and corporates in the taxed zones be controlled or cut off? What are the legal impediments to such action, and how costly would it be to undertake?
- The large volumes reported across foreign exchange products are often based on very thin margins. To what extent would trading strategies—for example, dynamic hedging, which requires constant readjustment of foreign exchange positions—be cut back in the face of a small tax?
- There would be substitution of trades in money market instruments to produce an effective foreign exchange transaction. To block these, the tax would have to be extended to a wide range of products. To what extent would the loss of liquidity in these and in the foreign exchange markets reduce trading volumes? To what extent would the decline in volume affect money centre bank profits?

Notes

1. This strong assumption papers over what is probably the most daunting of the issues that militate against the imposition or workability of a tax on foreign exchange transactions. Even if there is a willingness to provide development funding among industrial countries, they are unlikely to generate funds

by taxing the profitable foreign exchange business of the politically well-placed banking industry, especially since they have expended so much effort in shaving basis points off of their market spreads to attract high-wage business to their financial centres.

2. Tobin (1978) proposed such a tax. A recent symposium in the *Economic Journal* (January 1995) outlines the issues involved in this discussion, containing articles by Eichengreen, Tobin and Wyplosz (1995), Garber and Taylor (1995) and Kenen (1995).

3. Some registered securities are location-specific, as are book entry systems and depositories. Specifically, the depository for government securities is usually most naturally located in the country of issue. Trading and settlement, however, can proceed in offshore books. Only when a trade occurs between a party using offshore accounts and a counter-party using onshore accounts will the details of the trade be reported to the onshore tax authority. That government securities are more tied to the issuing country relative to other securities is not an advantage for imposing a transactions tax. Such a tax on government securities will be reflected in a lower issue price for the securities, so it will be paid from the general tax base.

4. Globally, turnover was estimated at $880 billion in 1992. See BIS (1993). See also Goldstein and others (1993) and Garber and Spencer (1994). Preliminary press reports of the results of the 1995 survey indicate that global volume has increased by about 20% since 1992, with London's volume surging to solidify its position as the premier trading centre. See Statistical Appendix in this volume, table A.1.

5. This is reflected in the average deal size, which for the US dollar was approximately $6 million overall. Deals were smaller in the spot market, because the proportion of transactions with end-users was higher. In the derivatives markets, deals tended to be higher: for example, the average size of an over-the-counter deutsche mark–pound sterling option was $32 million.

6. See Board of Governors of the Federal Reserve System, Federal Deposit Insurance Corporation and Office of the Comptroller of the Currency (1993).

7. Proponents of a transactions tax in the recent literature see this disparate effect as a benefit. The reduction of volume in short maturity markets is viewed as a desirable goal because of the perceived assumed relation between volume at the short end and market volatility. See, for example, Eichengreen, Tobin and Wyplosz (1995).

8. This section is adapted and developed from Garber and Taylor (1995).

9. The percentage might vary by type of contract to account for some products requiring more transactions for their support because of necessary hedging activity or differing maturities. Here, I will consider only a uniform tax, however.

10. Effectively, this amounts to a 20 basis point tax if it is collected by tax authorities from both counter-parties.

11. For spot and forward contracts, the delivery feature is clear. For derivatives, it is not so clear—for example, a foreign currency option may entail a delivery of only domestic currency in amounts contingent on the movement of the exchange rate. Such a product might be exempted from being directly taxed—a hedging operation to cover the risk by engaging in explicit foreign exchange transactions would ultimately pay the tax, however, if it were undertaken in the taxed jurisdictions.

12. For example, if an untaxed bank sells French francs for dollars, it must deliver the francs over the French payment system. To the extent that it has a net negative franc position of its overall transactions, it must obtain franc good funds for settlement, possibly by borrowing from a French bank. This simple credit transaction is not identified explicitly with a foreign exchange transaction and is therefore not taxed.

13. For this operation to be a successful substitute for a spot transaction, the institutions of Treasury bill settlement in the two currencies must be compatible. For example, dollar Treasury bills sold outright are settled on the same day of the transaction, but yen Treasury bills are settled in three business days. A swap of yen for dollar Treasury bills will permit the recipient of the dollar Treasury bill to immediately obtain dollar good funds through outright sale. The recipient of the yen Treasury bill will have to wait three days to obtain yen deposits in an outright sale, which is longer than the two days necessary in a straight spot foreign exchange transaction. To obtain yen funds in two days, the recipient of the yen Treasury bill would have to sell it outright and engage in an overnight repurchase agreement for the Treasury bill. This transaction is an additional complication. The Japanese and German money markets are particularly illiquid relative to dollar products and probably could not accommodate being substituted for a large volume of foreign exchange trades under current institutional arrangements. Of course, if foreign exchange transactions adopted this device, the institutions for settlement would presumably change to accommodate them.

14. Spreads on foreign exchange spot transactions in major currencies are on the order of 4 to 9 basis points. Spreads on dollar Treasury bill transactions are 2 basis points. Even with only a 2 or 3 basis point tax on spot foreign exchange, there would be a benefit in using Treasury bill transactions to circumvent the tax.

15. The available supply of Treasury bills might not permit trades to be made in accustomed volumes, however. For example, in Japan, outstanding Treasury bills amounted to only 11 trillion yen in December 1994, far below the daily volume of foreign exchange transactions. The supply of actual

Treasury bills would have to be used only for net settlements. Gross transactions could be netted through a mechanism similar to FXNET or even through a multilateral netting operation to minimize the necessity of using Treasury bills in final settlement.

16. Merton (1995) points out 11 different ways of taking a levered position in Standard and Poor's 500 stocks though the use of various kinds of derivatives.

References

BIS (Bank for International Settlements). 1992. *Recent Developments in International Interbank Relations*. Basle.

———. 1993. "Central Bank Survey of Foreign Exchange Market Activity in April 1992." Basle. March.

Board of Governors of the Federal Reserve System, Federal Deposit Insurance Corporation, and Office of the Comptroller of the Currency. 1993. "Derivative Product Activities of Commercial Banks." Joint Study Conducted in Response to Questions Posed by Senator Riegle on Derivative Products. Washington, D.C. January 27.

Eichengreen, Barry, James Tobin and Charles Wyplosz. 1995. "Two Cases for Sand in the Wheels of International Finance." *Economic Journal* 105 (January):162–72.

Garber, Peter M. and Michael G. Spencer. 1994. "Foreign Exchange Hedging with Synthetic Options and the Interest Rate Defense of a Fixed Exchange Rate Regime." IMF Working Paper 94–151. Washington, D.C.

Garber, Peter M. and Mark P. Taylor. 1995. "Sand in the Wheels of Foreign Exchange Markets: A Skeptical Note." *Economic Journal* 105 (January):173–80.

Goldstein, Morris, David Folkerts-Landau, Peter Garber, Liliana Rojas-Suarez, and Michael Spencer. 1993. *International Capital Markets: Part I. Exchange Rate Management and International Capital Flows*. World Economic and Financial Surveys. Washington, D.C.: International Monetary Fund.

Kenen, Peter B. 1995. "Capital Controls, the EMS and EMU." *Economic Journal* 105 (January):181–92.

Merton, Robert C. 1995. "Financial Innovation and the Management and Regulation of Financial Institutions." NBER Working Paper 5096. Cambridge, Mass.

Tax Administration Agency. 1994. *Tax Administration Agency Annual Reports* 1985-93.

Tobin, James. 1978. "A Proposal for International Monetary Reform." *Eastern Economic Journal* 4(July-October):153–9.

Walmsley, Julian. 1992. *The Foreign Exchange and Money Markets Guide.* New York: John Wiley and Sons, Inc.

Institutional Arrangements for a Tax on International Currency Transactions

Stephany Griffith-Jones

Support for a Tobin tax and, more generally, for taxes that dampen financial volatility, has increased in recent years, due to several episodes of serious financial instability and their resultant high costs to the real economy. In particular, the October 1987 crash lead distinguished economists like Joseph Stiglitz and Lawrence Summers to propose new taxes on securities transactions (see Stiglitz 1989; Summers and Summers 1990).

Furthermore, recent volatility in world financial markets, particularly the 1992 crisis of the European exchange rate mechanism (ERM) and the 1994 Mexican peso crisis, have generated interest in policy instruments that could reduce destabilizing capital flows—and thus the volatility of variables such as the exchange rate. In the context of this broader debate, interest has grown in James Tobin's 1978 proposal for a tax on foreign currency transactions.[1]

At the same time, the present financial constraint on the UN has led to the suggestion that the burden of financing UN programmes be

The author wishes to acknowledge discussions with academic colleagues and with specialists in international institutions, and especially the useful suggestions on legal aspects made by Carlos Espert and Maria Elena Toledo. Valuable comments were received at the October 10 meeting, with special thanks to Andrew Cornford, Barry Eichengreen and Inge Kaul for their comments.

shifted from national to global sources (see, for example, Kaul 1995). Such a shift would allow the UN to more effectively promote "international public goods" and fight "international public bads"—activities that are increasingly important in a world that is becoming more and more interdependent. The Tobin tax seems to be a prime candidate for raising such revenues globally, given its potentially high yield. This view—that the Tobin tax could become an important source of revenue for the UN—was put forward in the *1994 Human Development Report,* and the United Nations Development Programme (UNDP) is currently carrying out a more in-depth study of its feasibility. This article focuses on the institutional arrangements needed to implement a tax on international currency transactions.

The objectives of a Tobin tax

The idea of killing two birds with one stone, that is, implementing a Tobin tax that would both diminish volatility in capital flows and raise substantial revenue for global institutions, such as the UN and the World Bank, is clearly appealing. A uniform, constant Tobin tax may be too blunt an instrument for assuring that sand in the well-greased wheels is thrown at global financial markets in the right amount and at the right time to prevent or reduce speculative attacks on particular currencies.

A Tobin tax would be useful for discouraging speculative flows in general—there is evidence that it could affect destabilizing short-term speculation more than stabilizing long-term speculation, and as a result, reduce the variance of the exchange rate (see Frankel 1996). But its proposed level (even at 0.5%) would not be high enough to discourage speculation if speculators assume that they could (with a high probability) make large profits—or avoid large losses—during a major devaluation (for example, 10% or more). Although a 0.5% Tobin tax could discourage speculation in such a case, the disincentive would be marginal.

By discouraging short-term speculation in general, however, the Tobin tax could help to avoid the build up to crises. Evidence shows that a reduction of speculation in more normal times will lessen the number of incidents of larger-scale speculative instability. Furthermore, a 0.5% Tobin tax could eliminate the attractiveness of a 5% devaluation expected with 20% probability—the expected benefit of the transaction is 1%, that is, (0.2) (5%), which would exactly offset the cost of a 0.5% tax paid twice in a round trip (see Eichengreen and Wyplosz 1995). But major speculative attacks on currencies usually occur when speculators and other market actors expect a large devaluation (for example, more than 10%) and expect it with a fairly high probability (for example, 50%). The expected benefit of a transactions tax (more than 5%) would, in those cases, be much higher than the additional cost (1%) that a Tobin tax would imply. It would thus seem more appropriate to use the Tobin tax as one of several policy instruments that could be deployed to discourage speculative or unsustainable short-term capital flows.

Indeed, in considering capital flows to developing countries, the International Monetary Fund (IMF) and the G-7 countries have recently suggested several policy measures designed to prevent Mexico-style crises (see, for example, Halifax Summit 1995). These include sound fiscal and monetary policies and improved early warning systems, developed through improved surveillance of national economic policies and financial market developments. The IMF has also begun to recognize that measures taken by recipient countries to discourage unsustainable short-term capital inflows have a valuable role to play.[2] Such measures include taxing short-term inflows, imposing reserve requirement deposits on liabilities associated with short-term borrowing in foreign currencies (as in Chile) and even setting quantitative limits on inflows (as in Indonesia, Malaysia, and other Asian countries).

But these measures may be insufficient. In addition, regulatory authorities of source countries may need to actively discourage unsustainable short-term capital inflows to countries with very large current account deficits. It has been suggested that, for example, securities regulators in source countries could discourage or limit securities and other private short-term flows going to fund current account deficits in a developing or transition economy, where this deficit is too large— such as more than 4% of GDP (see Griffith-Jones 1995). The instruments described above or others can be specifically tailored and, ideally, suitably adapted to different circumstances in which discouraging short-term flows is necessary. They would therefore be fairly sharp policy instruments—complemented by a Tobin tax, which would also discourage short-term inflows (and outflows).

Another alternative would be to define a minimum Tobin tax and allow individual countries or groups of countries to raise it in times of excessive inflows or speculative outflows.[3] This idea is conceptually attractive. But given that the objective is to implement a tax that is as universal as possible, many countries would have to agree to allow a few to raise the tax (and on how to distribute the increased revenue); such a proposal may not be practical. The above-suggested option, in which a Tobin tax acts as a general disincentive to short-term flows, and sharper instruments (such as higher taxes, reserve requirements or other measures, possibly including regulations adopted by recipient or source countries) are tailored to specific circumstances, seems better to adopt. This option would be particularly compatible with using the Tobin tax as an instrument to raise revenue to help fund global institutions.

Precedents for taxing financial transactions

Before looking at practical issues related to levying the Tobin tax (either on a national or market basis), it is helpful to analyse international experience with taxing financial transactions. Several countries successfully tax financial transactions—the United Kingdom, for example (see Appendix B to Frankel 1996). Not only does the United Kingdom tax collect a very high yield (£830 million, about US$1,300 million, in fiscal year 1993, with higher yields in other years), but the United Kingdom Treasury manages to retain that high yield in one of the most sophisticated financial markets in the world—one in which market players are most likely to find mechanisms to evade the tax.

The UK securities transactions tax is known as a stamp duty. It began as a tax on the transfer of a financial instrument from one owner to another—the transfer could be made effective (legally) once a stamp was put on the instrument. It therefore originally taxed registration of ownership. But loopholes arose. For example, investors did not have to pay stamp duty when they bought and resold shares within the same two-week London Stock Exchange account period, thus avoiding the transfer of registered ownership. Furthermore, the stamp duty was not applicable to transactions in "renounceable letters of allotment or acceptance", which are traded instead of the shares during the six months after shares are first issued to the public. In 1986, the UK tax authorities closed such loopholes by introducing a stamp duty reserve tax, which was set at the same rate as the stamp duty and was payable in the two cases mentioned above.

This example illustrates how tax authorities, if agile, can cover loopholes. Furthermore, it points to the fact that most loopholes are discovered after a tax is imposed. Thus sufficient flexibility must be left in the design of the Tobin tax so that it can be modified after it is implemented. This flexibility and the capacity to respond to major loopholes must be incorporated from the start. Flexibility is particularly crucial in the medium and long term, as long-run elasticities of substitution are higher than short-run elasticities (see Kane 1987). Thus governments must be able to update any tax on financial transactions to avoid erosion of the tax base through financial innovation.

The UK stamp duty is applied to transactions in ordinary shares and in assets convertible to shares (such as convertible bonds, to use US terminology), while the conversion option is exercisable. Futures and options are not taxable, but the exercise of an option is treated as the purchase of a share and is taxable. Transactions in shares of investment trusts (closed-end funds in US terminology) are taxable, as are transactions carried out by managers of investment trusts. Purchases and redemptions of units in unit trusts (open-ended funds in US terminology) are taxed as if they were the transactions in the underlying shares. The UK stamp duty applies to both primary and secondary transactions. In new shares, the issuer pays the tax, whereas in secondary trading, the purchaser pays the tax. The rate of the duty was highest, at 2%, between its creation and 1963, and again between 1974 and 1984. Since 1986, it has been at 0.5%.

The British stamp tax does not distinguish between domestic and foreign investors. It is a tax on the transfer of legal ownership of UK shares. Transactions in some non-UK shares, mainly Australian, Irish and South African, are settled in the London Stock Exchange. The stamp duty is payable at the South African and Australian rates for South African and Australian shares, while the UK and Irish authorities share stamp duty revenues for purchases of Irish shares through UK brokers. The latter sets an interesting precedent for the Tobin tax in demonstrating that tax authorities from different countries can easily tax financial transactions involving actors of different nationalities and showing how the tax proceeds can be shared.

Looking at financial transactions taxes in other countries, such as the Swedish transactions tax levied directly on registered Swedish brokerage services, we see that such taxes do not yield substantial revenue when they tax a transaction that has close untaxed substitutes—as in the Swedish case. The UK experience shows that a tax on financial transactions is far more effective for generating revenue if substitution of the transaction is impossible or very difficult.

Practical issues concerning a Tobin tax

More work is needed to persuade critics or sceptics that the Tobin tax will help to reduce volatility. Statistical work may play a role here. Furthermore, critical arguments must be examined carefully. For example, some argue that taxes on financial transactions may increase volatility because they reduce market liquidity (Lo and Heaton 1993). But perhaps the best way of taking the Tobin tax forward is to focus on how it would be implemented. Several practical issues must be addressed: What coverage should a Tobin tax have? What type of transactions should be taxed? How can international agreement best be reached? How would such a tax be implemented? What would be the role of national governments and international institutions?

Before briefly discussing some of these issues, it is interesting to point out that a recent IMF study on financial transactions taxes, although sceptical of the ability of a Tobin tax to reduce volatility, is fairly optimistic about the ease with which a framework for administering the Tobin tax could be established (Shome and Stotsky 1995). Establishing an administrative framework would be facilitated by the relatively well-structured foreign exchange market, the limited number of licenced participants and the fact that most transactions are executed by registered dealers, and that foreign exchange transactions in all relevant markets rely heavily on automated processing and on telecommunications networks. Furthermore, tax collection would be facilitated in that most relevant transactions occur in a small number of countries. In 1992, Japan, the United Kingdom and the United States accounted for 55% of all countries' turnover. Adding Germany, Hong Kong, Singapore and Switzerland, raises this figure to about 78% of total trading.

Spahn (1995) further develops how automated processing and telecommunications networks could simplify tax administration. He emphasizes that tax assessment rules could be built into existing computer algorithms. Indeed, he concludes very convincingly that, "generally speaking, there do not seem to be major administrative problems associated with the operation of a Tobin tax, although specific difficulties may arise in detail, in particular for the derivatives markets. The main riddle relates to international cooperation and legal enforcement."

International agreement on the tax

Ideally, a Tobin tax would be applied universally. If all countries (or at least all major countries and financial centres) did not agree to apply the tax, foreign exchange operations would be booked through countries where the tax was not levied.[4] Thus the best way forward calls for international agreement and for national governments to charge the tax on relevant transactions carried out within their jurisdiction.

International agreement will probably have to take the form of a convention, ratified by all participating countries. One country—or more—would propose such a convention. Then, other countries would have to approve it, subject to ratification by their parliaments. Such a convention could be approved for an indefinite or for a limited period (such as five or ten years), after which it would be reviewed. It is important to stress that an international convention begins to operate when the fifteenth country approves it.

Alternatively, rules could be established by an international organization, such as the IMF. Indeed, if there was sufficient agreement among the major member countries, it would be possible to amend the IMF Articles of Agreement so that all countries would have to impose a Tobin tax—as Tobin himself suggested. But because changing the IMF's Articles is a major exercise, it would seem far more likely that major countries could reach an agreement among themselves.

Forming an international agreement, which includes all the major economies and the major financial centres, seems much more feasible politically. Indeed, it seems far less likely that major players would be willing to give up part of their sovereignty on tax matters to an international organization. But the agreement option does have the disadvantage that it will make universal participation more difficult to ensure, thus creating an incentive for transactions to migrate to non-taxing countries. This problem would, however, be far less serious if all of the major countries (financial centres) agreed to impose the Tobin tax. Moving a large portion of foreign exchange operations from a major financial centre to an offshore tax haven would probably be too costly and too risky to be worthwhile. Furthermore, the countries implementing the Tobin tax could design measures to keep this from happening. National tax authorities are not powerless against tax-evading financial operators, as shown by the way UK tax authorities have modified the UK stamp duty on registration of securities (see Froot and Campbell 1993). Because the UK stamp duty generated an incentive to create bearer instruments, the government levied the tax at triple the rate on bearer instruments, even when traded abroad. This measure has reportedly been effective in reducing evasion. Similarly, in Sweden, the transactions tax on the purchase and sale of equities, applied in the mid- and late 1980s, imposed a tax equal to three times the round trip tax on equity applied to funds moved offshore.

The successful UK stamp duty sets an encouraging precedent for imposing a higher tax on all transactions with non-taxing sites, as Kenen (1996) suggests. He rightly claims that the Tobin tax for operations with tax-free trading sites would have to be far higher than the normal Tobin tax. This higher rate would be particularly effective for avoiding the creation of special tax-free trading sites.

The need for an international administrative organization

Even if the Tobin tax were implemented by international agreement, the IMF or another international organization should still play a major coordinating and supervisory role. Alternatively, or additionally, an autonomous intergovernmental commission could be set up for such a purpose. Two choices must thus be made. First, should this job be performed by an existing international financial organization, or should a new agency or commission be created? Second, if an existing organization is thought to be more desirable, which international institution should be selected?

Before deciding on the best institutional option, it is important to outline the basic functions of such a body. Kenen (1996) suggests three key tasks: drafting a tax code, interpreting and amending the code and collecting the part of the tax revenue that is to be used for international purposes. This institution would also help to decide how the revenue would be distributed, though governments would make the ultimate decision.

On balance, it seems preferable to use an existing international institution because there is much resistance, especially among several major industrial governments, to creating new international public institutions. (One of the main reasons for this resistance is that new institutions cost more money. However, a Tobin tax could raise so much revenue that this argument is somewhat weakened.) In addition, an established international institution is more likely to have the authority to impose and monitor the tax, and to have the financial expertise to centralize the collection and distribution of funds, particularly those used for international purposes. Because, as Kenen points out, an existing institution may want to claim too much of these resources, it would be useful to complement its operation with a small, autonomous inter-governmental global tax commission, in which, for example, proposals for distributing the tax proceeds would be made and discussed. This commission could be established in the context of the UN, but it may need to invoke weighted majority voting, particularly so as to encourage and ensure the participation and collaboration of the major countries and financial centres.

Three different international institutions could be chosen to serve this role: the IMF, the Bank for International Settlements (BIS) or the World Bank. The choice is not straightforward—none of these (or any other) institutions have an explicit mandate for, or experience with, collecting international taxes. Indeed, there is no global Treasury. But the IMF has strong advantages for this task in that its membership is practically universal, its views are influential among many countries and it could use its powers to encourage its member countries to collect the tax (though the use of such measures seem unlikely to gain political support). Furthermore, the IMF has considerable expertise in international financial matters. More broadly, one of the IMF's central purposes is to promote international monetary cooperation—the IMF is committed to maintaining exchange rate stability and orderly exchange arrangements among its members. As the Tobin tax seeks similar objectives, it would seem appropriate for the IMF to play a role in its implementation. But the IMF does not have expertise in international taxation (though it has expertise in national taxation), and in some of its analyses, the IMF is somewhat sceptical about the ease of implementation.

The BIS has the advantage of being influential among industrial countries, particularly with the central banks of those countries. It also has less formal links with many central banks in developing and transition economies. The BIS has considerable expertise in international finance—in fact, it was originally established to administer financial settlements. But its main disadvantage is that its formal links are with the G-10 countries, which excludes several major financial centres, like Singapore and Hong Kong. Furthermore, the BIS has developed links with industrial countries only through their central banks—not through their Treasuries. This would make it even more problematic for the BIS to play a supervisory role.

A third institution that could take the lead is the World Bank. Like the IMF, it has the advantage of nearly universal membership, and its views are influential among developing countries. It also has considerable expertise in dealing with international and national financial markets (in some respects, far more than the IMF, because it borrows from these markets to fund a large proportion of its operations). Given its development mandate, it would probably be one of the institutions using the proceeds of a Tobin tax. But it is less clear that a global, public, development finance institution should be involved in raising global tax revenue. For reasons cited by Kenen (1996), it would therefore seem that the IMF would be the most appropriate choice, with the World Bank being a second possibility. Also, an important criterion for deciding which institution should take the lead is the enthusiasm of the management and staff for undertaking such a job.

Major policy decisions (such as the determination of whether or not to establish the tax, the tax rate, how transactions with non-taxing financial centres will be taxed, broad coverage of transactions, broad use of the tax and so on) would have to be made by finance ministers or central bank governors (or their representatives) of participating governments. A first meeting of such a group could, for example, precede or follow the Annual Meeting of the IMF and World Bank, during which most of the senior financial figures of all countries meet.

When the broad blueprint is designed (including the key institutional aspects), the leading financial institution, with the help of the special intergovernmental commission, would make more detailed proposals. Once implemented, the commission would make decisions on more technical matters. After defining and approving a detailed blueprint, the legal process of establishing an international convention would proceed. The convention must be approved by a sufficient number of major countries, after which the intergovernmental commission could start to collect taxes, in cooperation with national tax authorities. Once a year, for example, on the day preceding or following the IMF/World Bank Annual Meetings, progress on implementation could be evaluated and major outstanding issues could be discussed. If major decisions must be made in the interim, this could be done by circulation, or, in special circumstances, a meeting could be convened.

National and international arrangements for levying the tax

Although the rules for a Tobin tax would be set internationally, national tax administrations would assess and collect the tax. National foreign exchange markets are composed of two parts: the interbank or wholesale market (which is the largest market) and the retail market. Kenen (1996) designates three separate steps in the interbank market: a deal is struck, a deal is booked and a deal is settled.

For several reasons, mainly related to reducing evasion, Kenen convincingly recommends that the tax be levied at the moment the deal is struck. Indeed, even without a Tobin tax, booking operations are transferred to centres with little taxation and regulation.[5] But, first, it must be established that it is legally possible to tax the transaction at the moment when the deal has been struck (but neither booked nor settled). Second, it must be determined what would happen when deals are struck but later cancelled. And third, it must be established that levying the tax when the deal is struck is avoidance proof—that dealers cannot find a way to directly book and settle the transaction.

Applying the tax at such an early stage could be made easier by adding an electronic routing slip to the transaction, which would track the tax record and its payment until the transaction was settled on a central bank account. At that moment, the central bank could discount the tax from the amount being settled and transfer part of the amount to its national Treasury and part to the international organization collecting the proceeds. A special account, created for each country, would be established in the organization. Countries would deposit their Tobin tax proceeds in this account—for example, every three months the share of the tax designated for international use would be deposited. The organization would then distribute the proceeds of the tax to organizations and governments, according to a previously defined formula.

Kenen (1996) also suggests that the Tobin tax be levied on a market basis, rather than on a national basis. This arrangement would have the tax paid to the bank's host country, that is, the country where the dealing site is located. It would work particularly well if all the major foreign exchange markets imposed a Tobin tax. Universal agreement may require an incentive scheme whereby the governments levying the tax could keep a non-trivial share of the revenue.

An important precedent arises from the supranational value added tax (VAT) that helps fund the European Union's (EU's) structural funds. EU national governments keep 10% of the proceeds that they collect from this tax. But this incentive can have a regressive affect on the international distribution of the Tobin tax, as the countries with large international financial centres typically have per capita incomes well above the world average.

The solution would be to use a composite redistribution formula for which part is kept on the basis of the volume of transactions and revenue collected (a percentage sufficiently large to provide financial centres with an incentive to join the scheme and set it up properly, but sufficiently small to allow most of the proceeds to be used more equitably); part is distributed to national governments, according to criteria such as the size of their IMF quota (this would favour smaller and developing countries); part is allocated to institutions like the UN, the IMF, and the World Bank; and an extremely small part is used to fund better regulation of financial markets generally, so that they become more efficient, and costly financial crises are avoided. Often, such regulation is not undertaken because national regulating agencies are underfunded.

Defining a formula for distributing revenue that is both attractive enough to the major financial centres and equitable enough to reduce poverty seems crucial for universal approval. Another element that must be carefully clarified is accountability in spending. Developing-country governments and international organizations must identify the uses for which tax revenues are intended and specify criteria for monitoring and ensuring accountability.

Banks would have to collect the tax on all of their foreign exchange transactions with customers. If deals involved two banks, each would pay half the tax to avoid double taxation (unless one bank is not collecting the tax). Difficulties may arise with cross-border transactions among non-bank institutions. Spahn (1995) suggests that these could be overcome through an international licensing system for all foreign exchange market participants (including brokers, securities companies, pension funds and so on). Licensing, which could be centralized in an institution like the BIS, would become the legal basis for imposing the tax. But because of the large number of foreign exchange market operators, licensing could become complex and costly. Nevertheless, it is important to have relatively full coverage, not so much because of the size of transactions made by non-banks, but because excluding them could encourage transactions to be channelled through them.

Regarding implementation of the tax, one important issue is how to organize auditing to avoid tax evasion. A first level of auditing must be undertaken by national governments and is particularly crucial in the large financial centres. A significant amount of coordination (probably more than now exists) will be required among national tax authorities to limit tax avoidance. A second level of auditing may be required to ensure that national governments effectively transfer the established proportion to their account with the international organization. The second level may be particularly necessary in the initial stages, given that there are no precedents for a global tax, and therefore no tradition of national governments giving up their tax proceeds to an international organization. Especially in the third level, but also in the second level of auditing, the chosen international organization and the special intergovernmental commission would need to support—and in some cases carry out—the auditing.

The type of transactions taxed

Another important practical issue concerns which transactions to tax. The original 1978 proposal called for applying the tax to all spot foreign exchange transactions. Since this proposal was made, the increased volatility of exchange rates—and more general financial deregulation— has encouraged an explosion of instruments, broadly known as derivatives, to transfer risks (such as exchange rate and interest rate risks), as well as exploit the profit opportunities that these fluctuations offer. It is paradoxical that these instruments create additional problems for applying a Tobin tax—which would help to curb large oscillations in exchange rates and therefore diminish the need for derivatives. The problem of derivatives can be handled, although they do complicate the design of a Tobin tax in that operations could be switched from cash to equivalent operations in the derivatives market to avoid the tax.

The fact that derivatives are not an insurmountable obstacle to imposing taxes on financial transactions is illustrated by the existence of national securities transactions taxes in jurisdictions where derivatives are highly developed. Take one of the most successful securities transaction taxes, that in the United Kingdom, for example (see Froot and Campbell 1993). The UK stamp duty has a fairly high revenue yield: £830 million (about US$1,300 million) in fiscal year 1993. How does the United Kingdom deal with options? Futures and options transactions are not taxable, but the exercise of an option is treated as a purchase of ordinary shares at the exercise price and is therefore taxable.

Taxing future contracts, though desirable, is not easy.[6] Even deciding which transactions to tax is difficult, because fluctuations in cash flows in futures trades relate not to notional values but to the contract's value. A tax imposed on the notional value at a rate of 0.5% would be so onerous that it could destroy the futures market, which would be undesirable. As an alternative, lower rates could be applied to options. Or, a per-contract tax could be structured to reduce distortions of investors' choices over cash market or futures trading. But such a tax would be difficult to calibrate. Another alternative would be to not tax futures trades at all, as is the case with the UK stamp tax. The fact that the UK stamp tax is levied on neither futures nor options (except on options when they are exercised), and that there is no major flight from spot transactions into futures or options, further justifies Kenen's suggestion that it may not be essential for a Tobin tax to be levied on futures and options, particularly if the main purpose of this tax is to raise revenue, rather than curb speculation. Not imposing a tax on some derivatives transactions may also be sensible in that it may be legally difficult to tax certain types of derivatives.[7]

A final issue relates to whether certain groups of traders should be exempted from the tax because they perform an important role in markets, for example market-makers, who set prices and stabilize markets, or financial intermediaries more generally, because they provide liquidity to the banking industry. Exempting such institutions would stimulate evasion by encouraging the channeling of tax-free transactions by and through intermediaries. As a consequence, it would be advisable to tax all foreign exchange transactions, including those made by intermediaries. Given the low level of the tax being proposed (Kenen 1996 suggests a rate as low as 5 basis points), the negative effects on these intermediaries would be marginal.

Conclusion

My analysis indicates that Felix (1995) is correct in arguing that the Tobin tax is "an idea whose time has come". It would be useful as part of a battery of instruments to reduce the volatility of capital flows and their consequent negative effects. And it would be particularly valuable for funding the UN and other global institutions, as well as for providing additional revenue to governments.

Although many practical problems arise in trying to levy, for the first time, a global tax on such complex operations as foreign exchange transactions, the practical problems seem to have fairly straightforward solutions. The main challenges are to form an agreement among a sufficiently large number of governments (including the governments of the countries with large financial centres) to levy a tax and design its main features. Another important challenge is to develop the level of international cooperation needed to implement those agreements. To achieve cooperation, an existing international institution, preferably the IMF, should take the lead. And its work should be complemented by a small, autonomous intergovernmental global tax commission, which could be affiliated with the IMF, but stand as an independent entity.

Notes

1. See, for example, Felix (1995) and Spahn (1995). Also, for an important re-statement of the Tobin tax, see Eichengreen, Tobin and Wyplosz (1995).

2. See IMF (1995). For a previous analysis, supporting such measures, see, for example, Ffrench-Davis and Griffith-Jones (1995), and Agosin and Ffrench-Davis (1996).

3. Such a proposal, consisting of a two-tier rate structure—with a low-rate transactions tax plus an exchange surcharge, applied during phases of speculative trading—is developed by Spahn (1995).

4. Eichengreen, Tobin and Wyplosz (1995) stress that the tax would have to be "universal . . . and would have to apply to all jurisdictions".

5. Interview material.

6. For a good discussion, see Hubbard (1993). See also IMF (1995).

7. I thank Professor David Williams for this point.

References

Agosin, Manuel and Ricardo Ffrench-Davis. 1996. "Managing Capital Inflows in Latin America." This volume.

Eichengreen, Barry, James Tobin and Charles Wyplosz. 1995. "Two Cases for Sand in the Wheels of International Finance." *Economic Journal* 105 (January): 162–72.

Eichengreen, Barry and Charles Wyplosz. 1995. "What Do Currency Crises Tell Us About the Future of the International Monetary System?" Paper prepared for FONDAD conference, "Can Currency Crises be Prevented or Better Managed?" Central Bank of Holland, Amsterdam. September.

Felix, David. 1995. "The Tobin Tax Proposal: Background, Issues and Prospects." *Futures* 27(2): 195–213

Frankel, Jeffrey. 1996. "How Well Do Foreign Exchange Markets Function: Might a Tobin Tax Help?" This volume.

Ffrench-Davis, Ricardo and Stephany Griffith-Jones. 1995. *Coping with Capital Surges: The Return of Finance to Latin America.* Boulder, Col.: Lynne Rienner Publishers.

Froot, Kenneth and John Y. Campbell. 1993. "Securities Transaction Taxes: What About International Experience and Migrating Markets?" Catalyst Institute. Chicago.

Griffith-Jones, Stephany. 1995. "How Can Future Currency Crises Be Prevented or Better Managed?" Paper prepared for FONDAD conference, "Can Currency Crises be Prevented or Better Managed?" Central Bank of Holland, Amsterdam. September.

Halifax Summit. 1995. Communiqué. June 15–17.

Hubbard, R. Glenn. 1993. "Securities Transaction Taxes: Can They Raise Revenue?" Catalyst Institute, Chicago.

IMF (International Monetary Fund). 1995. *International Capital Markets: Developments, Prospects and Policy Issues.* Washington, D.C.

Kane, Edward. 1987. "Competitive Financial Regulation: An International Perspective." In Richard Portes and Alexander K. Swoboda, eds., *Threats to International Financial Stability.* Cambridge, U.K.: Cambridge University Press.

Kaul, Inge. 1995. "Beyond Financing: Giving the United Nations Power of the Purse." *Futures* 27(2):181–88.

Kenen, Peter. 1996. "The Feasibility of Taxing Foreign Exchange Transactions." This volume.

Lo, Ann and J. Charles Heaton. 1993. "Securities Transaction Taxes: What Would Be Their Effects on Financial Markets and Institutions?" Catalyst Institute. Chicago. December.

Shome, Parthasarathi and Janet Stotsky. 1995. "Financial Transaction Taxes." IMF working paper. Fiscal Affairs Department. August.

Spahn, Paul Bernd. 1995. "International Financial Flows and Transactions Taxes: Survey and Options." IMF Fiscal Affairs Working Paper 60. Washington, D.C.

Stiglitz, Joseph E. 1989. "Using Tax Policy to Curb Speculative Short-term Trading." *Journal of Financial Services Research* 3(2/3):101-15.

Summers, Lawrence H. and Victoria P. Summers. 1990. "When Financial Markets Work Too Well: A Case for Securities Transaction Tax." In D. Siegel, ed., *Innovation and Technology in the Markets.* Chicago: Probus Publishing Company.

United Nations Development Programme. 1994. *Human Development Report.* New York: Oxford University Press.

Lessons from Individual Country Experiences

Managing Capital Inflows in Latin America

Manuel R. Agosin and Ricardo Ffrench-Davis

Towards the end of the 1980s, private capital inflows began to return to Latin America (see Calvo, Leiderman and Reinhart 1993; Ffrench-Davis and Griffith-Jones 1995; and Ocampo 1994). Undoubtedly welcome, the reversal of the drought in capital inflows of the 1980s has relieved the binding foreign exchange constraint under which most countries laboured during the debt crisis. But both the magnitude of the new capital flows and their composition have caused problems for which the recipient countries have by and large been ill-prepared.

The large size of the recent capital inflows relative to the recipient countries' economies has led to a number of problems and policy dilemmas. The first problem is that of absorption. If capital inflows are to contribute to long-term development, they must lead to a significant increase in the investment rate, something that is difficult to achieve and that, in fact, has not taken place in most countries in the region (except Chile).

Large inflows also pose difficult dilemmas to policy-makers. Without intervention in foreign exchange markets and in the absence of capital controls, the real exchange rate will appreciate, which may be undesirable from the point of view of other important policy objectives (for example, encouraging export growth and diversification, raising investment rates or meeting targets for the current account deficit consistent with sustainable capital inflows). But intervention in the foreign exchange market tends to swell the domestic money supply and increases the difficulty of controlling inflation.

Sterilized intervention, which is practised by several countries in the region, is not without its problems. The central bank winds up accumulating large foreign exchange reserves with returns below those on central bank debt (which must be issued to conduct the required sterilization operations). Moreover, sterilized intervention tends to keep domestic interest rates high, encouraging further capital inflow.

Much of the recent inflow has taken the form of short-term capital or capital with short-term horizons. Although in some countries foreign direct investment (FDI) has been important, in all countries there have been two components of capital inflows that are clearly short-term: portfolio flows and short-term lending or deposits. Portfolio flows usually are not thought of as short-term capital, but in practice they are. Portfolio investors typically operate with imperfect information, seek short-term capital appreciation and are prone to bandwagon effects, either in taking positions or in liquidating them. This pattern was clearly in evidence in the recent Mexican crisis.

Short-term bank credits can also be very volatile, as they respond to differentials in interest rates adjusted for exchange rate expectations and country risk premiums. In the absence of capital controls in a financially open economy, the equilibrium domestic interest rate must equal the foreign interest rate plus expected exchange rate depreciation (pesos per dollar) plus the country risk premium demanded by foreign asset holders. That is, for inflows to take place, the domestic interest rate must exceed the international rate (in the case of Latin America, mostly on the dollar) by a margin sufficiently large to compensate for the expected depreciation of the recipient country's exchange rate and the country risk premium.[1]

These conditions have prevailed in many countries in Latin America since the late 1980s. Domestic interest rates have remained high as a result of high inflation and restrictive monetary policies, and dollar interest rates have declined, reaching a 30-year low in 1992 and 1993. The two other conditions for interest-arbitraging capital inflows have also been met. As countries began to emerge from the debt crisis and began to be regarded as more creditworthy, country risk premiums declined and expectations for the real exchange rate turned from real depreciation to appreciation. In some cases, improving terms of trade contributed to the change in expectations.

Expectations of exchange rate appreciation increase expected yields (in foreign currency) on domestic assets, and declines in country risk premiums reduce the minimum yield required to trigger foreign investments.[2]

As a result, most countries in the region began to receive very large volumes of foreign private capital—countries that have undertaken significant pro-market reforms (Argentina, Chile, Mexico) and countries where such reforms are more incipient or have not yet begun (Brazil, Ecuador, Venezuela). But flows to reforming countries have been particularly large because, as argued below, the reforms themselves tend to attract foreign capital as long as they are perceived to be credible.

The policy response to massive capital inflows has varied widely among countries in the region. At one end of the spectrum are Argentina and Mexico. Argentina has adopted a currency board approach to monetary policy, with a fixed nominal peg to the dollar and a passive monetary policy that simply monetizes increases in reserves (and contracts the money supply when there are reserve losses). In addition to other market-oriented reforms, Mexico has liberalized its capital account, dismantling most of its previous controls on capital movements. At the other extreme are Chile and Colombia, countries that have attempted to discourage short-term capital inflows while maintaining liberal policies towards long-term inflows and have also resorted to sterilized intervention in order to slow real exchange rate appreciation.

Brazil, Chile and Colombia have had a tradition of capital controls. Since the mid-1970s, however, Chile has maintained a fairly open capital account, and recent policies represent a move towards greater pragmatism. In the 1990s, Colombia has moved to liberalize substantially its foreign exchange transactions, and its authorities see the recent imposition of reserve requirements on short-term inflows as a temporary measure (Urrutia 1995). All three countries have been applying taxes or reserve requirements to foreign borrowing—Chile since 1991, Colombia since 1993 and Brazil more recently—that increase the cost of such borrowing and represent an attempt to throw some sand in the wheels of international capital inflows.

This paper examines the phenomenon of massive capital inflows in four countries—Brazil, Chile, Colombia and Mexico—its effects on their economies and the policy approaches the countries used to deal with those effects. The paper also draws some policy lessons.

Recent capital inflows: magnitudes and composition

In the 1990s, capital inflows to Chile, Colombia and Mexico have been large relative to gross domestic product (GDP) (figure 7.1). In all three countries, capital inflows have surged from much lower (or even negative) levels in the mid- to late 1980s. The surge has been particularly impressive in Mexico: whereas in the late 1980s there were net *outflows* of foreign capital of almost 1% of GDP, in 1991–93 net *inflows* represented more than 8% of GDP. Net inflows receded in 1994, and private

Figure 7.1 Balance of payments of four Latin American countries

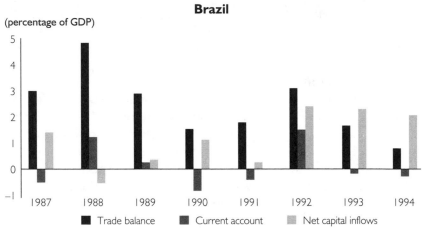

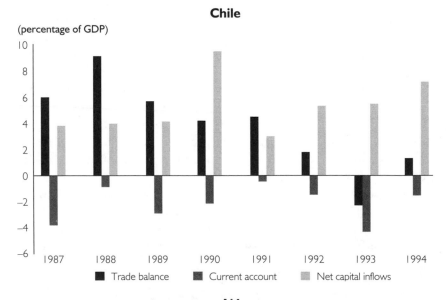

flows turned negative once again as the Mexican crisis began to unfold in December 1994.

In Chile and Colombia, the other two countries with large recent inflows, the foreign capital surges have also been important and will probably turn out to be longer-lived. In Brazil, the volume of capital inflows relative to GDP has been more modest. But relative to Brazilian foreign trade, inflows have been very large, especially over the past couple of years. After some policy swings, in mid-1995 the central bank authorities moved to impose taxes on foreign borrowing and portfolio foreign investment.

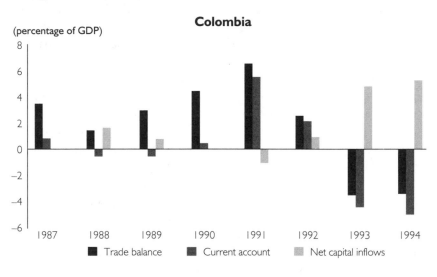

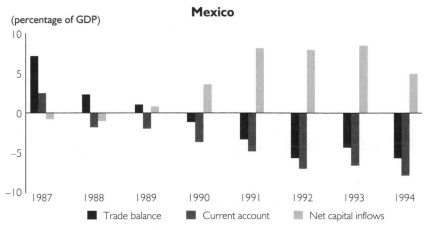

Source: Central Bank of Chile, Banco de la República (Colombia) and Comisión Económica para América Latina y el Caribe (CEPAL).

A major difference between Chile and Mexico, the two countries where capital surges have been sustained for the longest period, has been in the relationship between capital inflows and current account deficits. In Mexico, capital inflows were increasingly matched by equivalent current account deficits; in Chile, by contrast, the current account deficit remained much smaller than the net inflows of capital, which have mostly gone to swell foreign exchange reserves. In Colombia, capital inflows (at least, officially recorded inflows) are a more recent phenomenon—they represent a considerably smaller proportion of GDP, and they have been fairly evenly matched by current account deficits.

The composition of flows is also instructive (table 7.1). In Mexico, the largest item by far has been portfolio capital (purchases of stocks, bonds and money market instruments by non-residents and repatriated flight capital taking these forms). In Brazil, the growth in portfolio inflows has also accounted for a large share of the increase in inflows in recent years. In Chile, they have shown a tendency to rise, but they have been overshadowed by net FDI inflows in 1991 and 1992. In Colombia, portfolio inflows had been negligible until recently, but they have grown rapidly since 1992, when they were liberalized. FDI has been significant, although considerably less important than in Chile.

Short-term foreign borrowing has been an important source of capital inflows in Chile, owing mainly to overwhelming expectations of currency appreciation and a large interest rate differential favouring peso-denominated assets. In Mexico, too, during 1990–92, there were significant inflows of short-term borrowing, although quantitatively they were less important than in Chile. In Colombia, bank lending, both short-term and long-term, and repatriated flight capital taking the form of deposits with the banking system have become quite important since 1992. Moreover, there is evidence that such flows may be hidden in some current account services transactions (see Cárdenas and Barrera 1994).

The ability to deal with capital surges may have something to do with the composition of inflows. Policies towards inflows also affect their composition. When the supply of foreign capital takes the form mostly of FDI, its impact on key domestic prices is smaller than when the capital on offer is mostly liquid. Imports of capital equipment, a significant component of FDI, do not put pressure on domestic currency or foreign currency markets. But policies to discourage the more liquid forms of capital inflows may themselves account for the prominence of FDI in countries such as Chile, and the absence of such policies could be an important explanation for the much greater share of portfolio capital in Mexican inflows.

Table 7.1 Net inflows of foreign capital to Brazil, Chile, Colombia and Mexico, 1987–94
(percentage of GDP)

	1987	1988	1989	1990	1991	1992	1993	1994
Brazil								
Foreign direct investment	0.4	0.8	0.2	—	—	0.3	–0.1	..
Medium- and long-term credits	–3.3	–3.0	–1.3	–0.3	–0.4	..	..	..
Portfolio flows	–0.1	0.1	–0.1	0.1	0.9	3.6	2.7	..
Short-term credits	0.1	–0.3	–0.2	–0.2	–0.4	..	..	..
Other	4.4	1.9	1.8	1.5	—	–1.5	–0.4	..
Total	1.5	–0.5	0.3	1.1	0.2	2.5	2.4	2.1
Chile								
Foreign direct investment	5.5	6.3	6.9	6.1	3.1	1.8	3.2	4.2
Medium- and long-term credits	1.8	1.3	0.8	0.9	0.7	1.2	1.4	2.3
Portfolio flows	—	—	0.3	1.2	0.8	1.1	2.3	2.0
Short-term credits	–1.4	–0.8	1.1	2.9	1.9	2.4	1.7	1.0
Other	–2.1	–2.8	–5.1	–1.6	–3.4	–1.0	–3.0	–1.9
Total	3.8	4.0	4.1	9.6	3.0	5.4	5.6	7.6
Colombia								
Foreign direct investment	0.8	0.4	1.4	1.2	1.0	1.6	1.6	2.5
Medium- and long-term credits	0.2	0.1	–0.7	–0.4	—	0.1	1.7	4.4
Portfolio flows	..	..	..	..	..	..	..	..
Short-term credits	–0.2	–0.6	–1.4	—	–1.3	1.4	2.9	0.6
Other	–0.5	1.5	1.4	–0.5	–0.7	–2.3	–1.5	–2.5
Total	—	1.5	0.6	0.2	–1.0	0.8	4.6	5.1
Mexico								
Foreign direct investment	2.3	1.5	1.5	1.1	1.7	1.6	1.4	..
Medium- and long-term credits	–2.0	–0.8	–0.5	2.7	2.7	1.9	—	..
Portfolio flows	–0.3	1.0	0.2	–2.2	3.2	4.3	7.7	..
Short-term credits	–3.4	–0.4	–0.5	1.2	1.2	1.8	0.2	..
Other	2.7	–2.0	—	0.7	–0.3	–1.5	–0.3	..
Total	–0.7	–0.8	0.7	3.5	8.5	8.0	8.9	5.1

.. denotes not available; — denotes zero or close to zero.
Note: Both credit items are private flows. Other flows are mostly official capital transactions. In Mexico, portfolio flows include foreign purchases of government securities and money-market instruments issued by banks. In Chile, other flows are mostly debt amortizations and, particularly in 1987–90, include large figures of counterpart of debt-equity swaps recorded in FDI.
Source: Central Bank of Chile, Banco de la República (Colombia) and CEPAL.

In 1990–94, Chile and Mexico had similar levels of net capital inflows. As a share of GDP, total inflows averaged 6.2% in Chile and 6.8% in Mexico. In Chile, the predominant form of inflows has been FDI, which, because of its long-term horizon, is fairly stable. But in Mexico, portfolio investments have overshadowed all other forms of funding. These flows are notoriously volatile. Stock markets tend to overshoot their equilibrium levels, and this is exactly what appears to have happened in Mexico. Unsustainably large inflows bid up asset prices above the levels justified by the underlying fundamentals. At the same time, they sowed the seeds for their subsequent reversal, as the current account deficit they helped produce (through real currency appreciation) led eventually to a change in market participants' expectations about investments in Mexican assets.[3] Interestingly, Chile and Brazil have recently acted to discourage this type of foreign investment.

In sum, the recent surge in foreign capital inflows into Latin America has taken a wide variety of forms. Different countries have fared quite differently with regard to the volume and composition of flows. Generally, there have been both long-term and short-term components in the surge of foreign capital. The most problematic flows, because of their volatility and pro-cyclical nature, have been interest-arbitraging flows and portfolio investments. Therefore, an exclusive concentration on short-term bank credits and deposits may well miss some of the most important flows: portfolio investments. In all four countries studied, these flows, which are new to the region,[4] have been extremely significant, and in one (Mexico), they have dominated capital inflows.

As already noted, one of the major effects of the foreign capital surge has been a significant real appreciation of the exchange rates of the recipient countries (table 7.2). The trend has affected all countries, even Chile and Colombia, which deployed a panoply of measures to discourage temporary capital inflows. Without these disincentives to capital inflows, the appreciations could have been even steeper. In fact, appreciation has been more moderate in countries with policies to discourage short-term inflows (Chile and Colombia) than in those that

Table 7.2 Real exchange rate for exports in Brazil, Chile, Colombia and Mexico, 1986–94

(1990 = 100)

	Brazil	Chile	Colombia	Mexico
1986	160.7	88.4	77.0	130.4
1987	156.8	96.3	85.2	135.2
1988	143.2	102.0	86.5	110.0
1989	108.4	96.4	88.8	103.2
1990	100.0	100.0	100.0	100.0
1991	118.5	98.9	101.0	91.1
1992	127.7	95.3	90.0	84.1
1993	115.4	96.6	87.0	79.8
1994	92.9	96.5	74.8	81.9
1995	71.2	93.0	73.3	120.5

Note: Values correspond to the real exchange rate of each country with respect to its principal trading partners, weighted by the relative importance of exports to each partner.
Source: CEPAL, Balance Preliminar de la Economía Latinoamericana y el Caribe—1995, Santiago, December 1995.

actively welcomed all forms of foreign capital (Argentina and Mexico). Brazil also experienced a sharp exchange rate appreciation until 1995, mainly because of fairly permissive policies towards foreign capital inflows. As discussed below, there have recently been important policy changes towards more active management of inflows.

Actual capital flows to recipient countries and their composition are a result of the interplay of supply and demand. In some countries (such as Chile and Mexico), the potential supply has been quite large. But in Mexico, actual capital flows are likely to have been very close to the amounts that financial markets were willing to supply, because the Mexican authorities actively welcomed the inflows. In Chile, by contrast, policies effectively discouraged a broad category of inflows. In the absence of such policies, actual inflows might have been considerably larger. Chilean policies, of course, have not been without cost or undesired side effects. Domestic interest rates have remained high, making the task of discouraging short-term inflows more difficult.

The policy response

As already noted, there have been two polar responses to the foreign capital surge. At one end of the spectrum, Argentina and Mexico have responded rather passively to the sharp increase in the supply of foreign capital. In fact, in both countries, inflows have been viewed as a sign of international confidence in the broad set of pro-market reforms pursued by the authorities, which have included trade liberalization, the opening of the capital account and massive privatizations. The policy package has also included dramatic reductions in inflation and fiscal consolidation.[5]

At the other end of the spectrum, Chile, Colombia and Brazil have followed a more pragmatic policy approach. These countries have adopted strategies to deal with the foreign capital surge that contain three elements: disincentives to short-term inflows, foreign exchange market intervention and sterilization of the monetary impact of rising reserves.

Chile

In the 1990s, Chile adopted a battery of policies aimed towards the surge in capital inflows. The central bank has attempted to discourage short-term and speculative capital inflows while maintaining open access to the economy for FDI. It has also sought to partially insulate the domestic economy from the impacts of capital inflows by intervening in foreign exchange markets to prevent an excess supply from unduly appreciating the real exchange rate and by almost completely sterilizing the monetary effects of the rapid accumulation of international reserves (see Ffrench-Davis, Agosin and Uthoff 1995).

The main consideration of exchange rate policy has been to protect the growth model adopted by the authorities, which is based on the expansion and diversification of exports. If exports are to continue to be the engine of growth for the Chilean economy, the level and stability of the real exchange rate are crucial. This objective could have been jeopardized if capital inflows caused excessive exchange rate appreciation and greater future volatility when net flows reversed. Sterilized intervention was deemed necessary so as not to fall short of the central bank's inflation targets.

The Chilean authorities opted to regulate the foreign exchange market in order to prevent large misalignments in the real exchange rate relative to its long-term trend. Their decision to make the long-term fundamentals prevail over short-term factors influencing the exchange rate assumes (correctly) that there is an asymmetry of information between the market and the monetary authorities: the authorities have a better knowledge of the factors driving the balance of payments and a longer planning horizon than agents who operate intensely at the short-term end of the market. However, in the face of uncertainty, rather than a unique price, the authorities have used an exchange rate band centred on a reference price; this price is linked to a basket of three currencies in which the dollar, the deutsche mark and the yen are represented with fixed weights according to their share in Chilean trade.[6]

Chilean exchange rate policy has undergone substantial change. The fixed nominal exchange rate used in 1979–82, in the context of an increasing and eventually complete liberalization of capital account transactions, was abandoned after the crisis of 1982, during which GDP declined by 15%. In 1983–89, the authorities used a strict crawling peg with a floating band of 2% (increased to 3% in 1988 and to 5% in mid-1989). The "official" rate was devalued daily, in line with the differential between domestic inflation and an estimate of external inflation. On many occasions, discrete nominal devaluations were added, helping to achieve a remarkable real depreciation following the 1982 crisis (119% between 1981 and 1988).

The excess supply of foreign exchange began to accumulate in mid-1990. The changes in global markets, the increasing international approval of Chilean economic policies, the high interest rates in Chile and the fact that the uncertainty stemming from the 1988 plebiscite and from President Aylwin's induction into office was quickly dispelled all stimulated a growing inflow of capital to Chile. These events were quickly reflected in a real appreciation of the market exchange rate. Beginning in July 1990, the market rate moved from the top to the floor of the band. The strong inflows of capital continued, with the central bank making large purchases of foreign exchange in the market. Recurrent runs on the dollar and in favour of the peso were reinforced by expectations of a revaluation (and drops in domestic interest rates), which hampered monetary policy.

In early 1991, the strict crawling peg system was modified. To introduce exchange rate "noise" with the aim of discouraging short-term flows, the rate was abruptly revalued by a small amount on three occasions and then, in compensation, devalued in the following months. Since the first two exchange rate changes were unanticipated by the market, they were an effective tool for temporarily stemming the excess supply of foreign exchange. But the measure could not be repeated too often, because the market would come to anticipate the revaluation, and the policy would lose its effectiveness.

In June 1991, in addition to a small (2%) revaluation of the official rate and a drop in the import tariff from 15% to 11%, a non-interest-bearing reserve requirement of 20% was established on external credits. The reserves had to be maintained with the central bank for a minimum of 90 days and a maximum of one year, which meant that the impact fell mostly on short-term flows. At the same time, a stamp tax on domestic credit, at an annual rate of 1.2% on operations of up to one year, was extended to apply to external loans. In July, an alternative to the reserve requirement was allowed for medium-term credits, which consisted of paying to the central bank an amount equivalent to the financial cost of the reserve requirement. The financial cost was calculated by applying LIBOR plus 2.5% to the amount of the reserve requirement. The reserve requirement, the option of paying its financial cost and the tax on foreign credits all have a zero marginal cost for lending that exceeds one year and are particularly onerous for lending at very short maturities.

Pressures on the foreign exchange market continued in the ensuing months, owing partly to capital inflows (interest rates were low and declining in the United States, Chile's principal international capital market) and partly to a favourable current account. In January 1992, the official exchange rate was revalued by 5%, and the floating band in the formal market was expanded to 10%. To deter interest arbitrage by creating more uncertainty for short-term transactions, in March 1992, the central bank initiated dirty floating within the band.

In the ensuing months, interest rates continued to decline, exerting pressure on the central bank. But since the Chilean economy was booming, the central bank wanted to increase rather than lower domestic interest rates in order to maintain macroeconomic equilibrium. To avoid encouraging arbitrage, it decided to augment the reserve requirements on capital inflows. In May 1992, it raised reserve requirements on external credits to 30%, later extending them to time deposits in foreign currency. In October, the central bank increased the period for which the deposit had to be maintained to one year regardless of the maturity of the loan. At the same time, the spread charged over LIBOR in the option of paying the financial cost of the reserve requirement was raised from 2.5% to 4%.

In July of the same year, the dollar peg of the official rate was replaced by a peg to a basket of currencies as the new benchmark exchange rate. Given the instability of international exchange rates, these measures were intended to make interest rate arbitrage between the dollar and the peso less profitable by introducing greater exchange rate uncertainty for speculative dollar-denominated capital flows.

Since 1991, an attempt has been made to ease capital outflows as a way of alleviating downward pressure on the exchange rate (for details see Ffrench-Davis, Agosin and Uthoff 1995). But because the rate of return on financial assets remains considerably higher within than outside Chile, these measures are unlikely to ease the pressure on the exchange rate and, in the short run, may instead act as an incentive to additional inflows (Williamson 1992; Labán and Larraín 1993). Moreover, in the long run, such policies risk leaving too many doors open for outflows, which could be massive if the market becomes nervous and expectations shift to currency depreciation. A careless financial liberalization could pose significant obstacles to exchange rate policy and macroeconomic management, generating sources of instability. The recent Mexican crisis is a clear example of this.

Disincentives to short-term capital inflows have not prevented a significant real appreciation of the currency.[7] The appreciation was strongest between early 1991 and late 1992. Although there was a lull during 1993, owing to a sharp decline in export prices, the trend towards exchange rate appreciation reasserted itself in 1994. The terms of trade recovered strongly and, as already noted, there was a surge of both FDI and portfolio capital inflows. Faced with the need to continue purchasing large quantities of foreign exchange in the market to keep the dollar from piercing the floor of the floating band, the central bank revalued the central point of the band by 10% in November 1994.

In the first quarter of 1995, there was a lull in the trend towards currency appreciation, mainly as a consequence of the Mexican crisis, which temporarily dried up portfolio capital inflows. But the pressures towards appreciation reasserted themselves in the middle of the year. To stem these pressures, in July 1995, the central bank extended the reserve requirement obligation of 30% to foreign financial investments into the country, particularly the purchases of Chilean stocks by foreigners (so-called secondary American depository receipts, or ADRs).[8]

The definitive study on the efficacy of the measures used for deterring short-term flows and preventing excessive exchange rate appreciation has yet to be written. But there is some econometric evidence that they have worked rather well. A recent study indicates that the combination of disincentives to short-term inflows and the reforms of the exchange rate regime significantly reduced the inflow of short-term, interest-arbitraging funds (Agosin forthcoming).

Some observers have claimed that the efficacy of measures to discourage capital inflows is only temporary, because private sector operators will find ways to evade them. In principle, they can evade restrictions in three ways. First, they can underinvoice imports or overinvoice exports. Second, they can delay payment for imports or accelerate export receipts. And third, they can bring in funds through the informal foreign exchange market.[9] Although some evasion is inevitable, there is no hard evidence of large-scale evasion of the measures to discourage short-term capital inflows. In fact, short-term flows have tended to decrease as a share of GDP (see table 7.1). In the absence of the policy measures taken, they might have been considerably larger.

The imposition of reserve requirements on portfolio flows also appears to have been timely. In 1994 alone, gross inflows of portfolio capital represented about 3.5% of GDP. Thus the extension of reserve requirements to these inflows can be considered a pre-emptive strike to deal with an incipient problem that was already causing difficulties in policy management and could become even more important in the future. Although significant, the internationalization of the Chilean stock exchange was just beginning relative to, say, the Mexican market.

What have been the financial costs imposed on foreign borrowing by the reserve requirements and taxes on foreign lending? Table 7.3 shows the financial costs estimated in two ways: by assuming that medium-term borrowers pay the financial costs of the reserve requirements rather than leave funds on deposit, and by calculating the tax on foreign borrowing that is implicit in the reserve requirements, which impose extra interest costs.

Under the option of paying the financial cost (fc) of the reserve requirements, the tax equivalent (as a percentage of the value of the loan) is as follows:[10]

$$(1) \qquad\qquad fc = e(r + s) + t,$$

where e is the rate of reserve requirement, r is LIBOR, s is the central bank spread and t is the tax rate on foreign borrowing.

Under the option of placing funds on deposit with the central bank to comply with the reserve requirements, the tax equivalent on foreign borrowings with one-year maturities is as follows:

$$(2) \qquad\qquad \tau = \frac{re + t}{1 - e}$$

Both options have an almost identical implicit tax rate for one-year loans.[11] The implicit tax rate on foreign borrowing increases dramatically as maturities shorten because of two factors: the fixed tax of 1.2% and, since late 1992, the requirement that reserves be kept for one year regardless of the maturity of the loan.

Table 7.3 Chile: Implicit taxes on foreign borrowing, 1991–94
(annualized percentage rates)

	1991 II	1992 I	1992 II	1993	1994
Reserve requirement	20	20	30	30	30
Minimum reserve period (months)	3	3	3	12	12
LIBOR	5.5	4.5	3.6	3.4	5.0
Spread	2.5	2.5	2.5	4.0	4.0
Financial costs	2.8	2.6	3.0	3.4	3.9
Tax:					
annual	2.9	2.6	3.3	3.2	3.9
6-month	4.5	4.2	5.1	6.5	8.0
3-month	7.9	7.5	8.9	13.6	16.9

Note: For formula used to calculate the financial costs see below.
Source: Authors' calculations, based on data of the Central Bank of Chile.

**Table 7.4 Chile: Revenues from explicit and implicit taxes
on capital inflow, 1991–94**
(millions of US dollars)

	Tax on foreign loans	Interest paid in lieu of reserves	Interest earned	Total
1991	4.7	2.2	—	6.9
1992	28.8	16.6	19.4	64.8
1993	34.2	38.0	39.4	111.6
1994	42.5	64.4	65.3	172.2
Total	110.2	121.2	124.1	355.5

— denotes zero or close to zero.
Source: Authors' calculations, based on data of the Central Bank of Chile.

The Treasury or the central bank collects revenues through the stamp tax on foreign loans, interest paid by borrowers of foreign funds in lieu of meeting reserve requirements and the bank's earnings on the interest-free reserve requirements. The amounts are not terribly large: from the time reserve requirements and the stamp tax were imposed through the end of 1994, estimated revenues were $356 million, or about 0.7% of 1994 GDP (table 7.4). These policies should therefore be judged by their prudential and regulatory value rather than by their revenue-earning value.

Colombia

Colombia has put in place dramatic economic policy reforms since 1990, including a thorough trade liberalization in a very short period (essentially 1990–92), a liberalization of the rules and regulations towards FDI and a controlled opening of the capital account of the balance of payments (liberalization of foreign exchange transactions, greater freedom to borrow abroad and authorization of portfolio flows).[12] These policy changes were preceded by a fairly steep real exchange rate depreciation (see table 7.2), which gave the economy a cushion to face the stresses associated with the capital inflows that have often accompanied pro-market reforms in Latin America.

Faced with strong inflows that were putting pressure on the real exchange rate, in 1991 Colombia replaced the strict crawling peg that it had used together with effective foreign exchange controls since 1967 with a system combining foreign exchange market intervention and sterilization in a single operation. To cope with the abundance of foreign exchange, the Banco de la República purchased foreign exchange with "exchange certificates", or bonds denominated in dollars with a one-year maturity. The redemption price of these bonds, the "official exchange rate", was fixed daily by the bank. At the moment of issue, these certificates could be sold in the secondary market at a discount. The Banco de la República kept the market discount within specified limits that, in effect, constituted a band for the market exchange rate. If the discount reached 12.5%, the bank entered the market to purchase certificates; when the discount reached a minimum of 5.5%, the bank sold certificates (see Cárdenas and Barrera 1994).

In early 1994, the exchange certificates were replaced with an explicit floating band of 15% with a sliding central parity. Towards the end of 1994, the central parity was revalued by 7%, and its rate of devaluation was predetermined for the year ahead (a sort of "tablita") and fixed at 13.5% a year.

Other measures, including reserve requirements and taxes on short-term capital inflows, have also been used to deal with the excess supply of foreign exchange.[13] For example, in April 1991, authorities began to charge a commission of 5% on foreign exchange sold to the Banco de la República. In addition, a retention fee of 3% was imposed on non-export foreign exchange receipts (exporters were later given a drawback on the fee). In July 1992, the fee was raised to 10%. In that same month, to curtail the inflow of foreign capital through the tourism account, a limit of $25,000 was set for permitted exchanges of foreign currency by each tourism establishment. And in late 1992, the monetary authorities switched from attempting to control the monetary aggregates to discouraging interest rate arbitrage by setting limits on lending interest rates.

In September 1993, the authorities replaced this system with a fairly complex reserve requirement mechanism subjecting all credits of less than 18 months to a 47% reserve requirement for the duration of the loan.[14] The certificates issued by the authorities against the reserves could be repurchased at a discount that depended on the date of repurchase. This mechanism is equivalent to the Chilean scheme of paying the financial cost of the reserve requirement. Credits with maturities of less than six months and those for the purchase of capital goods were initially excluded from reserve requirements. However, longer-term credits that were partially amortized before 18 months were subject to reserve requirements on the portions amortized, if the amortizations represented at least 30% of the credit.

In March 1994, reserve requirements were extended to all credits with a maturity of less than 36 months. The period during which the deposits had to be maintained was changed, and borrowers were given the option of constituting deposits of 12, 18 or 24 months. Reserves on 12-month deposits had to be equivalent to 93% of the foreign credit; on 18-month deposits, 64%; and on 24-month deposits, 50%. There was also an option of reselling the certificates of deposit to the Banco de la República at a discount. If loans had maturities in excess of 36 months and at least 40% was amortized before 36 months, reserve requirements had to be constituted against the amounts amortized.

In August 1994, reserve requirements were extended to all loans of up to 60 months' maturity. Longer-term loans were exempted, except for amortizations within the first 60 months (when such amortizations are at least 40% of the credit). For trade credits of between four and six months, reserve requirements were set at 30%.

In addition, banks must maintain net asset positions in foreign exchange, which severely limits their borrowings in foreign exchange for the purpose of lending in pesos. This measure not only helps prevent inflows, and therefore excessive real exchange rate appreciation, but also protects bank balance sheets and liquidity when the flows are reversed and the exchange rate is depreciating.

Although capital inflows have been large, they are still reasonable relative to GDP, and the current account deficit is moderate. Without the measures taken, inflows might have been much larger, in view of the general expectations of currency appreciation stemming from both the economic reform and the good prospects for the Colombian current account.[15] Although there is no hard evidence on the effects of the reserve requirement mechanism used in Colombia, perhaps one of its results has been the lengthening of maturities on foreign borrowing and the near disappearance of short-term borrowing since late 1993. Thus Colombia has probably avoided (or at least smoothed) the boom-bust cycle that tends to accompany economic reform combined with a capital surge (see Urrutia 1995).

Because of the way that the reserve requirement system has operated—becoming prohibitive for funds affected—actual tax-like proceeds seem to have been low. It is estimated that less than $100 million was deposited as reserves.

Brazil

Brazil has undergone more policy shifts with regard to capital inflows than either Chile or Colombia. Until the adoption of the Plano Real in 1994, hyperinflation and broad macroeconomic disequilibrium prevailed. In recent years, there have been several capital surges, and Brazil has responded with policies that have evolved towards more active management of flows.

In 1991, several measures were adopted to stimulate capital inflows, particularly to the stock exchange. Several additional taxes on foreign funding were eliminated, placing tax rates at the same levels as those applying to residents' financial transactions. In addition, Brazilian firms recovered voluntary access to external sources of finance.

In 1992, a huge current account surplus developed as a result of a three-year recession between 1990 and 1992. Despite the recession, inflation averaged more than 1,000% a year. There were growing capital inflows, particularly for privatizations, the purchase of bonds and stock market transactions. Brazil chose to continue depreciating the real exchange rate (by 28% in 1990–92) and accumulating reserves. Reserves were used partly to reduce interest payment arrears, as agreed in the renegotiation of the external debt.

In 1993, hyperinflation and large capital inflows continued, with portfolio inflows reaching $12 billion. The central bank continued purchasing foreign currency but allowed some exchange rate appreciation. By mid-1993, taxes were imposed on financial inflows, along with minimum-length maturity terms on foreign borrowing. But the reactivation of demand, the lagged effects of import liberalization and the appreciation of the exchange rate led to a sharp change in the current account, which went from a large surplus in 1992 to a small deficit in 1993. Despite an increase in the deficit in 1994, capital inflows were even larger, and reserves continued to accumulate. Between 1992 and 1994, the central bank increased its international reserves by $31 billion.

In conjunction with the launching of the Plano Real, the bank retired from the market, with the result that the exchange rate appreciated sharply (by about a third) in a short period. The plan was successful in reducing inflation, from roughly 40% a month to nearly 2%. Imports rose strongly, a significant trade deficit was generated in the second half of 1994, and a worrisome current account deficit emerged. After some confusing ups and downs, the "Tequila effect" helped Brazil to make a policy shift; beginning in the second quarter of 1995, exchange rate policy became active, a band was established and dirty floating within the band was adopted.

Several restrictions on inflows were gradually introduced or reimposed. In August 1995, a tax of 5% was imposed on loans in foreign currency and on interbank operations between Brazilian and foreign institutions. Foreign exchange sales on the open market were taxed at the rate of 7%. The tax rate for foreign purchases of fixed-income instruments, previously 5%, was raised to 7%. In September, a capital gains tax of 15% on stock market transactions that had applied only to residents was extended to non-residents.

Mexico

Mexico adopted a more laissez-faire approach to the surge in foreign capital. In fact, the Mexican capital account has been dramatically liberalized since the mid-1980s, partly in connection with Mexico's signing of the North American Free Trade Agreement (NAFTA). The capital account liberalization was part of a broad effort to liberalize the economy, which included a drastic trade liberalization, accession to the General Agreement on Tariffs and Trade (GATT) and the Organisation for Economic Co-operation and Development (OECD), privatization of state enterprises and the liberalization of FDI policies (see Lustig 1992; Ten Kate 1993; and Ros 1994). In addition, there has been a serious—and largely successful—effort at fiscal consolidation. Mexico presents a classic case of the effects of an economic reform perceived as credible by international capital markets. With the globalization of international financial markets, such reforms encourage capital inflows that are unsustainable in the long run and that, through overshooting, sow the seeds for their later reversal.

In Mexican policy relating to the capital account of the balance of payments, the changes have almost all been in the direction of opening up and liberalization—both for long-term flows such as FDI and for short-term flows such as foreign borrowing or purchases by non-residents of stocks, bonds and money market instruments. The rules and regulations towards FDI were liberalized beginning in 1984: new sectors were opened to foreign investors, restrictions on majority foreign ownership were relaxed in several sectors and the administrative procedures for the approval of projects were simplified. Since 1989, investments of less than $100 million in fully owned subsidiaries have received automatic approval.

Before 1988, foreign portfolio investment was strictly regulated and actively discouraged in Mexico. The liberalization of financial markets after 1988 made an important contribution to the surge in foreign portfolio investments (Ros 1994). In 1989, Mexican firms were allowed to issue special shares for purchase by foreigners. At the end of 1990, foreigners were allowed to purchase Mexican bonds and money market instruments. The possibility of placing ADRs on the New York Stock

Exchange (with the associated purchases by foreigners in the Mexican market of the same securities) and the rapid growth of investments in Mexican securities by Mexico mutual funds were made possible by almost simultaneous regulatory changes in Mexico and the United States (Culpeper 1995).

In 1990, Mexican commercial banks began to issue short-term dollar-denominated certificates of deposit. Faced with massive inflows from this source, in April 1992, the monetary authorities decided to put a 10% cap on the share of foreign liabilities in the total liabilities of banks. They also set a liquidity coefficient of 15% for dollar liabilities, requiring that this share be invested in low-risk or risk-free assets (Gurría 1995). But these measures were insufficient to stem the inflows from this source.

Mexico made important changes in its exchange rate regime in November 1991, eliminating controls and the dual exchange rate system that had operated in Mexico since 1982. Banco de México introduced a widening exchange rate band, with a fixed floor and a ceiling that depreciated by a fixed peso amount every day. Until the crisis of late 1994, the monetary authorities had undertaken active sterilized intervention in the foreign exchange market. Until March 1994, the bank had made large net purchases of foreign exchange, at a rate close to the bottom. Nevertheless, the peso appreciated steadily from its lows after the devaluations of 1986–87 (see table 7.2). During the rest of 1994, as a result of adverse political developments (the Chiapas insurrection and the assassination of presidential candidate Colosio) and a rise in US interest rates, given rising external liabilities of Mexico accumulated between 1992 and 1994, the still growing current account deficit began to exceed new capital inflows, and the bank made large sales of foreign exchange. At the same time, faced with growing investor nervousness, the government switched from issuing peso debt (Cetes) to issuing dollar-indexed short-term securities (Tesobonos). This shift ended up adding to the depth of the economic and financial crisis after the crash of the peso in December 1994.

During the period of capital inflows, Mexican inflation was reduced, but remained above international inflation. Thus the real exchange rate appreciated persistently. The real appreciation continued until March 1994, when the rate jumped from the floor to the ceiling of the band. Then, after the onset of the crisis in December 1994, the peso was officially devalued by 15%, and shortly thereafter the exchange rate was left to float freely upward. After December 20, 1994 the correction was swift, with a 100% rise in the nominal price of the dollar in less than three months. Inflation in 1995 jumped to more than 50%, gross investment dropped by one-third and GDP fell by 7%.

What accounted for the boom-bust cycle and the associated massive inflows of portfolio capital, followed by equally massive outflows? What was the role of poor macroeconomic management? In particular, did inadequate fiscal restraint play an important part, as has been suggested by those who unwaveringly support capital account liberalization? Or, can the blame be assigned to inadequate regulation of the more volatile forms of capital inflows, which have a propensity to overshoot their equilibrium levels? The answers to these questions are crucial to policy-making in an increasingly globalized international financial system.

The main explanation seems to be that both policy-makers and international portfolio investors came to hold overly optimistic expectations about Mexico's prospects in the wake of economic reforms, and that this led to excessive capital inflows and excessive domestic spending. Neutralizing inflows as large as those of Mexico in recent years is no doubt a difficult and costly task. The inflows alone tend to unleash a spending boom, centred on importables, as the ensuing appreciation of the exchange rate leads to higher real incomes in terms of tradables. The increase in the money supply, arising from incompletely sterilized increases in reserves, has similar expansionary effects. In the meantime, the stock of external liabilities can accumulate very rapidly. In Mexico, they rose by more than $90 billion between 1991 and 1994. Most of these liabilities were short-term or very volatile. Therefore, disincentives to capital inflows are unavoidable in circumstances such as those faced by Mexico in the first half of the 1990s.

Policy and economic performance

Have countries that have used disincentives to short-term capital inflows performed better in terms of growth and stability than countries, such as Argentina and Mexico, that have been more permissive? Of course, a simple inspection of growth rates, inflation and similar variables will not provide a sure answer, since these variables respond to a large variety of influences, of which capital inflows are only one. Moreover, countries that have allowed their real exchange rates to appreciate in response to large capital inflows have in effect experienced lower rates of inflation for a while. That was certainly the case for Mexico (table 7.5). And in Argentina, inflation rates are now at or

Table 7.5 Latin America: GDP growth rates, inflation rates and cumulative current account deficits

(percent)

	Brazil	Chile	Colombia	Mexico	Latin America and the Caribbean
GDP growth rates					
1980–90	1.7	2.8	3.7	1.7	1.2
1990–94	2.3	6.3	4.3	2.6	3.6
1995ᵃ	4.2	8.5	5.3	–7.0	0.3
Cumulative current account deficit (percentage of GDP)					
1991–94	–0.5	10.4	2.4	25.4	9.7
Inflation rates					
1991	476	18.7	26.8	18.9	200
1992	1,149	12.7	25.2	11.9	419
1993	2,489	12.2	22.6	8.0	888
1994	929	8.9	23.0	6.9	337
1995ᵃ	22	8.3	20.0	52.0	25

a. Preliminary.
Source: CEPAL, Statistical Yearbook for Latin America and the Caribbean 1994, CEPAL, Economic Survey of Latin America and the Caribbean 1994–1995; and CEPAL Preliminary Overview of the economy of Latin America and the Caribbean, 1995, Santiago, December 1995.

even below international levels, owing to the use of the exchange rate as the nominal anchor. But the costs of maintaining a fixed nominal exchange rate and fully free international capital movements are proving to be very high: in 1995, unemployment reached nearly 20% of the labour force, GDP dropped by 4.4% and gross investment fell by one-fifth.

Despite the caveats about a naked-eye inspection of economic performance indicators, it is suggestive that, in the 1990s, Chile and Colombia have experienced higher or steadier rates of GDP growth than Mexico (and Argentina). At the same time, inflation rates in these two countries have been somewhat higher than in Mexico, where inflation eventually converged towards international levels, while inflows were positive. But when inflows were reversed, causing depreciation of the exchange rate (which probably overshot its long-term "fundamental equilibrium" level), Mexican inflation shot up to levels much higher than those experienced in either Chile or Colombia.

An indicator of financial sustainability is the cumulative current account deficit. In this respect, the figures in table 7.5 are telling. Even though the volume of foreign capital inflows in Chile as a share of GDP was quite similar to that in Mexico, Chile effectively used a much smaller amount. The cumulative disequilibrium of Mexico's external accounts during 1990–94 was two and a half times that in Chile's external accounts. From this perspective, the Mexican crisis looks inevitable, and Chile's success in maintaining broad macroeconomic balances and avoiding large cycles is easy to explain.

Policy lessons

The evidence on the latest surge in foreign capital inflows into Latin America suggests that it is essential to have in place a policy apparatus that distinguishes between long-term, stable capital inflows such as FDI and those that are considerably more volatile and that have adverse effects on long-term growth. Volatile flows include short-term financial credits to banks and large domestic firms, short-term deposits by non-residents in the domestic financial system and purchases of stocks and bonds by non-residents. These transactions seek to arbitrage interest rate differentials or to obtain quick capital gains. These flows cause very sharp increases (bubbles) in domestic asset prices and unsustainable exchange rate appreciations that are later reversed when the effects on domestic relative prices and the current account balance become evident (see Devlin, Ffrench-Davis and Griffith-Jones 1995). Then, an overshooting ensues in the other direction, with asset prices falling and the real exchange rate depreciating more than is justified by the underlying fundamentals.[16]

In attempting to differentiate between volatile short-term investments and long-term, more stable inflows such as FDI (or long-term borrowing from multilateral institutions), the cleanest option is to impose a small tax on inflows. Such a tax is prohibitively expensive for very short-term round-tripping but a negligible cost for long-term investors. In Latin America, Chile's approach comes closest to such a device. Brazil also began implementing a tax on credits in foreign currency in August 1995. As discussed above, the non-interest-bearing reserve requirement system is a close equivalent to a tax on inflows. In Chile, the implicit tax can be quite steep on very short maturities. Colombia also uses a reserve requirement system. But it seems to be less effective than the Chilean system, in which the reserve requirement applies to all credits regardless of maturity and is therefore difficult to evade.

These policies are quite similar in effect to the tax proposed by Tobin on foreign exchange transactions (see Tobin 1978 and 1994): both are attempts to throw sand in the wheels of speculative international capital flows. But there are significant differences between the approaches followed by the more activist Latin American countries and the Tobin tax. The Tobin tax is far more comprehensive, since it would be imposed on all foreign exchange transactions, not merely on certain categories of capital inflows. The Tobin tax would also be much smaller than the explicit and implicit tax rates on capital inflows in Latin America. While proposals for the Tobin tax range from 0.15% to 0.5%, the tax rates on capital inflows have been several times larger.

The Mexican case affords an interesting contrast to the experiences of the three other countries analysed in this paper. Mexico has used few controls on foreign capital inflows. Indeed, it has gone the other way, dismantling those in place before the liberalizations of the second half of the 1980s. Those restrictions had been quite effective in limiting foreign portfolio investments in Mexico. The results are clear: unnecessary fluctuations of the exchange rate, large swings in output and employment, and low economic growth.

The problems posed by foreign portfolio investments must be appropriately tackled. It is unclear that developing countries have much to gain from this form of internationalization of finance.[17] Firms able to issue stock in international markets can obtain finance at much lower cost than in domestic capital markets—clearly a positive thing. But allowing foreign portfolio investors to purchase stock in domestic markets results only in a change in the ownership of existing assets, and the problems of volatility and overshooting associated with these investments are likely to be as acute as (or even more acute than) those associated with other forms of short-term capital flows.

When portfolio investors discover a new emerging market, massive capital inflows follow until foreign investors acquire the desired stocks of portfolio capital. These inflows, in turn, can appreciate the exchange rate to a point at which the resulting current account deficits become unsustainable. In due course, capital inflows turn into outflows, and the exchange rate overshoots in the opposite direction. Disincentives to portfolio inflows can be used to dampen the speed at which the desired stock is approached. These disincentives can take several forms: taxing capital gains on transactions in domestic stock (the option chosen by Brazil beginning in September 1995), placing limits on the share of firms' capital that can be owned by non-residents (the approach adopted by the Republic of Korea), auctioning quotas for such investment, taxing the purchase and sale of stock by non-residents and placing reserve requirements on such transactions (the Chilean policy since July 1995).

Even FDI might need to be slowed. As the recent Latin American experience shows, such inflows can be quite massive. After many years of underinvestment, owing mainly to the effects of the debt crisis, multi-national companies engaged in a typical process of stock adjustment. While stocks of FDI are adjusting to their desired levels, flows can be massive indeed. Small economies have difficulty absorbing these large inflows. So, a case could be made for auctioning the rights to make foreign direct investments, placing investment applications on an informal queue or choosing from all the projects on offer those most likely to enhance development. All these options entail a much more pragmatic approach to FDI than the uncritical embrace of recent years.

The measures discussed in this paper should not be considered revenue-earning. Only for Chile was a calculation of the revenue impact of these measures feasible, and for Chile the revenue from taxes on capital inflows or from their equivalents are small. Thus in developing countries, where international financial transactions are minuscule by international standards, these measures should be adopted essentially for their regulatory and prudential value. The surge in foreign capital inflows in recent years has shown, however, that such inflows can be enormous by national standards and, if countries do not adopt appropriate policy measures, that they can have very disruptive effects on the domestic economy.

Appendix: Calculating the implicit tax in Chilean disincentives to capital inflows

The Chilean monetary authorities have used two main mechanisms to discourage capital inflows: a tax of 1.2% on all foreign loans regardless of their maturity and reserve requirements for a period of up to one year on foreign borrowing, bank deposits in foreign currency and, recently, some portfolio inflows. Until October 1992, reserve requirements had to be maintained for a period that fluctuated between 90 days and one year. The regulations were changed in October 1992 to require reserves to be maintained on deposits for a full year, regardless of the maturity of the loan.

There are therefore three elements that raise the cost of foreign borrowing to Chilean agents: to meet the reserve requirement, they must borrow more funds than they need; they must pay the foreign credit tax; and for loans with maturities of less than one year, they must maintain reserves on deposit for longer than the maturity of the loan.

This appendix examines three cases. Case 1, the simplest, assumes that the foreign loan is for one year and that the reserve requirement is also for one year. Case 2 assumes that the loan is for less than one year and that reserves must be maintained for the life of the loan (essentially as under the regulations in force from June 1991 until October 1992). Case 3 assumes that the loan is for a fraction of the year and that reserve requirements must be left on deposit for a full year (as under the regulations in force since October 1992).

Case 1

In case 1, foreign borrowing is made more expensive by the effect of the reserve requirements and the tax on foreign borrowing. The implicit tax on foreign borrowing (τ_1) is equal to the difference between the effective annual borrowing costs ($\hat{r}$) and the international interest rate (r):

(A1)
$$\tau_1 = \hat{r} - r$$

and

(A2)
$$\hat{r} = \frac{r + t}{1 - e}$$

where t = the fixed tax rate (in this case, 1.2%) and e = the reserve requirement rate, therefore:

(A3)
$$\tau_1 = \frac{r+t}{1-e} - r = \frac{t+re}{1-e}$$

Case 2

In case 2, the interest rate (i) applied for a shorter period is related to the annual interest rate by the following compound interest rule:

(A4)
$$r = (1+i)^n - 1,$$

where n is the number of such periods in a year (for example, $n = 12$ for a one-month loan).

In this case, $\tau_2 = \hat{r}_2 - r$, where

(A5)
$$\hat{r}_2 = (1 + \frac{i+t}{1-e})^n - 1.$$

Case 3

In case 3, the non-interest-bearing reserve deposit must be left for a full year even though the loan itself is for a fraction of the year. Again, the interest rate is calculated (based on the year equivalent) for the period of the loan. There are n such periods in a year.

The real cost of borrowing ($\hat{i}_3$), including the cost of the reserve requirement and the tax, is:

(A6)
$$\hat{i}_3 = \frac{i+t}{1-e} + \frac{e}{1-e} [(1+i)^{n-1} - 1].$$

On an annualized basis, the real cost of borrowing ($\hat{r}_3$) is:

(A7)
$$\hat{r}_3 = (1 + \hat{i}_3)^n - 1.$$

As in the other cases, the implicit tax (on an annualized basis) is the difference between the real cost of borrowing and the international interest rate:

(A8)
$$\tau_3 = \hat{r}_3 - r.$$

Notes

1. If there are to be interest-arbitraging capital inflows, the following condition—which is behind the paper's analysis of recent changes in the incentives to capital movements—must hold: $i = i^* + E(dep) + cr$, where i is the domestic nominal interest rate, i^* is the foreign interest rate, $E(dep)$ is the expected rate of depreciation of the domestic currency, and cr is the country risk premium.

2. The emerging markets mania of recent years in international stock markets can be interpreted as a dramatic reduction in perceived country risk premiums (only for countries with more developed domestic stock markets, of course).

3. For theoretical discussions of this phenomenon in the context of international bank lending decisions, see McKinnon (1991) and McKinnon and Pill (1995).

4. Portfolio capital, especially the placement of long-term bonds in the London market, was an extremely important form of international finance in Latin America before the First World War. But the recent massive investment in Latin American equity is in fact a new phenomenon.

5. The main difference in the responses of Argentina and Mexico has been in the degree to which central banks have sterilized increases in international reserves. While Mexico practised partial sterilization, Argentina's currency board approach to exchange rate and monetary policy, in force since April 1991, precludes it altogether. After the "Tequila effect" of late 1994, however, some flexibility was introduced in order to soften the effects of the loss of reserves on aggregate demand and on the liquidity crunch threatening the survival of many domestic banks.

6. For a comparative analysis of bands in Chile, Israel and Mexico, see Helpman, Leiderman and Bufman (1994). For an analysis of Chile, Colombia and Israel, see Williamson (forthcoming).

7. Chile was coming out of a profound debt crisis that was accompanied by a sharp exchange rate depreciation. Consequently, there was room for some appreciation. But because Chile was moving from a restricted to an overabundant supply of external savings, the authorities wanted to avoid an overadjustment of the exchange rate. A troublesome feature of emerging markets is that as investors' expectations change to optimism, they seek to reach a new desired stock of investment in the emerging market over a short period. This implies excessively large inflows for a time. Obviously, these are transitory flows rather than permanently higher periodic inflows.

8. For an analysis of this issue, see Ffrench-Davis, Agosin and Uthoff (1995).

It is not difficult to impose reserve requirements on foreign portfolio investments. If the funds that will be used for the investment are deposited with a Chilean bank, the foreign deposit is liable to reserve requirements. For funds that do not go through a Chilean bank, the reserve requirement can be imposed when the asset is registered in the name of an agent with a foreign address. Funds being converted into ADRs must also be registered with the central bank.

9. Potentially, short-term funds could be registered as FDI. But this could be a costly option, since Chilean law requires that FDI remain in the country for one year before repatriation. The loans associated with FDI are subject to the reserve requirement. Since the average maturity of these loans is about seven years, the incidence of the restriction is low.

10. A more formal derivation is shown in the appendix, which also gives various formulae for the implicit tax on maturities of less than one year.

11. Short-term borrowers do not have the option of paying the financial costs of borrowing and must meet reserve requirements.

12. A discussion of the Colombian trade policy reform can be found in Ocampo (1993). Policies towards the capital account are described in Cárdenas and Barrera (1994). For an account of the liberalization of FDI regulations, see Steiner and Giedion (1996).

13. The importance attributed by the monetary authorities to the excess supply of foreign exchange and the appreciation of the Colombian peso since 1991 suggests that the capital inflows recorded in the balance of payments seriously underestimate their real magnitudes.

14. This information was kindly provided by Dr. Miguel Urrutia, general manager, Banco de la República.

15. Recent petroleum investments will transform Colombia into a major oil exporter in a few years.

16. At the microeconomic level, these fundamentals are, of course, the future earnings prospects of firms. At the macroeconomic level, they include sustainable current account positions and long-term capital flows.

17. For a discussion of this issue, see CEPAL (1995a, chapter 10) and Stiglitz (1994).

References

Agosin, Manuel R. Forthcoming. "El retorno de los capitales extranjeros a Chile." *El Trimestre Económico.*

Calvo, Guillermo, Leonardo Leiderman and Carmen Reinhart. 1993. "Capital Inflows and Real Exchange Appreciation in Latin America: The Role of

External Factors." *IMF Staff Papers* 40(1).

Cárdenas, Mauricio and Felipe Barrera. 1994. "Efectos macroeconómicos de los capitales extranjeros." In José Antonio Ocampo, ed., *Los Capitales Extranjeros en las Economías Latinoamericanas.* FEDESARROLLO and the Interamerican Development Bank. Bogotá.

CEPAL (Comisión Ecónomica para América Latina y el Caribe). 1994. *Statistical Yearbook for Latin America and the Caribbean 1994.* Santiago.

———. 1995a. *America Latin America and the Caribbean: Policies to Improve Linkages with the Global Economy.* Santiago.

———. 1995b. *Balance Preliminar de la Economía Latinoamericana y el Caribe— 1995.* Santiago, December.

———. 1995c. *Economic Survey of Latin America and the Caribbean 1994–1995.* Santiago.

———. 1995d. *Preliminary Overview of the economy of Latin America and the Caribbean.* Santiago, December.

Culpeper, Roy. 1995. "Resurgence of Private Flows to Latin America: The Role of North American Investors." In Ricardo Ffrench-Davis and Stephany Griffith-Jones, eds., *Coping with Capital Surges—The Return of Finance to Latin America.* Boulder: Lynne Rienner Publishers.

Devlin, Robert, Ricardo Ffrench-Davis and Stephany Griffith-Jones. 1995. "Surges in Capital Flows and Development: An Overview of Policy Issues." In Ffrench-Davis and Griffith-Jones, eds., *Coping with Capital Surges—The Return of Finance to Latin America.* Boulder: Lynne Rienner Publishers.

Ffrench-Davis, Ricardo, Manuel R. Agosin and Andras Uthoff. 1995. "Capital Movements, Export Strategy, and Macroeconomic Stability in Chile." In Ffrench-Davis and Stephany Griffith-Jones, eds., *Coping with Capital Surges— The Return of Finance to Latin America.* Boulder: Lynne Rienner Publishers.

Ffrench-Davis, Ricardo and Stephany Griffith-Jones, eds., 1995. *Coping with Capital Surges—The Return of Finance to Latin America.* Boulder: Lynne Rienner Publishers.

Gurría, José Angel. 1995. "Capital Flows: the Mexican Case." In Ricardo Ffrench-Davis and Stephany Griffith-Jones, eds., *Coping with Capital Surges— The Return of Finance to Latin America.* Boulder: Lynne Rienner Publishers.

Helpman, Elhanan, Leonardo Leiderman and Gil Bufman. 1994. "A New Breed of Exchange Rate Bands: Chile, Israel and Mexico." *Economic Policy* 19(October):259–93.

IMF (International Monetary Fund). 1995. "Evolution of the Mexican Peso Crisis." In *International Capital Markets—Developments, Prospects, and Policy Issues.* Washington, D.C.

Labán, Raul and Felipe Larraín. 1993. "Can a Liberalization of Capital Outflows Increase Net Capital Inflows?" Documento de Trabajo 155 Instituto de

Economía, Pontificia Universidad Católica de Chile, Santiago.

Lustig, Nora. 1992. *México—The Remaking of an Economy.* Washington, D.C.: The Brookings Institution.

McKinnon, Ronald I. 1991. "The International Capital Market and Economic Liberalization: The Overborrowing Syndrome." In McKinnon, ed., *The Order of Economic Liberalization—Financial Control in the Transition to a Market Economy.* Baltimore: Johns Hopkins University Press.

McKinnon, Ronald I. and Huw Pill. 1995. "Credible Liberalization and International Capital Flows: The 'Over-Borrowing' Syndrome." Department of Economics. Stanford University. Processed.

Ocampo, José Antonio. 1993. "Economía y economía política de la reforma comercial colombiana." Serie Reformas de Política Comercial 1. CEPAL. Santiago.

———. ed. 1994. *Los Capitales Extranjeros en las Economías Latinoamericanas.* FEDESARROLLO and the Interamerican Development Bank. Bogotá.

Ros, Jaime. 1994. "Mercados financieros y flujos de capital en México." In José Antonio Ocampo, ed., *Los Capitales Extranjeros en las Economías Latinoamericanas.* FEDESARROLLO and the Interamerican Development Bank. Bogotá.

Steiner, Roberto and Ursula Giedion. 1996. "Características, determinantes y algunos efectos de la inversión extranjera directa en Colombia." In Manuel R. Agosin, ed., *Inversión Extranjera en América Latina.* Santiago: Fondo de Cultura Económica.

Stiglitz, Joseph E. 1994. "The Role of the State in Financial Markets." In *Proceedings of the World Bank Annual Conference on Development Economics 1993.* Washington, D.C.: World Bank.

Ten Kate, Adriaan. 1993. "Structural Adjustment in México: Two Different Stories." In Manuel R. Agosin and Diana Tussie, eds., *Trade and Growth: New Dilemmas in Trade Policy.* London: Macmillan.

Tobin, James. 1978. "A Proposal for International Monetary Reform." *Eastern Economic Journal* 4(July-October):153–9.

———. 1994. "A Currency Transactions Tax: Why and How?" Università La Sapienza, Rome.

Urrutia, Miguel. 1995. "La cuenta de capital durante un proceso de liberalización económica." Paper presented at the seminar, "Seventy Years of the Central Bank of Chile." August 21. Santiago.

Williamson, John. 1992. "Acerca de la liberalización de la cuenta de capitales." Estudios de Economía. 19(2):185–197.

———. Forthcoming. "How to Manage Exchange Rates: Lessons from Israel, Chile and Colombia." Washington, D.C.: Institute for International Economics.

The Republic of Korea's Experience with Managing Foreign Capital Flows

Yung Chul Park

For more than twenty years since the Foreign Exchange Management Act was enacted in 1961, the Republic of Korea maintained strict capital controls to prevent capital flight and to allocate its limited foreign exchange resources to export and other strategic industries. But recognizing the inefficiency of these regulations and given the worldwide trend towards economic liberalization, Korea has been liberalizing capital account transactions since the early 1980s. In December 1994, it launched the Plan for Foreign Exchange System Reform to accelerate this process and to prepare for membership in the Organisation for Economic Co-operation and Development (OECD). The plan envisages a capital account regime that, by 2000, will be as liberal and open as those in industrial economies.

When capital account transactions are liberalized, Korean firms will be able to gain access to foreign financial resources at a lower cost than available domestically—thereby improving their competitiveness and efficiency. Easing the flow of capital inherently means exposure to the

The author would like to thank Ki-Young Chung, Chi-Young Song, Chan-Woo Chung, Gong-Pil Choi and participants of the UNDP Meeting on Proposals for an International Currency Transaction Levy for their helpful comments. The author is alone responsible for all errors.

risk of speculative flows, which could disrupt domestic financial markets and destabilize the economy. Thus, too large a capital inflow would likely appreciate both the nominal and real exchange rate, which, in turn, would worsen the competitiveness of Korean export-oriented industries. Moreover, domestic financial markets are underdeveloped, and domestic financial institutions are not competitive. Korea's financial sector in general, and many financial firms in particular, would find it difficult to compete in an open financial market. Faced with these potentially difficult problems, the government has been searching for measures to reduce negative effects without losing the benefits of liberalization. This paper reviews the ongoing process of capital account liberalization and its effects on the Korean economy and then analyses possible policy measures to deal with problems that may arise.

Liberalization of the capital account

Since the early 1960s, developments in the current account dictated the way in which capital controls were implemented. For example, if the current account deteriorated, restrictions on capital outflows were tightened, while those on inflows were loosened. In the first half of the 1980s, the current account remained in deficit, though the deficit was getting smaller. In an effort to ease difficulties in financing the current account deficit, the Korean government tightened regulations on capital outflows, mainly by restricting residents' overseas investments. It also adopted several measures to ease inward capital movements.[1] In 1981, for example, foreign investors were allowed to participate in the Korean stock market through the investment trust funds set up exclusively for them, while in 1985, Korean firms were allowed to raise foreign capital by issuing convertible bonds, bonds with warrants and depository receipts.[2]

The easing led to a sharp increase in borrowing from abroad by domestic firms and banks, and in 1986, the current account recorded a surplus, which continued to grow until 1989. This surplus resulted from the recovery of the world economy and the rapid appreciation of the Japanese yen, which improved the competitiveness of Korean exports. Foreign exchange reserves, only $2.8 billion at the end of 1985, reached $12.6 billion a year later, and $15 billion by the end of 1989. In order to reduce excessive foreign exchange holdings, the government abolished all restrictions on residents' foreign direct investment (FDI) below $1 million and permitted residents to purchase foreign real estate for business purposes. But commercial loans by domestic firms, except public enterprises, were not allowed, and issuance of bonds and depository receipts by residents was also restricted.

In 1990, the current account balance fell into deficit again because of rising domestic wages, real appreciation of the Korean won and deterioration of the world economy. The current account worsened in 1991, generating a deficit of $8.7 billion, which was more than four times the level of the preceding year. The amount of foreign exchange reserves held by the Bank of Korea fell markedly. Facing difficulties in financing the mounting current account deficit, the Korean government was once again forced to liberalize the capital account by amending the Foreign Exchange Management Act (FEMA) in 1991.

Under the amended FEMA, those transactions classified as capital inflows were liberalized first, although the positive system of capital control—in which only those transactions specifically allowed are listed—remained intact.[3] Residents could raise funds by issuing securities abroad under certain conditions. Restrictions on direct investment by non-residents were almost completely lifted. Most importantly, effective from January 1992, foreign investors were allowed to invest directly in the Korean stock market, although with a number of restrictions, including a 10% limit on the amount of a firm's listed stock that non-resident investors as a group could hold.[4]

As a result of these liberalizing measures, foreign capital inflows, mainly in the form of portfolio investment, surged in 1991. Net foreign capital inflows in 1990 were only $1.3 billion, but jumped to $5.7 billion in 1991, and then again to $9.6 billion in 1993. Net foreign portfolio investment accounted for 51% and 180% of the increases in total net foreign capital inflows in 1991 and 1993, respectively. During this three-year period, the cumulative current account deficit was $12.9 billion, whereas foreign portfolio investment amounted to $21.9 billion—generating a large surplus in the overall account.

A sudden increase in foreign capital inflows on top of the improvement in the current account threatened the stability of domestic financial markets and the economy. Several steps were taken to liberalize outward capital movements and thus to reduce the overall account surplus. Domestic institutional investors, such as securities firms, insurance companies and investment trust companies, were allowed to invest in foreign securities without any restrictions, and in February 1994, the mode of controlling residents' direct investment abroad was changed from a positive to a negative system, that is, a system whereby all transactions are allowed save those that are specifically restricted.

Even though many controls on foreign exchange and cross-border capital transactions had been removed or relaxed, the foreign exchange system was still criticized for being too restrictive, and, among other things, critics claimed that the rigid control undermined the international competitiveness of domestic firms. In response to these complaints and the foreign pressure for further deregulation, the Korean government unveiled a new Plan for Foreign Exchange System Reform in December 1994. The Plan attempts, in three stages, to completely liberalize current and capital account transactions (with a few exceptions) and to develop an efficient domestic foreign exchange market over a five-year period. It espouses a gradual liberalization process, with the speed of liberalization adjusted to the state of the economy. One of the focal points of the reform is the adoption of a negative system. Another is the priority given to the removal of restrictions on capital outflows rather than inflows. A third is the deregulation of capital account transactions closely related to investment in the real sector prior to cross-border financial transactions.[5] Implementation of the first stage of the capital account liberalization, which focuses on the decontrol of capital outflow, began in February 1995. For example, the limit on the amount that domestic pension funds can invest in overseas securities was abolished, and domestic residents were allowed to hold overseas deposit accounts for the first time.

For a number of reasons, the Korean authorities have been reluctant to rapidly liberalize the capital account. Although liberalization could generate efficiency gains for the economy, these are relatively small or insignificant, and at best realized in the long run, whereas macroeconomic instability that may result from the sudden opening up of financial markets could be devastating.

In a number of countries, capital account liberalization has increased the volatility of financial markets, including the foreign exchange market. Furthermore, little is known as to how a small semi-open economy like the Republic of Korea, caught in disequilibrium characterized by a domestic interest rate twice as high as the rate prevailing in international financial markets, would move to a new equilibrium if restrictions on capital account transactions were removed suddenly and completely. Presently, domestic financial markets are underdeveloped, and domestic financial institutions have little competitive advantage over their foreign counterparts.

Trends in foreign capital flows

Since 1991, there has been a large increase in foreign capital flows. The large interest rate differential between domestic and foreign financial markets and the country's favourable economic prospects have made the Republic of Korea one of the most attractive emerging markets, and the capital account decontrol triggered a massive inflow. Over the last five years, net foreign capital inflows amounted to $32.1 billion—more than ten times total net inflows for the entire 1980s.

Foreign capital inflow mainly took the form of loans, especially public loans, until the first half of the 1980s (figure 8.1). The share of private capital inflows was relatively small because, even then, domestic firms and financial institutions had difficulties borrowing from abroad without government guarantees. During the second half of the 1980s, with the emergence of a current account surplus and its subsequent expansion, the capital account recorded a net outflow. Despite the strong performance of the Korean economy, the inflow of foreign direct investment was moderate, largely because of restrictions on the types of investment allowed.

Figure 8.1 also shows that portfolio investment dominated foreign capital inflows in the 1990s. Foreign loan repayments continued, and inward foreign direct investment showed a trend similar to that seen in the second half of the 1980s. The surge in portfolio investment during this period resulted largely from opening the Korean stock market (in

Figure 8.1 Trend and composition of foreign capital inflows in the Republic of Korea

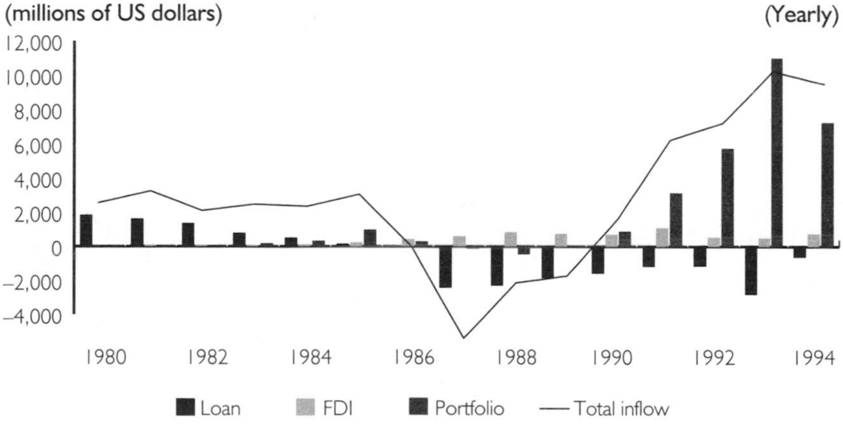

Source: Bank of Korea: *Balance of Payment.* Various issues.

1992) and allowing domestic firms to issue securities abroad to take advantage of lower interest rates in international financial markets. In addition, the opening of the Korean stock market came just as the strong economic performance in developing countries in general encouraged international institutional investors to increase their holdings of emerging market securities.[6]

The major type of foreign portfolio investment, even after the stock market opening in 1992, was issuance of securities by Korean firms in international capital markets (figure 8.2).[7] The dominance is particularly noticeable between 1994 and 1995, when the Korean stock market performed relatively poorly.[8] Moreover, foreign stock investment and resident borrowing from abroad has exhibited an inverse relationship, largely because the Korean authorities attempted to stabilize total capital inflows by adjusting the inflows of securitized capital raised by domestic firms and financial institutions to changes in foreign investment in Korean equities. From January 1992 through July 1995, the standard deviation of the rate of monthly change in total foreign portfolio investment was 146%, while that of foreign stock investment was 494% and that of resident issuance of securities in international capital markets was 383%. This figure implies that an increase (decrease) in foreign stock investment was offset by a decrease (increase) in resident security issuance, thereby reducing the volatility of total foreign portfolio investment.

Figure 8.2 Trend and composition of foreign portfolio investment in the Republic of Korea

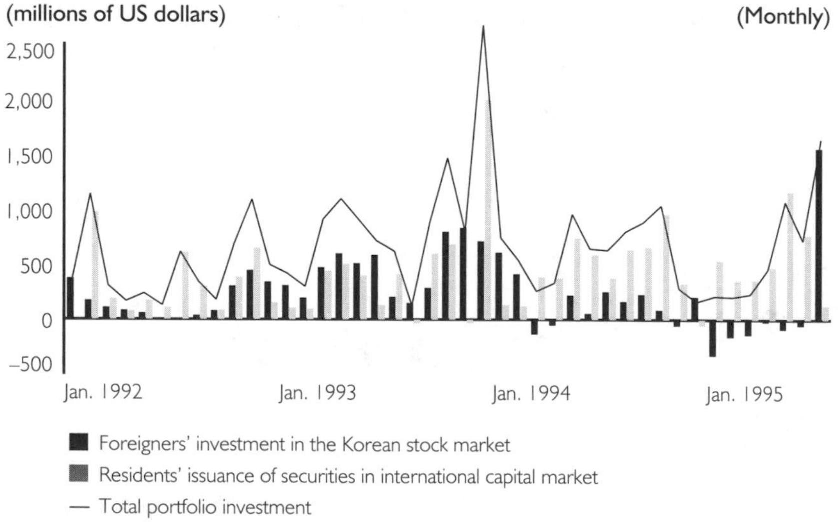

(millions of US dollars)   (Monthly)

Foreigners' investment in the Korean stock market
Residents' issuance of securities in international capital market
— Total portfolio investment

Source: Bank of Korea: *Balance of Payment.* Various issues.

In a new financial environment in which financial derivatives proliferate, it is difficult and may not be meaningful to make any distinction between short-term and long-term portfolio investment. However, foreign stock investment may be classified as short-term because it can be withdrawn quickly. From January 1992 to July 1995, net inflows of foreign capital invested in the Korean stock market accounted for about 38% of total net foreign capital inflows—implying that more than one-third of the foreign capital invested in the Korean economy could leave the country at any time.

Because Korean policy-makers were aware of the problem of financial market volatility related to capital inflow and the resulting difficulties in managing macroeconomic policy, they were cautious about opening up domestic financial markets. Indeed, these difficulties have been the government's principal arguments for opening the financial market slowly. Furthermore, in recent years, the current account deficit was relatively small and thus was the need for foreign financing. The ratio of current account deficit to GDP in the Republic of Korea between 1990 and 1994 was only 1.3% on average, while those of Thailand and Malaysia were 6.7% and 4.8%, respectively. Consequently, the impact of capital inflow on the Korean economy has been small compared with that of other Asian countries.

Capital account liberalization and financial market volatility

In order to examine the effect of capital account liberalization on key macroeconomic variables, I have carried out a number of simulation exercises of capital account deregulation in an open-economy Keynesian model.[9] These exercises show that, initially, the nominal exchange rate appreciates sharply, overshooting a new equilibrium level that satisfies an interest parity condition consistent with a deregulated capital account regime. Both the nominal and real exchange rates continue to appreciate, and the current account deteriorates before foreign capital inflows cease. During the adjustment period, domestic interest rates remain relatively stable, but output growth and employment suffer greatly, because export industries lose competitiveness. Only through a protracted slowdown and a large increase in the current account deficit over a long period does the economy reach a new equilibrium.[10]

In several countries, capital account liberalization also increased the volatility of financial variables, such as the exchange rate, domestic interest rates and stock prices, during and after the transition period. In order to examine whether financial markets have become more volatile as a result of the liberalization in Korea, I estimated GARCH variance of these financial variables and foreign capital flows.[11] The volume of capital inflows has increased since 1990, but there is no evidence that inflows have become more unstable since liberalization (figures 8.3 and 8.4). In fact, the variance of net capital inflow was higher during 1987–89, when capital inflows were tightly controlled.

Figure 8.3 Inflow and outflow of foreign capital in the Republic of Korea
(millions of US dollars)

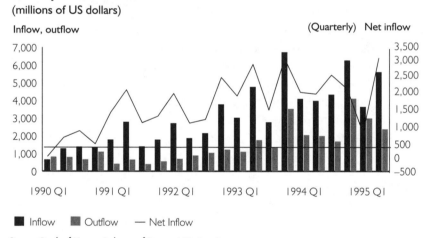

Source: Bank of Korea: *Balance of Payment.* Various issues.

Figure 8.4 GARCH variance of net capital inflow, 1986–95

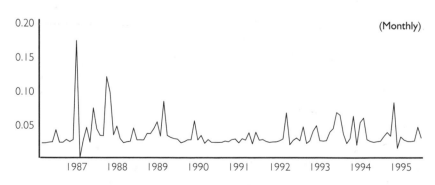

Source: Author's calculations.

200

Variance estimates do not indicate any correlation between the volatility of the won–US dollar rate and the movement of foreign capital throughout the period (figure 8.5). The volatility of the exchange rate against the US dollar has increased since early 1995. This increase is explained by the fact that the government refrained from intervening in the foreign exchange market, suggesting that volatility may have been suppressed by intervention until 1994.

Large, persistent increases in volatility of the interest rate (the yield on three-year bank-guaranteed corporate bonds) can be seen in 1992–93 and in 1995. The first increase mainly reflects domestic interest rate liberalization, but the second is partly attributable to an increase in foreign capital inflows. After the opening of the stock

Figure 8.5 GARCH variance

Won–dollar exchange rate (March 1990–September 1995, daily)

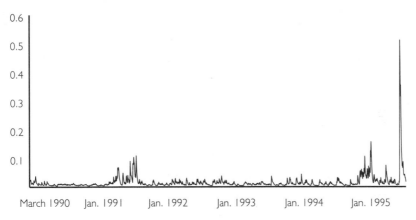

Interest rate (January 1990–September 1995, daily)

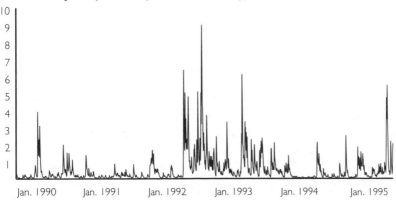

Figure 8.5 GARCH variance (cont.)

Stock returns (January 1990–September 1995, daily)

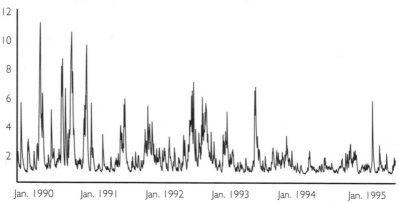

Source: Author's calculations.

market in 1992, the volatility of the rate of return on stocks using the Korea Stock Price Index actually fell, yet large swings remained.

Has the presence of foreign capital increased the turbulence of the stock market in Korea? Are foreign investors more informed traders who tend to buy when the price is low and sell when the price is high, or who are more sensitive to optimism and pessimism than Korean players? That is, are foreign investors more likely to speculate than local investors? To answer these questions, I estimated monthly turnover rates for the three different groups of investors: domestic institutional investors, domestic individuals and foreign investors (figure 8.6). The turnover rate is the ratio of the monthly volume of transactions to total holdings of equities. On average, there is no discernible difference between domestic institutional and foreign investors, although individual domestic investors with the highest turnover rate tend to be more frequent noise traders than the investors in other two groups.

But the variability of the turnover rates of the three different groups of investors tells a somewhat different story. When the variability is measured by the ratio of the standard deviation of turnover rates to the average turnover rate for the entire period, the variability of domestic institutional investors is the highest (0.547), followed by foreign investors (0.477) and individual domestic investors (0.351). This difference is related to the fact that the volume of each sale or purchase of stocks by either domestic institutional or foreign investors is likely to be larger than that of individual domestic investors, although they are less frequent traders.

Has the stock market opening been associated with any significant increase in the volatility of the rate of return on stocks? The rate of return is positively correlated with the monthly volume of net foreign equity investment (figure 8.7). But there is no such relationship between the volatility of the monthly volume of net foreign equity investment and that of the rate of return on stocks, suggesting that the

Figure 8.6 Trend in the monthly turnover rate in the Korean stock market

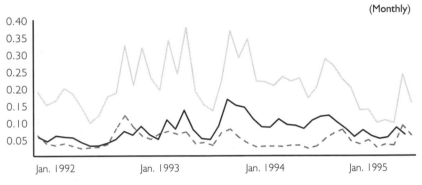

- - Foreign investors
— Domestic individual investors
— Domestic institutional investors

Source: Author's calculations.

Figure 8.7 Trend of stock returns and net foreign equity investment

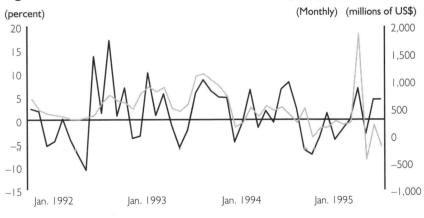

— Stock returns
— Net foreign equity investment

Source: Bank of Korea: *Balance of Payment.* Various issues; Bank of Korea: *Monthly Bulletin.* Various issues.

presence of foreign capital has not necessarily increased the volatility of Korea's stock market (figure 8.8).

It is true, however, that foreign equity investment has increasingly exerted a stronger influence on changes in stock prices in Korea. Cross-

Figure 8.8 Volatility of stock returns and net foreign equity investment

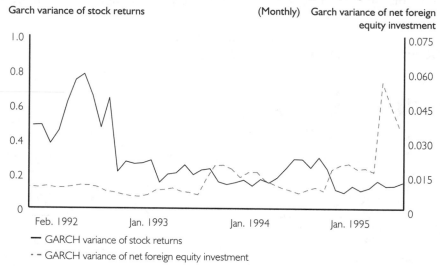

Garch variance of stock returns   (Monthly)   Garch variance of net foreign equity investment

— GARCH variance of stock returns
- - GARCH variance of net foreign equity investment

Source: Author's calculations.

Figure 8.9 Cross-correlation coefficients between volume of foreign stock investment and rate of return on stocks

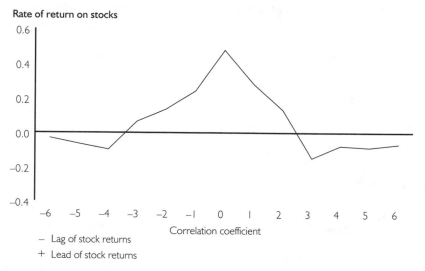

Rate of return on stocks

Correlation coefficient

− Lag of stock returns
+ Lead of stock returns

Source: Author's calculations.

correlation coefficients between the monthly volume of foreign stock investment and the rate of return on stocks show that a change in foreign equity investment at time t is affected by changes in the rate of return during the two preceding months ($t-1$ and $t-2$) and will influence stock prices for the following two months ($t+1$ and $t+2$). As a group, foreign investors have emerged as one of the market leaders in the Republic of Korea (figure 8.9).

The period under consideration is not long enough to conduct any meaningful empirical examination, and, more importantly, during the period, government authorities were actively sterilizing capital inflows. But although it is difficult to reach any meaningful conclusions, the existing pieces of evidence do not suggest that capital market liberalization has made domestic financial markets more volatile.

Policy responses to capital inflows

Since the mid-1960s, the main engine of Korea's economic growth has been the rapid expansion of exports and investment arising from increases in foreign demand. Reflecting the export-oriented development strategy, the degree of openness [measured as (exports + imports)/GDP] has been very high for the last ten years (table 8.1). Therefore, Korean policy-makers have been very careful not to allow Korean products to slip behind in competitiveness. Between 1990 and 1993, their foreign exchange rate policy was geared to maintaining a weak Korean won regardless of whether the overall balance was in surplus or deficit. As a result, the Korean won depreciated, even when a large amount of foreign capital inflow generated an overall account surplus.

The overall account recorded a deficit between 1990 and 1991 because of a large deficit in the current account, leading to a depreciation of the won against the US dollar (table 8.1, figure 8.10). Since 1992, the won has been experiencing strong upward pressure because of a large overall surplus. Both a large increase in foreign capital inflows and an improvement in the current account have contributed to this surplus. Still, the Korean won continued to depreciate until the end of 1993, implying that the Bank of Korea actively intervened in the foreign exchange market to reduce the upward pressure.[12] This intervention can be seen from the increase in the Bank of Korea's net foreign assets by $8.6 billion during 1992–93, when the overall account surplus was $11.4 billion.[13]

Table 8.1 Major economic indicators

	1990	1991	1992	1993	1994	1995.1Q^a	1995.2Q^a
Rate of change (%) in							
GDP	9.5	9.1	5.1	5.8	8.4	9.9	9.6
CPI ^{b}	8.6	9.3	6.2	4.8	6.2	4.6	4.9
M2	21.2	18.6	18.4	18.6	15.6	14.3	14.6
Interest rate (%)^c Nominal	16.5	18.9	16.2	12.6	12.9	15.1	14.8
exchange rate (%)$^{d,\,e}$	707.8	733.4	780.7	802.7	803.5	786.7	761.3
Real effective exchange rate (%)$^{d,\,f}$	101.4	104.8	113.2	120.8	126.4	133.0	142.0
Current account (CA)	−2,179.4	−8,727.7	−4,528.5	384.6	−4,530.8	−3,569.5	−2,519.6
CA/GDP	−0.9	−3.0	−1.5	0.1	−1.2	−0.4	−0.3
Capital account (KA)	3,881.2	4,227.0	8,342.6	6,878.6	9,024.9	2,517.2	2,452.5
KA/GDP	1.5	1.5	2.7	2.1	2.4	0.3	0.3
Overall balance	−273.9	−3,740.8	4,898.1	6,542.2	2,821.7	−1,446.4	−139.0
Openness^g	61.9	60.7	60.8	59.8	74.0	83.7	86.7

a. Year-on-year rate of change in GDP, CPI, M2.
b. Consumer Price Index.
c. Yield on three-year bank-guaranteed corporate bonds.
d. Period averages.
e. Exchange rate of the Korean won with respect to the US dollar.
f. A rise in real effective exchange rate indicates a depreciation of the Korean won.
g. (Export + Import)/GDP x 100.
Source: Bank of Korea: *National Account.* Various issues; The Bank of Korea: *Monthly Bulletin.* Various issues.

Since 1994, the Korean won has appreciated continuously against the US dollar, mainly because of the marked appreciation of the yen-dollar exchange rate, which has led to a large depreciation of the real effective exchange rate of the won since 1992. Between 1992 and the second quarter of 1995, the real effective exchange rate of the won depreciated 28%, and all of this depreciation was accounted for by the yen appreciation with respect to the US dollar. The strong yen has contributed to a sharp increase in export earnings, meaning that the central bank authorities could let the won appreciate to a degree without risking the erosion of price competitiveness of Korean export industries. Together with a large capital inflow, export expansion resulted in an overall account surplus of $2.8 billion in 1994. Although the surplus was large, the Bank of Korea did not consider it necessary to intervene in the foreign exchange market, as long as the yen remained strong.

Turning to monetary policy, the Bank of Korea resorted to active sterilization in order to absorb the impact of foreign capital inflows on the money supply. The foreign exchange intervention augmented the central bank's net holdings of foreign assets, thereby increasing the money supply, which is the most carefully monitored intermediate target of monetary policy. To offset the increase, the monetary authorities required that financial institutions purchase monetary stabilization

Figure 8.10 Exchange rate and balance of payment in the Republic of Korea

(billions of US dollars)

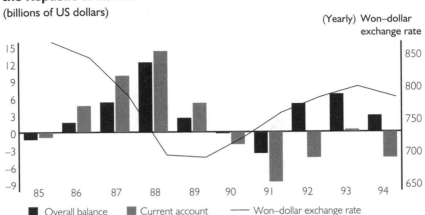

(Yearly) Won–dollar exchange rate

■ Overall balance ■ Current account —— Won–dollar exchange rate

Source: Bank of Korea: *Balance of Payment Monthly Bulletin.* Various issues.

bonds (MSBs). According to Kim (1991), the Bank of Korea sterilized about 90% of the increase in net foreign assets during the 1980s.

The amount of the central bank's net foreign assets changed each period between 1986 and the first quarter of 1995, even after the market average exchange rate system (MARS) was adopted in 1990 (figure 8.11). This implies that the Bank of Korea continued to intervene in the foreign exchange market to stabilize the foreign exchange rate. During 1992–93, the Bank of Korea's intervention was most active because of the large increase in foreigners' portfolio investment. Also, changes in net foreign assets and changes in net domestic assets have been inversely related, suggesting that the Bank of Korea actively mopped up the increase in money supply resulting from the foreign exchange market intervention.

Sterilization has kept Korea's money supply growth under control— it has been decelerating continuously since 1990, as has inflation, as measured by the CPI (see table 8.1). Korea avoided serious inflation, but because of the crowding-out effect caused by the massive sterilization, interest rates have gradually risen since 1993. And the large gap between the interest rate in Korea and that in the industrial economies—a major reason for capital inflows—has persisted.

Sterilization through sales of MSBs has additional costs: an increase in interest payments on MSBs will ultimately produce inflationary pressure. Indeed, interest payments on MSBs explain more than 70% of the increase in the monetary base since 1990. The Bank of Korea thus faces significant difficulties in continuing to use sterilization to manage foreign capital inflows.

Figure 8.11 Trend of changes in net domestic assets and net foreign assets in the Republic of Korea, 1985–95

(billions of won)

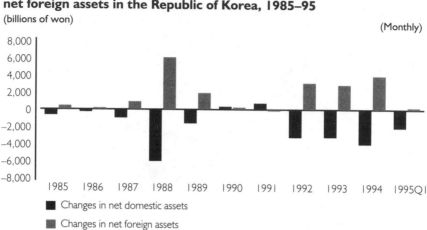

Source: Author's calculations.

Capital flows into Korea have been small relative to GDP and thus easily managed through sterilization. Since the plan to accelerate capital market liberalization will undoubtedly result in a large inflow, it will be difficult to rely on sterilization as much as before. Hence other policy measures must be considered to moderate some of the negative effects of a large capital inflow. If sterilization is no longer a variable solution, fiscal policy could complement monetary and exchange rate policies. For example, by running a budgetary surplus, the government can mitigate both inflationary pressures and the appreciation of the real exchange rate. Thailand provides a good example of how reduced government expenditure can help to mitigate the effects of capital inflows on the money supply. When Thailand recorded its largest-ever capital account surplus in 1991, a government budget surplus equal to about 5% of GDP absorbed more than 20% of the increase in money supply. In Korea, however, rigidities in the budget and the need to invest in social infrastructure make it very difficult to maintain a large budget surplus. Further, the budget is usually set on the basis of medium- to long-term considerations. Overall, Korea's fiscal policy lacks the flexibility needed for timely intervention when dealing with capital inflows.

Encouraging capital outflows is also effective in reducing the magnitude of net inflows—thus it must be made easier for domestic investors to hold foreign assets. Korea has already removed many restrictions on outflows and plans to lift the remaining controls in the near future. As of mid-1995, domestic residents have had significant freedom to invest abroad.

The amount of direct investment abroad by domestic residents has increased considerably since the mid-1980s: in 1986, it was $110 million. It increased to $820 million by 1990 and reached $2.075 billion in 1994. The portfolio investment portion is minuscule, mainly because of low returns on portfolio investment abroad relative to returns in Korea. The low level also reflects domestic financial institutions' lack of necessary investment skills.

When a relatively high interest rate in domestic financial markets discourages portfolio investment abroad, central bank swap arrangements could be used to provide additional incentives. The swaps involve the central bank selling foreign reserves for domestic currency when reserves increase beyond a certain level (because of capital inflows). The buyers are foreign exchange banks or non-bank financial institutions that are required to invest the reserves abroad for a specified period. When the buyers sell the foreign currencies back to the central bank for domestic currency, the central bank makes good any losses from exchange rate fluctuations and the difference between domestic and foreign interest rates. The subsidies given to the swap participants are the cost of managing the money supply.

The Bank of Korea has not used swaps, but the legal framework is in place to do so. Germany employed them to stabilize its money supply in the 1970s, and Malaysia, the Philippines and Singapore have also used them. Because pressure on the money supply from the foreign sector is transferred abroad during the swap period, a swap can help to stabilize domestic money supply and interest rates without issuing monetary stabilization bonds—as Korea has been doing.

Another approach for the Bank of Korea is to lend foreign currency funds to domestic financial institutions, mainly investment banks, to finance their portfolio investment abroad. This method can be more cost-effective than a swap, but it exposes the central bank to investment risk. The risk can be mitigated by restricting investment to less risky assets such as government securities.

Direct policy measures for managing capital inflows

Employing a mix of monetary, fiscal and exchange rate policies together with deregulation of capital outflows may not be enough to counter surges in capital inflows. For a more effective response, therefore, the Korean authorities may consider using other direct control measures, such as imposing limits on banks' borrowing from abroad and foreign exchange transactions, a deposit requirement or a levy on foreign exchange transactions.

Prudential regulation of financial institutions

Given the progress made in capital account liberalization, it has become more important to regulate financial institutions in a prudential manner, largely because of their structural weakness. Banking institutions hold large amounts of non-performing loans, most of which were made at the government's behest—so-called policy loans. These institutions have been regulated and protected, and thus they have had little incentive to learn advanced financial techniques. Thus, when Korean financial institutions are allowed to freely operate and raise financial resources abroad, they will be exposed to interest and exchange rate risk that they have little experience in dealing with. Further, liberalization of interest rates, which Korea has carried out, may increase the volatility of interest rates and lead to excessive competition among financial institutions.

As the restrictions that reduce the competitiveness and efficiency of financial institutions are lifted, Korea must adopt new regulations and methods of supervision that maximize effectiveness and control without being an excessive administrative burden on financial institutions. Government authorities also must induce financial institutions to increase capital, for example, through the issuance of new shares. Authorities may impose penalties on those that do not meet certain criteria on equity capital, such as the Bank for International Settlements (BIS) standard. As part of this, the issue of non-performing loans must be addressed.

Non-bank financial institutions in Korea have a deposit insurance system. A similar insurance system for commercial banks will be introduced in 1996. Although there is strong evidence that deposit insurance exacerbated the savings and loan fiasco of the 1980s in the United States, a properly designed system not only protects depositors, it also works as a supplementary tool in minimizing negative effects from financial deregulation.

The variable deposit requirement

Imposing a variable deposit requirement (VDR) on incoming capital— that is, setting reserve levels depending on the type of capital and its circumstances—reduces the volume of inflows and can thus reduce their negative effects. More specifically, the purpose of a VDR is to raise the effective rate of interest on incoming capital and thereby decrease demand for it. A VDR is more market efficient than quantitative restrictions, but, because it limits domestic firms' access to international financial resources, care is needed in its implementation.

Foreign capital inflow is classified in Korea as foreign borrowing by residents, FDI or foreign portfolio investment. FDI is generally long-term investment in the real sector and contributes to domestic economic development—it is thus not an inflow to be discouraged. Except for the stock market, Korean capital markets are largely closed to foreign investors, meaning that there is almost no foreign portfolio investment in debt, and thus foreigners generally cannot make profits from interest rate differentials. This leaves only foreign borrowing by residents as an area in which a VDR might be imposed usefully.

The deposit (reserve) ratio can be adjusted according to the volume of capital inflows, but should be kept constant across maturities. It is also straightforward to determine the ratio that fully absorbs the interest rate differential between home and abroad. The effective interest rate on foreign borrowing (R') equals the expected rate of depreciation during the borrowing period (Fx) plus the foreign interest rate (Rf) divided by 1 minus the reserve ratio (D). That is,

$$R' = Fx + \frac{Rf}{1 - D}$$

Substituting the domestic interest rate for the effective rate—that is, making it as expensive to borrow abroad as domestically—allows us to solve the equation for the reserve ratio (D). This is not unlike the banking practice of requiring compensatory balances on loans as a way of raising effective interest rates. Required reserves would be deposited in non-interest-bearing foreign-currency accounts at the Bank of Korea until they were needed to pay back the loan.

In Korea, the amount of foreign borrowing by residents is not significant compared with foreign direct investment and foreign portfolio investment. Until now, the government has directly restricted domestic firms and financial institutions from raising funds through commercial and bank loans abroad. But when this restriction is relaxed, the volume of foreign borrowing is expected to rise rapidly. A VDR works as an implicit levy on capital transactions, and can be imposed to reduce the inflow. Because it hinders access to foreign financial resources that can enhance Korean firms' competitiveness, use of a VDR should be limited to periods of heavy capital inflow caused by a rapid appreciation of exchange rates or a substantial increase in interest rate differentials.[14]

A levy on foreign exchange transactions

In recent years, foreign exchange transactions taxes, both explicit and implicit, have been extensively analysed as a means of mitigating speculative short-term capital flows. Imposing an explicit levy on foreign exchange transactions has been widely discussed but has not been imposed in any country.[15] There are several possible ways that it can be handled: the tax can be imposed on either the seller or the purchaser of the domestic currency, or on both. For foreign exchange transactions, it would be more effective to levy round trip taxes.

The tax rate can be adjusted depending on the degree of capital market opening and the level of short-term capital flows. It should be noted that the impact of a tax is related to the investment period. For example, when a 2% round trip tax is imposed (1% for each buy and sell), the annualized decrease in return on investment is about 0.2% over a ten-year period. But for a day trade, the decrease is about 124,600% at an annual rate.

An implicit levy requires foreign investors to make non-interest-bearing deposits in the central bank when they sell foreign currencies for domestic currencies. Examples include Italy during the 1970s and Spain in 1992.[16] Unlike an explicit tax, an implicit tax hampers long-term portfolio investments if the deposit period is as long as the investment period. This effect can be mitigated by having the same deposit period for all transactions—one just long enough to lower returns on short-term investments. Care must be taken in setting the reserve ratio, as it will discourage long-term investment if it is too high, while a too-low reserve ratio will not accomplish the purpose.

If a transactions tax is imposed on foreign exchange related to current account transactions, it increases costs for domestic traders and thus might decrease the competitiveness of domestic products. To avoid this, the tax could be confined to investments made by non-residents in domestic stocks, bonds and short-term financial instruments. It would be levied when foreign investors buy or sell won in connection with trading such instruments. Because foreign investors have to exchange foreign currencies through resident financial institutions in order to invest in the domestic financial market, it would not be difficult to administer the tax. Moreover, most foreign investors have to register and invest through designated financial institutions in Korea, so there are no immediate loopholes through which to evade the tax. However, sooner or later, financial markets are likely to find ways to do so.

A foreign exchange transactions tax increases transaction costs, which in theory should discourage movement of speculative short-term capital. However, many researchers are suspicious of their effectiveness. They argue that empirical studies have failed to demonstrate a relationship between transactions costs and volatility in domestic financial markets, implying that foreign exchange transactions taxes would not decrease the volatility of exchange rates or security prices. Examples of this line of research include Schwert (1993), Hakkio (1994) and IMF (1995a).

Even if it works, the transactions tax has shortcomings. It raises equity problems if applied only to transactions made by non-residents. By decreasing the return on Korean securities, it makes them less attractive to foreign investors. Further, because Korea wants to develop into an international financial centre, it must liberalize and internationalize its domestic financial market. A foreign exchange transactions tax is inconsistent with both. It would undoubtedly decrease the volume of foreign exchange transactions, which would hinder development of a domestic foreign exchange market.[17]

Nonetheless, a transactions tax might have desired effects in Korea. It can be flexibly applied—adjusted to the amount of short-term capital flows. And the revenue can be used to enhance the stability of the foreign exchange market.

Conclusion

Korea has gradually headed towards, now unavoidable, capital account liberalization, and its progress is expected to accelerate. This process, if well managed, will contribute to the development and globalization of the domestic economy, as well as to the enhancement of domestic financial market efficiency. It may also result in an increase in the volatility of short-term capital flows, which may disturb domestic financial markets and macroeconomic stability. The most efficient way to offset any negative effects, including maintaining price stability, is to enhance the soundness and robustness of the domestic economy. But when inflows surge, the Korean monetary authorities are most likely to consider some of the measures "to influence the level and characteristics of capital inflows such as taxes on short-term bank deposits and other financial assets, reserve requirements against foreign borrowing, prudential limits on banks' offshore borrowing, and limits on consumption credit" suggested in IMF (1995b).

Appendix: The foreign exchange rate system in the Republic of Korea

Korea's exchange rate system is a variant of the managed floating system, known as the market average exchange rate system (MARS), in which the exchange rate of the won with respect to the US dollar is primarily determined in an interbank foreign exchange market. Prior to the adoption of the MARS in March 1990, Korean authorities had maintained a multi-currency basket system. At present, there are 101 participants in the market, including the Bank of Korea, 25 domestic commercial banks, 5 specialized banks, 3 development banks, 15 merchant banks and 52 branches of foreign banks.

The average market rate, which is used as a daily basic rate for interbank transactions of the US dollar, is a weighted average of the market exchange rates related to all transactions of the previous day, with the weight being the volume of each transaction. The interbank market rate of the won against the US dollar in each business day is allowed to fluctuate within a specified band around the basic rate. The band is revised daily.

When the MARS was first introduced, the market exchange rate was allowed to vary within ±0.4% of the basic rate. Since then, the band has been gradually widened. At present, the band is ±2.25% of the basic rate. The Korean government plans to widen the band further and to remove it entirely in the near future. Although the band has been widened gradually, the won–US dollar exchange rate has not moved very much in either direction, even within the band. In fact, the intraday exchange rate of the won against the US dollar hit the band only once—in July 1995. This is mainly because the Bank of Korea does not allow a large change in the exchange rate, even within the band, through window guidance.

There are no commercial foreign exchange brokerage firms in Korea. As a result, most of the interbank transactions are intermediated by a public brokerage house: the Fund Trading Center at Korea Financial Telecommunication and Clearing. The public foreign exchange brokerage system may help the Bank of Korea to closely monitor developments in the foreign exchange market and to maintain stability of the market through effective supervision. But the supervision of the market is likely to create distortions because banks as market-makers may be discouraged from active price quotations, and the Fund Trading Center, as a public institution, has little incentive to develop new products or to serve the market in general.

215

Furthermore, the total volume of direct interbank foreign exchange transactions is trivial compared with the volume cleared through the Fund Trading Center. Even in the case of direct interbank foreign exchange transactions, detailed information on each transaction must be reported to the Fund Trading Center after it is completed.

The interbank won–US dollar exchange rate is affected mainly by the demand for and supply of the US dollar arising from international trade and financial transactions. The exchange rates of the Korean won against the currencies other than the US dollar are determined by the cross-rate. Assuming an arbitrage relation, they are calculated by multiplying the won–US dollar exchange rate by the exchange rates of other currencies with respect to the US dollar, as determined in the international foreign exchange market. The exchange rates quoted in the Tokyo foreign exchange market in the morning (08:40 am of each business day) are used to calculate the official exchange rates of the won with respect to the Japanese yen, British pound, German mark, Swiss franc and Australian dollar. They are announced in the morning of each business day along with the basic won–US dollar exchange rate.

Korean commercial banks and other financial institutions have been risk-averse in foreign exchange transactions. Foreign exchange trading is a relatively new business to them, and they do not have the necessary skills or experience. As a result, they try to minimize foreign exchange risks simply by maintaining a square position of foreign exchange holdings rather than exposing themselves to a speculative position. Moreover, the net foreign exchange position of market participants is also subject to limits. For example, a spot over-sold position of each bank at the end of each business day should not exceed 2% of its capital or $3 million, whichever is larger. Also, an overall over-sold position at the end of each business day is permitted up to $20 million or 30% of its daily average foreign exchange purchase in the previous month. An overall over-bought position is allowed up to $20 million or two times its daily average foreign exchange purchase in the previous month, whichever is larger. The position restriction is imposed in order to maintain stability in the foreign exchange market and to prevent excessive speculative foreign exchange trading. Because of the position restriction on top of the risk-averse behaviour of domestic banks, speculative trading in the local foreign exchange market has been relatively insignificant.

The Bank of Korea often intervenes in the interbank market through the sale or purchase of US dollars. It is conjectured that the main purpose of the intervention in the foreign exchange market is to stabilize the real effective exchange rate of the won in order to maintain the price competitiveness of Korean exports. The central bank intervention has been effective as a result of the thinness of the domestic foreign exchange market—the average volume of daily turnover in 1994 was only $2 billion.

Notes

1. The Korean economy faced difficulties in attracting foreign capital at that time because of continued depreciation of the Korean won and high country risk resulting from political instability. Park (1995) argues that these developments were responsible for the decontrol of capital inflow.

2. The Korea International Trust, the first trust fund specifically designed for foreign investors by a domestic investment trust company, the Hankuk Investment Trust Corporation, was established in 1981. The Korea Fund, the first overseas investment company specialized in investing in Korean stocks, was organized in Maryland and listed on the New York Stock Exchange in 1984. In response to increases in demand for Korean stocks, the Korea Europe Fund was established in Guernsey Island, England in 1987, and the Korea Asia Fund was established in the Cayman Islands in 1991. The Korea Europe Fund was listed on the London Stock Exchange and the Korea Asia Fund on the Hong Kong and London Stock Exchanges.

3. A negative system was adopted for current account transactions.

4. The limit was raised to 12% in December 1994, and again to 15% in July 1995.

5. See Korea Ministry of Finance and Economy (1994) and Korea Institute of Finance (1994) for more details.

6. Ishii and Dunaway (1995) argue that the improvement in the availability and reliability of financial information on firms in developing countries also contributed to the increase in foreign portfolio investment in emerging markets.

7. Since the share of foreign investment in the Korean bond market in total portfolio investment is very small because of strict restrictions on foreign participation, its trend is not shown separately but is included in total portfolio investment in figure 8.2.

8. The sudden and massive increase in foreigners' stock investment in July 1995 was due to the fact that the maximum limit of stock holdings by foreign investors was increased from 12% to 15% on July 1.

9. Simulation exercises were carried out with a Korea Institute of Finance quarterly forecasting model.

10. The adjustment period could be as long as several years depending on the assumed rate of capital inflow induced by the interest rate differential and how the expectation of the nominal exchange rate is formed.

11. The GARCH variance of a financial variable, R_t, is estimated by the following model,

$$R_t = a + bR_{t-1} + u_t$$
$$\text{where } u_t / \Omega_{t-1} \sim N(0, h_t), \text{ and}$$
$$h_t = w + \alpha u^2_{t-1} + \beta h_{t-1}.$$

12. See the appendix for a description of the foreign exchange rate system in the Republic of Korea.

13. The change in the central bank's net foreign assets docs not correctly estimate the amount of intervention. It may underestimate or overestimate the magnitude of intervention depending on the central bank's management of its foreign assets. Also, intervention in the foreign exchange market can be effective through the central banks' announcement or signaling, without actual trading, of foreign exchanges.

14. A VDR has been shown to be effective, at least in the short run. Australia used it when experiencing an overall balance of payments surplus but a current account deficit. In the early 1970s, a rapid increase in domestic interest rates due to a strict monetary policy generated expectations of an exchange rate appreciation and thus led to massive capital inflows. The Australian government imposed non-interest-bearing reserve requirements on every foreign borrowing over A$10,000. This reduced the amount of inflow. The reserve ratio, initially 25%, was adjusted depending on the amount of inflow.

15. Transactions taxes are used in other financial markets. For example, on the Korean Stock Exchange, when an investor sells, a tax is levied. Japan also taxes stock sales, although at a very low rate.

16. When the September 1992 European currency crisis hit, Spain, in an attempt to avoid a realignment of the peseta, imposed an implicit levy on the purchase of foreign currencies by domestic financial institutions. This levy was opposite in direction to the levy considered here.

17. Thailand and Indonesia are opposed, or at least reluctant to impose, a transactions tax because they feel it would reduce the amount of capital available for economic development. They are willing to accept some volatility in capital movements as long as foreign capital overall is contributing to economic development.

References

Bank of Korea. Various issues. *Balance of Payment.*
———. Various issues. *National Account.*
———. Various issues. *Monthly Bulletin.*
Hakkio, Craig. 1994. "Should We Throw Sand in the Gears of Financial Markets?" *Economic Review,* Federal Reserve Bank of Kansas City 79(2):17–31.
IMF (International Monetary Fund). 1995a. "Financial Transaction Taxes." Washington, D.C. Processed.
———. 1995b. *International Capital Markets: Developments, Prospects, and Policy Issues.* Washington, D.C.

Ishii, Shogo. and Steven Dunaway. 1995. "Portfolio Capital Flows to the Developing Country Members of APEC." In Moshin Khan and Carmen Reinhart, eds., "Capital Flows in the APEC Region." IMF Occasional Paper 122. Washington, D.C.

Kim, Gyuhan. 1991. "A Study on the Effectiveness of the Sterilization Policy in an Open Economy: The Case of Korea." *Studies in Financial and Monetary Economics* Vol. 28 (in Korean). March.

Korea Institute of Finance. 1994. *Foreign Exchange System Reform in Korea* (in Korean). Seoul.

Korea Ministry of Finance and Economy. 1994. *The Plan for Foreign Exchange System Reform* (in Korean). Seoul.

Park, Daekeun. 1995. "Financial Opening and Capital Inflow: The Korean Experience and Policy Issues." In Rudiger Dornbusch and Yung Chul Park, eds., *Financial Opening: Policy Lessons for Korea*. Korea Institute of Finance and International Center for Economic Growth.

Schwert, G. William. 1993. "Stock Market Volatility." *Journal of Financial Service Research* 46(May-June):23–4.

Revenue Raised by the Tobin Tax

On the Revenue Potential and Phasing in of the Tobin Tax

David Felix and Ranjit Sau

The recent surge of interest in James Tobin's 1978 proposal to tax global foreign exchange transactions is producing two distinct clusterings of tax and revenue estimates, each assigning a different primary function to the tax. If the tax is taken purely as a source of funding for the United Nations and its peacekeeping functions (for example, Walker 1993) or for financing the social development and environmental proposals emanating from recent UN summit conferences (for example, d'Orville and Najman 1995), estimates have moderate revenue goals and thus work with very low tax rates. Such estimates can disregard the effect that the tax has on the overall volume and structure of global foreign exchange trading, since even for high elasticity coefficients, the effects are likely to be minimal. Indeed, Peter Kenen, in his contribution to this volume (Kenen 1996), proposes that in the case of swaps, the small tax be applied to only one leg of the spot-forward round trip in order to further minimize the decline of swap volume.

The other clustering, represented in this volume by Jeffrey Frankel's contribution (Frankel 1996) and by this article, focuses on the principal motivation behind Tobin's proposal: to slow the speed of reaction of globalized financial markets in order to reduce exchange rate volatility and provide more freedom for governments to implement counter-cyclical monetary and fiscal policies. To meet this objective, the requisite rate has to be high enough to significantly alter volume and structure—notably, to reduce short-term foreign exchange trading. How high depends on the sensitivity of foreign exchange volume to the tax, and thus transaction costs and elasticity estimates are central to rate selection and revenue projections. Because the information used to generate elasticity estimates of a hypothetical tax is sparse, the projections are likely to differ substantially. But, surprisingly, although Frankel applies a much lower tax rate (0.1%) than we do (0.25%), our revenue estimates are fairly close. We get this result primarily because of the offsetting effects of the higher transaction costs and elasticity coefficients that we use compared with those that Frankel uses.

These revenue estimates are so large that a modest slice would meet the funding goals motivating the low-tax cluster. Advocates can thus choose between two promotional strategies. Which is likely to be more effective depends on whether global solidarity arguments for funding international institutions and activities through a low Tobin tax are more politically appealing than those that call for using a higher tax to facilitate macroeconomic stability. Given the current nationalistic and anti-tax political environment, we feel that "bottom line" arguments for the Tobin tax as a means to overcome slow economic growth, unemployment and global financial instability have a greater political appeal.[1] If so, those promoting global solidarity should not rule out concurrently supporting the broader case in the hope of earning a slice of the greater revenue, because that route could prove to be the only politically viable way to achieve their funding goals.

The size and structure of global foreign exchange transactions

The base for our estimates is the $880 billion in net global foreign exchange transactions per trading day. In 1992, the Bank for International Settlements (BIS) calculated this figure by correcting its 1992 gross global estimate of $1,354 billion for dual reporting (BIS 1993).[2] Preliminary reports from the 1995 BIS survey indicate that the daily global foreign exchange turnover in 1995 was nearly 48% higher than that in 1992.[3] In this paper, however, we use the more complete 1992 data, which, based on 250 trading days, amount to a global foreign exchange volume of $220 trillion.

Looking at such numbers in historical perspective, three relationships stand out (see table A.2 of the Statistical Appendix to this volume). First, the precipitous growth of foreign exchange transactions has been driven by international financial asset plays rather than by trade financing—global exports fell from 28.5% of global foreign exchange turnover in 1977 to 1.6% in 1995.[4] Second, contrary to predictions that floating rates and globalization of financial markets would permit countries to economize on official reserves, these have been rising globally relative to the value of exports. Countries have been pressed to hold large reserves as informal collateral to reassure inconsistent financial markets and deter currency runs. Third, notwithstanding the rise of official reserves, the power of central banks to intervene collectively in foreign exchange markets has dwindled. Global official reserves are now less than the value of one day of global foreign exchange turnover, a 93% decline from 1977.

The structure of the foreign exchange market is heterogeneous (see tables A.3 and A.5 of the Statistical Appendix). Spot transactions, though losing share in recent years to swaps and options, still made up nearly half the value of global foreign exchange transactions in 1992. Spots plus short-maturity round trips of two to seven days made up 81% of the 1992 transactions (see table A.5 of the Statistical Appendix). Transactions among dealers far exceeded those with non-dealers, accounting for 70% of global turnover in 1992 and 66% in 1995. Interdealer trading was especially dominant in spot and swap transactions. Only in outright forwards, a category of diminishing importance, did transactions with non-dealers dominate interdealer trades (see BIS 1993, table 1-A).

The dominance of interdealer trading is of recent vintage. Growth of transactions in the US foreign exchange market took off towards the end of the 1970s—from a small base and a much smaller multiple of the value of foreign trade and direct investment than was reached in the 1980s (see table A.2 of the Statistical Appendix). Moreover, the Euromarket, housed in London, grew even faster during that decade, overtaking New York by a substantial margin (see table A.4 of the Statistical Appendix). Currently, 80% of the London foreign exchange volume is handled by branches of foreign financial institutions, half of them from the United States. Thus an even greater ballooning of interdealer trading characterizes the London market.[5]

The phenomenal growth of interdealer trading was driven by four main factors: the augmented chain of interbank flows linked to each foreign exchange transaction with a non-dealer; the internationalizing of portfolios by non-bank financial institutions such as mutual, pension and hedge funds; the growth of hedging against exchange risk by multinational corporations (MNCs); and the rapid expansion of cross-currency speculation, both covered arbitraging of interest differentials by international banks and open speculation by all of the above.

The first factor relates to the need of a dealer bank to restore its foreign exchange balances following the sale or purchase of a foreign currency. Exotic new hedging instruments that dealers concocted have added new links to this chain of interdealer transactions. The increased desire of non-financial firms to hedge against exchange risk provided much of the demand for innovative instruments. Of the respondents to a 1992 survey of Fortune 500 corporations, 85% reported that they used derivatives for risk management. This figure was only 61% in 1986 (Dolde 1993). Participants in the survey gave exchange risk as their main concern.

Evidently foreign exchange (FX) risk bears much greater potential for harm than interest rate risk. For non-financial firms, FX risk may pose quantitatively greater threats to cash flow than does interest rate risk. For the FX risk may have large competitive effects, since FX movements necessarily subject some firms to an appreciating currency. In contrast, domestic interest moves in the same direction for all domestic competitors. Further, foreign and domestic interest rates are at least as likely to move in the same direction as in opposite directions. (Dolde 1993, pp. 18–19)

However, the cost of hedging rationed its use. Only 22% of the firms that hedged, hedged 100%, and that figure fell to 16% when the hedging firms developed a view about the direction of the exchange rate on which they were willing to gamble. Hedging was also inversely related to size. The firms in the sample that reported never having hedged were smaller firms, whose capital averaged only (!) $2.5 billion compared to $8 billion for the 85% that hedged. (Dolde 1993, pp. 23–24, exhibit 1)

Covered arbitraging of interest rates across currencies appears to be the largest single motivation for the ballooning of foreign exchange flows. As financial deregulation spread in the 1980s the "neutral zone"—the range of interest rate differentials within which arbitraging would not be profitable—shrank to equal the transaction costs of purchasing and selling forwards the requisite foreign exchange (Frankel

1989). Since such costs have become very low for multi-million-dollar transactions, dealer banks moving very large sums in and out of major currencies to exploit interest differentials between short-term government bonds, which barely exceed the narrowed neutral zone, now account for much of the global foreign exchange volume (Clinton 1988). But the general consensus over "much" dissolves when it comes to estimating "how much".

Part of the difficulty is that the line between hedging against and speculating on exchange and interest rate movements is blurred. Banks and MNCs are known to move from hedged to uncovered speculation when they have developed a confident view about the direction in which rates are moving.[6] Prior to the 1992 crisis, the view that the European exchange rate mechanism (ERM) was stable led many MNCs to move unhedged between Euro-currencies in pursuit of cheaper credit or higher return from their liquid reserves. Some lost badly when the mechanism collapsed in September 1992,[7] while others gained by moving quickly to speculate against the weaker European Community (EC) currencies.[8] Fortune 500 companies also increase hedging when they increase their debt leveraging, since leveraging increases their need to smooth cash flows (Dolde 1995). The misnamed hedge funds, on the other hand, leverage with short-term bank credit in order to engage in unhedged speculation.

These complexities plague efforts to separate those foreign exchange transactions that facilitate activities of the "real" economy from those devoted to socially questionable financial speculation. The former head of Deutsche Bank puts the former at 5% of the $1 trillion daily foreign exchange volume (Guth 1993). The New York Federal Reserve Bank's estimate is reported to be more generous: 18% (Wachtel 1995).

Precise separation of speculative from virtuous foreign exchange transactions is not, however, required for implementing a globalized Tobin tax. The tax would affect quick round-tripping related to speculation much more than delayed round-tripping related to foreign trade and investment, but would let the market do the separating. Estimating Tobin tax revenue thus reduces to estimating the response of the taxable foreign exchange volume to different tax rates. This is, of course, no easy problem, since there is not yet an experience base for directly estimating responsiveness. The estimate can be made roughly, however, with simulations that use different values for elasticities and transaction costs, provided those values can be shown to be plausibly related to characteristics of the heterogeneous foreign exchange market. We use this strategy here.

The tax base, formal estimating model and parameter values

Our estimating strategy is to model the annual global foreign exchange volume as though it was generated by a composite profit-maximizing firm. The values of the key revenue and cost parameters are weighted averages of those of the heterogeneous traders making up the global foreign exchange markets. By adding to transaction costs, a Tobin tax not only reduces the foreign exchange volume by an amount determined by the weighted average elasticity of volume with respect to costs, but alters its composition by squeezing hardest the low unit-profit, high elasticity transactions, such as covered interest arbitraging. The reduced volume is thus accompanied by a lower weighted average elasticity. If the final Tobin tax rate is phased in through a schedule of incrementally rising rates—a strategy we favour—the elasticity of foreign exchange volume with respect to the tax increments diminishes sequentially.

From the 1992 figure of $220 trillion of global foreign exchange transactions, we make two deductions. The first is 10% of the $220 trillion to account for official, and presumably tax exempt, foreign exchange transactions.[9] The second is approximately 25% of the $220 trillion to account for private transactions that elude the tax by one means or another. This leaves $144 trillion as the effective tax base, though the deductions are merely guesses.

The formal estimating model

We sketch first the demand structure of our global firm, which is shaped by two motives governing the global demand for foreign exchange—to facilitate international transactions in goods and services (transactions demand) and to speculate on expected movements of asset prices in different currencies (speculative demand).

Let Y denote world trade in goods and services, and $\mathbf{i}$ and $\mathbf{f}$ the vectors, respectively, of interest rates and inflation rates across the trading countries. Foreign exchange demand is motivated by the financing requirements for Y and by speculation on expected changes in $\mathbf{i}$, $\mathbf{f}$ and Y. The demand for V, the volume of foreign exchange turnover in a given period, is thus:

(1) $$V = V(p, Y, \mathbf{i}, \mathbf{f}),$$

where p is the "price" or fee charged by the firm per unit of foreign exchange supplied. We can rewrite equation 1 as an inverse demand function:

(2) $$p = p(V,Y,\mathbf{i},\mathbf{f}).$$

Total revenue, R, received by the firm is given by:

(3) $$R = pV.$$

Substituting equation 2 into equation 3 gives us:

(4) $$R = p(V,Y,\mathbf{i},\mathbf{f})\,V.$$

For our on-off estimate we treat Y, $\mathbf{i}$ and $\mathbf{f}$ as exogenous. The revenue function, equation 4, will therefore typically be a parabola in relation to the quantity variable, V. More precisely, if the demand function (equation 2) is linear in V, then R of equations 3 and 4 is clearly a parabola in terms of V. Since, in equilibrium, marginal revenue equals marginal cost for our maximizing firm, the equilibrium V will always fall in the region where marginal revenue is positive. The relevant part of the revenue curve can therefore be approximated by:

(5) $$R = gV^a \qquad 0 < a < 1,$$

where g and a are parameters.

Transaction costs, broadly defined to include search costs, subjective risk premia and dealer fees, are given by:

(6) $$C = tV^b, \text{ with } b > a,$$

where t is the unit transaction cost to the firm when $V = 1$, and b is a parameter. When $b = 1$, t becomes global average transaction costs. The Tobin tax would be an addition to p—a component of t. Profit, P, is given by:

(7) $$P = R - C.$$

The firm maximizes P with respect to V, given the value of t and the other parameters. The first-order condition for profit maximization requires that:

$$\text{(8)} \qquad\qquad \log V = \frac{\log t + \log b - \log a - \log g}{a - b.}$$

Hence, the elasticity of foreign exchange volume with respect to transaction costs is:

$$\text{(9)} \qquad\qquad \frac{d\log V}{d\log t} = \frac{-1}{(b-a)} = -E$$

By convention, E is expressed as a positive number.

In addition to foreign currency, other assets, such as Treasury bills, might be explicitly introduced, because as t rises with the Tobin tax, speculative activities will shift to other assets. This possibility is formally recognized in equation 1. A portfolio shifting would affect the elasticity coefficient, E. But according to Walras' Law, we can concentrate on the foreign exchange market.

We next hypothesize that although b is a parameter for the firm, it changes with volume and compositional changes of the foreign exchange market. That is,

$$\text{(10)} \qquad\qquad b = b(V, D),$$

where D is the weight average round trip or duration of the foreign exchange transaction normalized to uniform size. We contend that a decline in the foreign exchange volume raises average transaction costs, as does an increase in the average duration of foreign exchange round trips. Equation 10 is a step function (and thus not everywhere continuous and differentiable), but to oversimplify these contentions, we stipulate that $db/dV < 0$ and $db/dD > 0$.

If the contentions are valid, E, which equals $1/(b-a)$, will fall. This means that as the increments to the Tobin tax rate are phased in, the reduced annual global foreign exchange volume will become more stable, at least regarding further changes in transaction costs. The annual revenue from the tax will also become more stable.

Validation of the contentions

The two contentions used in the estimating model are generally considered valid in the financial literature. Currency trading is typically recognized as a decreasing-cost activity. To quote from an authoritative financial text by a Citibanker:

A more controversial feature of the new shape of the financial system is that the bulk of its participants now have a vested interest in instability because the advent of high-technology dealing rooms has raised the level of fixed costs. High fixed costs imply that high turnover is needed for profitability. But high turnover tends to occur only when markets are volatile. The analysts at Salomon Brothers put it clearly: 'Logically, the most destabilizing environment for an institutional house is a relatively stagnant rate environment.' (Walmsley 1988, p.13)[10]

Increasing the size of a foreign exchange transaction also generates scale economies. The quoted bid-ask spreads on trades of major currencies in the "wholesale" foreign exchange market (trades less than $50 million) over the electronic network are usually less than 0.1% (Bollerslev and Melvin 1994; Clinton 1988). The spreads are doubled for "retail" trades (less than $5 million) and can rise to more than 1.0% for small retail transactions.[11] Such numbers should, however, be taken only as relative orders of magnitude. Electronic quotes in the wholesale market are invitations to negotiate terms, while in the retail market, asymmetric information favouring foreign exchange dealers often allows them to add a monopolistic margin to the pricing.

That longer round trips increase transaction costs is backed by two general observations. First, risk increases with duration because lengthening the duration of a project increases the likelihood of exogenous shocks, causing things to go awry for one of the counter-parties. Second, the greater the volatility of expected returns from financial transactions, the higher are transaction costs, an observation that has been strongly validated econometrically for foreign exchange and other financial assets (Frenkel and Levich 1977; Overturf 1982; Aiyagari and Gertler 1991; Dixit 1992; Hubbard 1993; Bollerslev and Melvin 1994).[12]

From the standard premise of finance theory, which holds that economic agents are risk-averse, it follows that agents lengthen their investment horizon only when the expected return rises by more than the expected risk. It also follows that adding the same Tobin tax rate to the transaction costs of both low-risk/low-return and high-risk/high-return transactions will squeeze the profitability of short foreign exchange round trips more than long ones. The tax, along with reducing foreign exchange volume, will shift its composition towards longer duration round trips.

Four classes of foreign exchange transactions, all at the short end of the spectrum, are likely to be especially sensitive to a Tobin tax. In decreasing order of sensitivity they are: covered interest rate arbitraging, uncovered interest rate arbitraging, hedge fund speculating and open-end mutual funds that invest in foreign assets. The last is, however, a composite of regional open-end emerging market mutuals—whose elasticity with respect to a Tobin tax is likely to be high—and global, international and country funds, whose elasticity is likely to be moderate. The elasticity of spot transactions, although at the extreme short end of the duration spectrum, is also likely to be moderate.

Covered interest arbitraging

Covered interest arbitraging, primarily carried out by dealer banks, is motivated by differences between market interest rates on bonds and notes of identical maturity and credit risk denominated in different currencies. Typically, these are negotiable CDs of large banks and government securities of the major OECD countries, which are heavily traded and carry little credit and liquidity risk. A profitable arbitrage opportunity appears when the interest difference exceeds the discount on the forward exchange rate for the same maturity period as the bond plus the transaction costs. In the case of Treasuries, the costs include fees for selling a packet of bonds in currency A to purchase currency B, buying a packet of currency B bonds and concurrently selling B currency forward for A currency, plus search costs and risk premia. Both search costs and risk premia are small in the case of covered interest arbitraging, especially for Treasuries.

Transaction costs fix a neutral zone of interest rate differences, with profitable arbitrage opportunities appearing only when the differences exceed the size of the zone. The neutral zones for covered interest arbitraging in major currencies have shrunk substantially since the 1970s because of the lifting of capital controls, the advent of electronic transactions and the generation of scale economies from the expanding volume of transactions. Since the early 1980s, huge flows of foreign exchange transactions among dealers have been induced by small deviations of interest rate differences from the forward exchange rate discount. That is, interest rate arbitraging in the major currencies has become a profitable low-yield, low-risk, high-volume activity that exploits small deviations from narrowed neutral zones.

Because a moderate Tobin tax applied to each leg of the foreign exchange round trip would mean a proportionately greater widening of the small neutral zone, the post-tax interest rate deviations would have to exceed the forward exchange rate discount by a much greater percentage than is now the case to create profitable arbitraging opportunities. Thus with a 0.25% Tobin tax, annualized interest rates on 30-day Treasury bills could differ between countries by an additional 6% without triggering arbitraging flows. Such flows between major currencies could therefore drop substantially.

Uncovered interest rate arbitraging

The neutral zone impeding arbitraging with a weak currency partner, notably with developing countries, is much wider, mainly because the risk premium is much larger and forward exchange markets for hedging exchange risk are missing. The exchange risk is assessed as sizable, even in periods during which the weak currency's exchange rate is relatively stable, because of what the finance literature has dubbed "the peso problem", that is, remembrance of past exchange crises. And it shoots up when another crisis threatens—witness the rapid reversal of capital flows that preceded the December 1994 Mexican crisis. The Tobin tax would expand the neutral zone of weak currencies proportionately less than that of strong ones. Comparatively, however, the foreign exchange volume involved in weak currency arbitraging is much smaller, so that its less elastic response to a Tobin tax would do little to dampen the large initial global decline of interest arbitraging.

Hedge funds

Hedge funds are private unregulated coalitions of wealthy individuals and financial institutions, such as pension funds, whose capital contributions to the fund are combined with heavy short-term borrowing from banks to make runs on vulnerable currencies.[13] This is uncovered speculation, so the risks and the mean expected return to hedge fund investors are much greater than those for covered interest arbitraging. A modest Tobin tax added to an already wide neutral zone would act as a weak deterrent.

But two side effects from the reduction in global foreign exchange volume could considerably strengthen the tax's deterrent power. If the tax dampens exchange rate volatility, as its advocates believe it will, hedge funds would find fewer speculative opportunities. Further, reducing the volume of trading increases the power of central banks, with their limited reserves, to counter-speculate. If exercised, it would raise the risk of speculating. For example, the drop in the global foreign exchange volume from a 0.25% Tobin tax could raise the ratio of official reserves to foreign exchange volume by as much as 30%. A Tobin tax could thus widen the hedge funds' neutral zone by more than twice the tax rate by making foreign exchange speculation riskier and costlier.

International open-end mutual funds

The strategies of the open-end mutuals are shaped by two standard features: the commitment to give shareholders almost instant cashing-in rights and remuneration arrangements that heavily reward managers for expanding the fund's volume and increasing its net value per share. The reward arrangements drive managers away from holding low-return, highly liquid assets to meet the cashing-in commitment and towards market-timing strategies that emphasize loading up on current market favourites, whose rising values would allow them to be sold profitably were the demand for cash to rise. The result is high portfolio turnover, which in the case of regional, international or global mutual funds, also means frequent cross-currency trading.

The incidence of a Tobin tax would fall least on funds that are able, without abandoning market timing, to reduce cross-country trading in favour of selling and buying within each of the countries in their trading purview. European, international and global funds, whose purview includes countries with thick financial markets, would be far more able to do this than emerging market funds. Emerging markets are uniformly thin—only a handful of companies in each national market have shares that trade in large enough volume to meet the liquidity requirements of the mutual funds. Open-end emerging market mutuals are therefore predominantly regional or global, so that their market timing involves frequent portfolio shifting among weak currencies. Faced with a Tobin tax and the high risk of broadening their holdings in each of the emerging markets, such funds would be forced to stay longer with the large companies in their portfolio and cut back on new investment to avoid over-exposure in these companies. The overall investing rate of emerging market mutuals would probably decline much more than that of the other open-end mutual funds. (Appendix A illustrates this with reference to Latin American funds.)

Spot transactions

More than 72% of global spot transactions in 1992 were made among dealers (BIS 1993, table 1-A). Much of this pattern probably relates to the chain of interbank transactions set off as dealer banks readjust their foreign exchange inventories following transactions with customers.[14]

Some of this growth relates to hedging by final customers—MNCs, mutual funds and non-dealer financial institutions. But, mostly, it has been impelled by an increasing volume of covered interest arbitraging by dealer banks, who mainly use interdealer swaps for this purpose. As the Tobin tax reduces covered and uncovered speculation and hedging, the spot transactions linked to these activities should also decline. On the other hand, interdealer spot trading related to international trade and foreign investment financing would probably not decline much because of a Tobin tax, since the dealers would be able to pass along most of the accumulated taxes on interdealer trades to their non-dealer customers, whose demand for foreign exchange is fairly inelastic.[15] We therefore expect spot transactions to decline at first, but then to level off and perhaps even rise, should the tax reduce exchange rate volatility and thus encourage faster growth of trade and long-term investment.

The duration of round trips

In our model, b rises with the average duration of foreign exchange round trips, and a higher b means higher transaction costs and a less elastic response of the foreign exchange volume to changes in transaction costs. In 1992, the weighted average duration of global foreign exchange trades, standardized for size of transaction, was 8.7 days, with the dominance of short round trips of seven days or less largely determining the average (see Appendix B).

If the Tobin tax cuts down speculative flows, would it raise the average duration of round trips? Probably—such flows, covered and uncovered, tend to be short round trip forays, and the impact of the tax falls much more heavily on short than on long round trips. But interdealer and dealer-customer spot transactions, which pull down the average duration, would decline proportionately less than covered and uncovered speculative round trips. Average duration would consequently rise less. The published survey data are, however, too aggregated to support estimates of the extent to which average duration might increase.

Estimates of revenue and reduction of foreign exchange volume

We first compute revenue and volume reductions from a phased-in 0.25% Tobin tax, which, given its macroeconomic benefits and revenue potential, we tend to favour. We assume that the tax is levied by at least all of the major international money-centre countries, with each participating country collecting the tax from all private trading initiated within its jurisdiction, including trades booked offshore in non-participating countries by banks and other trading entities chartered within its jurisdiction. The initial tax base is the $144 trillion in foreign exchange transactions calculated earlier. We also assume that global output, trade and the US dollar's international and domestic purchasing power do not change during the four-period estimating interval. That is, the estimates do not incorporate guesses about trends of the real economy, the dollar exchange rate or US inflation that could affect the future size and purchasing power of the Tobin tax revenue. With this in mind, we offer the following interpretation of our estimates and their sensitivity to alternative parameter values (table 9.1):

- A phased-in tax of 0.25% applied to the 1992 foreign exchange volume would have produced $200 billion—more if pre-tax transaction costs were already high, and less if they were low. Because the 1995 global foreign exchange volume sans derivatives was 50% higher than in 1992—48% higher if cross-country derivative turnover is added (see the Statistical Appendix, footnote 2 and table A.1)—the tax revenue in 1995 would be closer to $300 billion.

- The revenue is only moderately sensitive to alternative values of pre-tax transaction costs. In table 9.1, tax revenue declines from $267.6 billion to $205.5 billion, or by 23%, when pre-tax costs are set 50% lower, that is, at 0.5% instead of 1.0%. The reason is that adding the Tobin tax uniformly to both the high and the low pre-tax costs narrows the percentage difference between them.

- The revenue estimates are not very sensitive to moderate differences in elasticities. Raising or lowering each period's E by 0.25 results in only a positive or negative 6.2% change in annual revenue if pre-tax transaction costs are 1.0%, and a positive or negative 12.8% change if pre-tax transaction costs are 0.5%. The 1992 annual tax revenue in table 9.1 thus ranges from a maximum of $284.3 billion to a minimum of $180.3 billion. The maximum is reached if pre-tax costs average 1.0%, and the initial elasticity is 1.25; the minimum is reached if pre-tax costs average 0.5% and the initial elasticity is 1.75. We think the ranges of parameter values are reasonable and conclude that a 0.25% Tobin tax would indeed generate annual revenue large enough to tempt deficit-plagued national governments and provide a considerable addi-

Table 9.1 Global revenue and foreign exchange turnover effects of a phased-in 0.25% Tobin tax

Transaction Cost	Foreign exchange volume ($ trillions)		Effect of dE= ±0.25 ($ trillions)	T-Tax revenue ($ billions)	Effect of dE= ±0.25 ($ billions)
	Taxable	Total			
Year 1 (T-tax = 0.1%, E = 1.5)					
t_1 = 1.1%	122.4	198.4	3.6	122.4	3.6
t_2 = 0.6%	100.8	176.8	7.2	100.8	7.2
Year 2 (T-Tax = 0.15%, E = 1.25)					
t_1 = 1.15%	115.5	191.5	4.8	173.3	7.2
t_2 = 0.65%	92.4	168.4	8.3	138.6	12.5
Year 3 (T-tax = 0.2%, E = 1.0)					
t_1 = 1.2%	110.6	186.6	5.8	221.1	11.7
t_2 = 0.7%	86.9	162.9	9.2	173.8	18.5
Year 4 (T-tax = 0.25%, E = 0.75)					
t_1 = 1.25%	107.0	183.0	6.7	267.6	16.7
t_2 = 0.75%	82.2	158.2	6.9	205.5	25.2

Note: Initial tax base is $144 trillion, and total volume is $220 trillion (1992 global foreign exchange volume); t_1 is 1% + the Tobin Tax; t_2 is 0.5% + the Tobin Tax; E is the elasticity of the annual foreign exchange volume with respect to transaction costs. It is assumed to diminish by increments of 0.25 per period from the initial value of 1.5; the dE columns give the change of volume (in $ trillions) and of tax revenue (in $ billions) if E is 0.25 higher or lower than the specified elasticity of each period.
Source: Authors' calculations.

tion to the financing of the UN's and other international agencies' social and economic development projects, should they be given a modest share of that revenue.

• A tax rate much higher than 0.25% would be destabilizing because it would cut foreign exchange volume too drastically—unless elasticity is very low. Plugging the 0.5% tax rate that Felix (1994) used into our estimating model with its relatively high elasticities reduces foreign exchange volume by almost half if pre-tax transaction costs are 1%, and completely wipes out the volume if the transaction costs are 0.5%.

To minimize shock, phasing in the tax would be advisable, although the four-year period is arbitrary. But since an extended political debate would undoubtedly precede adoption, there would be a prolonged "announcement effect", which would further reduce the shock to existing financial arrangements. While they were lobbying against the proposal, financial institutions would undoubtedly be preparing contingency plans should the lobbying fail, and might even begin anticipatory adjusting before the tax begins to be phased in.

Looking at the 1992 and 1995 tax receipts from a 0.25% Tobin tax for each country that collects the tax highlights some distribution problems impeding globalization (table 9.2). At first glance, countries housing major foreign exchange markets that are virtually offshore benefit the most from a globalized and effectively collected Tobin tax, assuming they kept the tax receipts. In Singapore, the United Kingdom and Hong Kong, where foreign exchange trading is chiefly carried out by foreign-owned dealing houses transacting among third-country currencies (see table A.7 in the Statistical Appendix), the tax would fall predominantly on foreigners. But trading volume would fall relatively more in these markets, as a disproportionately large share of their trading involves short round trip transactions that would be squeezed especially hard by the tax. They are likely to be very resistant to shrinking their oversized financial sectors by participating in a globalized Tobin tax regime and

Table 9.2 Annual revenue from a 0.25% Tobin tax applied to 1992 and 1995 global foreign exchange volumes
(billions of US dollars)

| | Pre-tax transaction costs | | | |
| | 0.5% | | 1.0% | |
	1992	1995	1992	1995
Industrial countries				
United Kingdom	55.3	89.0	72.2	115.9
United States	31.7	46.8	41.3	60.9
Japan	22.6	30.8	29.4	40.1
Switzerland	12.3	16.4	16.0	21.4
Germany	10.3	14.4	13.4	18.7
France	6.3	11.3	8.0	14.7
Australia	5.3	7.4	6.9	9.6
Denmark	5.1	5.7	6.6	7.9
Canada	4.4	5.5	5.7	7.2
Sweden	3.9	3.6	5.1	4.7
Netherlands	3.5	4.7	4.6	6.1
Other OECD	16.1	25.1	20.9	32.7
Group total	176.7	260.7	230.1	339.4
Developing countries				
Singapore	13.8	20.0	18.1	26.0
Hong Kong	11.3	17.1	14.7	22.3
South Africa	0.5	0.9	0.6	1.2
Bahrain	0.5	0.5	0.7	0.6
Other LDCs	2.6	2.9	3.4	3.9
Group total	28.8	41.4	37.5	54.0
Global total	205.5	302.1	267.6	393.4

Source: BIS (1993, 1995a, 1995b).

sharing the proceeds with countries with small foreign exchange markets—that is, most developing countries. Yet, as table 9.2 shows, without some redistribution of the tax receipts from the North to the South, the revenue receipts of most developing countries would be meagre.[16]

We also computed estimates using 0.1% and 0.05% tax rates. These estimates (shown in tables 9.3 and 9.4) are based on the same model used above, with the base elasticities of table 9.1 but no phasing-in. With the lower tax rates, the revenue pie shrinks globally and for each collecting country. It shrinks less, however, than the drop in the tax rate. With the 0.1% tax, revenue falls by 49% if pre-tax transaction costs average 0.5%, and by 54% if they average 1%, while for a 0.05% tax, revenue falls by 69% and 75%, respectively.

The relative distribution of the tax receipts in the two tables is impervious to the tax rates. But this may be an artifact of the estimating model

Table 9.3 Annual revenue from a 0.1% Tobin tax applied to 1992 and 1995 foreign exchange volumes
(billions of US dollars)

| | Pre-tax transaction costs | | | |
| | 0.5% | | 1.0% | |
	1992	1995	1992	1995
Industrial countries				
United Kingdom	27.0	43.7	32.9	53.1
United States	15.5	23.0	18.8	27.9
Japan	11.1	15.1	13.4	18.4
Switzerland	6.0	8.0	7.3	9.7
Germany	5.1	7.0	6.2	8.4
France	3.1	5.5	3.8	6.7
Australia	2.6	3.6	3.2	4.3
Denmark	2.5	2.9	3.0	3.4
Canada	2.1	2.6	2.5	3.2
Sweden	1.9	1.8	2.3	2.2
Netherlands	1.8	2.2	2.1	2.7
Other OECD	7.9	12.3	9.6	15.0
Group total	86.6	127.7	105.0	155.0
Developing countries				
Singapore	6.8	9.8	8.3	11.9
Hong Kong	5.5	8.4	6.7	10.3
South Africa	0.3	0.4	0.4	0.5
Bahrain	0.3	0.2	0.4	0.3
Other LDCs	1.3	1.7	1.6	1.9
Group total	14.2	20.5	17.4	24.9
Global total	100.8	148.2	122.4	179.9

Source: BIS (1993, 1995a, 1995b).

Table 9.4 Annual revenue from a 0.05% Tobin tax applied to 1992 and 1995 foreign exchange volumes
(billions of US dollars)

| | Pre-tax transaction costs | | | |
| | 0.5% | | 1.0% | |
	1992	*1995*	*1992*	*1995*
Industrial countries				
United Kingdom	16.4	26.6	17.7	28.7
United States	9.4	14.0	10.2	15.1
Japan	6.7	9.2	7.2	9.9
Switzerland	3.7	4.9	4.0	5.3
Germany	3.0	4.2	3.2	4.5
France	1.9	3.3	2.0	3.6
Australia	1.6	2.2	1.8	2.4
Denmark	1.5	1.7	1.6	1.8
Canada	1.3	1.6	1.4	1.7
Sweden	1.2	1.1	1.3	1.2
Netherlands	1.0	1.3	1.1	1.4
Other OECD	4.8	7.6	5.3	8.1
Group total	52.5	77.7	56.8	83.7
Developing countries				
Singapore	4.1	5.9	4.4	6.4
Hong Kong	3.4	5.1	3.7	5.5
South Africa	0.1	0.3	0.1	0.3
Bahrain	0.1	0.1	0.1	0.1
Other LDCs	0.8	1.0	0.9	1.1
Group total	8.6	12.4	9.2	13.4
Global total	61.1	90.1	66.0	97.1

Source: BIS (1993, 1995a, 1995b).

rather than reality, since the lower the rate, the less it will deter the short round-tripping associated with cross-currency arbitraging and open speculation. If so, the tax receipts of major offshore financial centres like London, Singapore and Hong Kong would decline less than the global average. Would this make them more amenable to sharing their receipts with other countries, industrial or developing? Who knows? What is clearer is that the potential macroeconomic pay-off from the Tobin tax in reducing speculative currency movements is substantially diminished at these lower tax rates. With a 0.25% tax, the difference in the annualized interest rates of one-month Treasury bills between countries could widen by 6% without setting off covered arbitrage flows. With a 0.1% tax, the annualized margin drops to 2.4%, and with a 0.05% tax, to 1.2%.

Comparisons of estimates using different parameters

Identifying the strategic factors that account for the revenue differences should help improve future estimations by indicating where more information about the modus operandi of global foreign exchange markets is especially needed. We turn first to Frankel's estimates, which, like ours, are directed at the sand in the gears objective of the Tobin tax.

Frankel's estimates

Frankel picks 0.1% as a feasible tax rate for reducing speculative transactions and raising a large amount of revenue. His estimating strategy uses the ratio of interdealer trading volume to dealer-customer trading volume in the major foreign exchange trading centres. In 1992, his ratio was 3.3:1. In 1995, it dropped to 3.0:1. Customers include both financial and non-financial entities, with financial entities now accounting for the larger share of dealer-customer trading (see table A.3 of the Statistical Appendix). He believes that the 0.1% tax would squeeze primarily dealer-financial customer trading, with negative feedback on interdealer trading. Applied to the 1995 global foreign exchange volume, the 0.1% tax might reduce that volume by 45% and raise an annual tax revenue of $176 billion.

This result is surprisingly close to our revenue estimates (in table 9.1), which are based on a phased-in 0.25% tax. Why? One reason is prima facie. Our estimates are based on the 1992 volume, Frankel's on the 1995 volume. Applying Frankel's approach to the 1992 volume reduces the annual revenue to $121 billion. But that still means that his 60% lower tax rate reduces annual revenue to only 25% below our lowest estimate.

Three factors help to counter the large tax rate difference. First, Frankel deducts 20% for exempted official trading and tax evasion from the global foreign exchange volume to arrive at the tax base, whereas we deduct 35%. Frankel's 0.1% tax is thus applied to a larger tax base than is our 0.25% tax. Both deductions are, however, pure guesses. Research could pin down the share of official trades in global foreign exchange transactions more accurately, but there is no database for refining estimates of the extent of evasion of a hypothetical global tax of unknown rate. Second, our elasticity assumptions differ. Frankel

241

uses 0.32, while we phase in a diminishing set ranging from 1.75 to 0.5, with the arc elasticity for the entire phasing-in ranging from 0.59 to 0.67. Using a 0.1% Tobin tax, Frankel's $121 billion revenue estimate corresponds to an elasticity of about 1.0 when plugged into our estimating approach (table 9.5). But pending actual experience with a Tobin tax, all elasticity assumptions are primarily judgmental, though more than pure guesses.

The judgment is shaped, however, by the third factor, pre-tax transaction costs, for which assumed values are directly testable. Frankel assumes that pre-tax costs are 0.1%, the typical spread on wholesale interdealer transactions. Since a 0.1% Tobin tax and a 1.0 elasticity coefficient wipes out all foreign exchange trading, Frankel's 0.1% transac-

Table 9.5 Tobin tax revenue and decline of the 1992 global foreign exchange volume under alternative tax rates and elasticities

	0.1% Tax[a]		0.05% Tax[b]		0.003% Tax[c]	
Elasticity	Volume decline[d]	Revenue[e]	Volume decline[d]	Revenue[e]	Volume decline[d]	Revenue[e]
Pre-tax transaction costs = 1%						
1.75	25.2	118.0	12.6	65.7	0.8	4.3
1.50	21.6	122.4	10.8	66.6	0.7	4.3
1.25	18.0	126.0	9.0	67.5	0.5	4.3
1.00	14.4	129.6	7.2	68.4	0.4	4.3
0.75	10.8	133.2	5.4	69.3	0.3	4.3
0.50	7.2	136.8	3.6	70.2	0.2	4.3
0.30	4.4	139.6	2.2	70.9	0.1	4.3
Pre-tax transaction costs = 0.5%						
1.75	50.4	93.6	25.2	59.2	1.5	4.3
1.50	43.2	100.8	21.6	61.2	1.3	4.3
1.25	36.0	108.0	18.0	63.0	1.1	4.3
1.00	28.8	115.2	14.4	64.8	0.9	4.3
0.75	21.6	122.4	10.8	66.6	0.7	4.3
0.50	14.4	129.6	7.2	68.4	0.4	4.3
0.30	8.8	135.4	4.4	69.8	0.3	4.3
Pre-tax transaction costs = 0.1%						
1.75	144.0	0.0	126.0	9.0	0.7	4.3
1.50	144.0	0.0	108.0	18.0	0.6	4.3
1.25	144.0	0.0	90.0	27.0	0.5	4.3
1.00	144.0	0.0	72.0	36.0	0.4	4.3
0.75	108.0	36.0	54.0	45.0	0.3	4.3
0.50	72.0	72.0	36.0	54.0	0.2	4.3
0.30	43.2	100.8	21.6	61.2	0.1	4.3

a. The rate suggested by Frankel (1996).
b. The rate used by Kenen (1996).
c. The rate proposed by Walker (1993).
d. Trillions of dollars.
e. Billions of dollars.
Source: Authors' calculations.

tion costs must be accompanied by an elasticity well below unity in order to produce more plausible consequences. We use higher pre-tax transaction costs of 0.5% and 1.0%, which allow us to estimate the effects of a 0.25% tax with higher elasticity coefficients. Higher elasticities also bring our revenue estimates closer to Frankel's, but we chose the higher pre-tax transaction costs primarily for conceptual reasons. The scope of transaction costs should, we believe, include the cost of carrying out the full array of financial exchanges needed to complete a primary transfer, as well as search costs and risk premia.[17] Hedged foreign exchange transactions, whether interdealer or dealer-customer, usually involve multiple financial exchanges.[18] Asymmetric information implies that for many customers, search costs are not trivial, and subjective risk premia are probably important for non-hedged transactors. In addition, dealer-customer spreads in retail transactions are reportedly much higher than 0.1%. Empirical research could substantially improve estimates of the weighted average size of pre-tax transaction costs, and thus the accuracy of estimates of Tobin tax revenue.[19]

There is also partial convergence between Frankel's and our assessment of the range of feasible sand in the gears Tobin tax rates. Both advise against applying the 0.5% or higher rates suggested by some Tobin tax advocates on the grounds that such high rates would disrupt foreign exchange trading so much that exchange rate volatility may not be reduced.[20] There may be disagreement, however, on what the upper limit of the range of feasible tax rates might be. In our estimates using a 0.25% tax rate, the maximum one-time reduction of global foreign exchange volume is 33%. Foreign exchange markets should be able to adjust to that reduction without going into terminal shock, 33% being less than the percentage increase of global foreign exchange trading in every triennium since 1977 (see table A.1 of the Statistical Appendix). Frankel suggests the upper limit is not far above 0.1%, but doesn't cite a specific number. Our disagreement about the limiting tax rate may, therefore, be of moderate proportions.

Revenue estimates with no "sand in the gears" tax rates

Two suggested no sand in the gears tax rates are 0.05%, used by Peter Kenen in his contribution to this volume (Kenen 1996), and 0.003%, proposed by British journalist, Martin Walker, to fund UN peacekeeping (Walker 1993). Plugging these rates into our estimating model shows that Walker was justified in disregarding elasticity effects, since they are negligible for pre-tax transaction costs ranging from 0.1% to 1.0%, even with high elasticity coefficients (see table 9.5).[21] The effect of a 0.05% tax, on the other hand, oscillates between being strictly revenue generating and throwing some sand in the gears. It is predominantly revenue generating when pre-tax transaction costs are 1.0%. But with pre-tax transaction costs of 0.5%, the sand in the gears effect, that is, significant volume declines, kicks in at higher elasticities, and become devastatingly large at elasticities of 1.0 or higher if pre-tax transaction costs are only 0.1%.

Conjectures on longer-term revenue prospects

Tobin tax revenue will evolve mainly according to two offsetting dynamics. Growth of international trade and long-term investment will raise foreign exchange volume and tax revenue, and the development of tax escape routes will lower it.

Likely growth effects

Felix (1995), a companion paper, concludes that a moderate sand in the gears Tobin tax would stimulate real growth globally—though not necessarily global economic integration—if the space it provides for national counter-cyclical macroeconomic policies to operate without triggering adverse capital flows and for the G-7 to implement joint exchange rate targeting is used sensibly. A world with less volatile exchange rates, whose constituent economies are able to operate closer to their full employment frontier, would be faster growing.

Taken by itself, full employment growth would stimulate international trade and investment through the channels emphasized by conventional international trade theory: positive income elasticities of demand for imported consumables and foreign tourism, international relocations of industrial capacity stemming from the successive realignments of relative factor scarcities, and so on. Full employment growth should also ease political pressures for import protection. Thus the global foreign exchange volume should rebound, pulling up Tobin tax revenue. However, although a Tobin tax may reduce exchange risk, it is discriminatory when it comes to the cost of capital, taxing foreign trade and investment projects, but not locally financed domestic projects. We cannot determine a priori which of these two offsetting forces would dominate, but if the import substitution bias is stronger, Tobin tax revenue would grow more slowly than domestic tax revenue.

The evasion problem

We agree with the conclusions reached by Kenen (1996) in his master-ful dissection of the evasion problem, in which he concludes that a glob-alized Tobin tax is quite enforceable and that avoidance efforts over time through asset substitution, offshore booking and the relocating of foreign exchange markets are containable. Kenen, however, carefully limits his conclusions to a 0.05% tax, whose purpose is funding inter-national agencies and programmes, and suggests that the conclusions might not hold for higher tax rates, since these would increase inge-nuity and efforts to avoid the tax.

Does this mean that higher Tobin tax rates with macroeconomic objectives are infeasible? Such an a priori dismissal is unwarranted, because the different objectives are also likely to evoke different polit-ical responses to the evasion problem. The intensifying of evasionary efforts is more likely to be countered by an intensifying of enforcement if the main function of the tax is macroeconomic improvement and if a large part of the substantial revenue is appropriated by national gov-ernments than if it is being collected primarily as a contribution to international solidarity. But that judgment, which reflects the sour post–cold war political climate, could hopefully change for the better.

Appendix A: The Tobin tax and emerging market mutual funds

Emerging market mutual funds, both open-end and closed-end, have, along with American Depository Receipts (ADRs) and Global Depository Receipts (GDRs), been the major channels through which the flow of foreign portfolio capital to Asia and Latin America has surged and ebbed. Net foreign portfolio inflow to these regions peaked at $88 billion in 1993, fell to $62 billion in 1994 and, in reaction to the Mexican crisis, ebbed further in 1995. The cresting and ebbing has been primarily centred in Latin America, where the net inflow crested at $54 billion in 1993 and dropped to $29 billion in 1994. Its further decline in 1995 accounts for most of the further ebbing of portfolio flows to both regions (IMF 1995).

Trying to attract open-end mutual funds is probably the most flawed component of the strategy of relying on portfolio capital inflows to finance faster economic growth in developing countries. The reason is that the modus operandi of these funds makes them excessively volatile sources of external funds.

Open-end mutuals, in general, must have portfolios with sufficient liquidity to enable them to meet their statutory commitment to allow shareholders to cash in with minimal delay. But managerial incentives primarily reward yield and volume. This encourages fund managers to eschew meeting the cashing-in commitment by keeping large holdings of low-return, safe liquid assets in the portfolio, favouring acquisitions that offer both high yield and a thick market. These can be sold quickly and profitably should liquidity needs require. The bias, in other words, is towards high portfolio turnover strategies that focus on market timing and avoid keeping assets for the long pull that may be temporarily out of favour in the financial market. Since the thin stock market of each developing country offers few company shares that meet the requisite criteria, the recent explosion of open-end mutual funds specializing in emerging market investing has been almost entirely in multi-country funds that encompass at least a region, such as Latin America, Asia, the Pacific or, in the case of international and global funds, all emerging market countries in varying combinations with OECD countries. Thus, to flow oscillations generated by interest rate movements in the industrialized countries and other external factors (Calvo, Leiderman and Reinhart 1993; Reisen 1993), the high turnover strategies of open-end emerging market mutuals add a further layer of volatility to the portfolio capital movements of each of the emerging market countries.

The quick entry and exit into other currencies required by timing strategies lead their managers to favour acquisitions in countries with minimal capital controls and other impediments to free capital movements. This generates a form of adverse selection by regional funds, as illustrated by a recent interview with the manager of the Scudder Latin American Fund, the largest of the Latin American funds. To recoup severe losses from the Mexican market collapse and the contagion effect on share prices in other Latin American markets, the manager reported that he was gingerly returning to a few of the heavily hit markets, notably Argentina's and possibly Peru's. Why not Chile's, whose share prices, little affected by the tequila effect, have continued rising nicely this year? His "fund can't afford to have a lot of capital invested in Chile because foreigners have to keep their money there for about a year" (Calian 1995).

The reference is to Chile's successful strategy, operative since 1991, of relying on a combination of zero interest deposits and transfer taxes to keep volatile capital flows from undermining the stability of its real exchange rate, which it views as central to its export-led growth strategy. The capital restrictions have been moderate, and foreign capital can avoid them by remaining in peso-denominated assets for at least a year (Ffrench-Davis, Agosin and Uthoff 1995). The restrictions are similar in principle and intent to the penalties for early withdrawal that most open mutual funds, including the Scudder Latin American Fund, impose on shareholders to deter them from market timing, since that could impose ill-timed asset liquidation on the funds. Bypassing stable Chile with its comparatively high yields for unstable Argentina because Argentina allows free and instant exit, implies that the market timing strategies of emerging market mutual funds, like Scudder's, incorporate extremely high liquidity premia. The international placements of open-end emerging market mutuals resemble hot money flows rather than development financing.

Appendix B: Computing the initial weighted average duration

To arrive at the initial average duration, D, of our representative firm, we exploited 1992 data from BIS (1993) to calculate a weighted average of the round trips per year of the different categories of foreign exchange transactions. As weights, we used the relative volumes of the transactions and divided that number into 365 days. The weighted average was then adjusted to make the size of each foreign exchange transaction the same. For the adjustment, we used information from the New York Federal Reserve Bank's 1992 survey of the US foreign exchange market (New York Federal Reserve Bank 1993).

The data show that spot transactions (settlements within two trading days) made up 47.3% of the 1992 net global foreign exchange volume. Forward transactions of seven days or less made up another 33.9%, forward transactions of greater than seven days but less than a year made up 18.2% of the volume, and forwards greater than a year made up 0.6% of the volume. We combined the spot and less-than-seven-day forwards and chose the mid-point of 3.5 days as the average turnover for that group. Similarly, 183 days, the mid-point of the forwards greater than seven days but less than one year, was chosen as the average turnover for that group. And eighteen months was chosen as the average turnover of the greater-than-one-year forwards. Weighted by relative shares of annual net foreign exchange volume, we get: $(365/3.5)$ x $0.812 + (365/183)$ x $0.182 + (2/3)$ x $0.006 = 84.7 + 0.4 + 0.004 = 85.1$ as the weighted average turnover per year. Dividing 85.1 into 365 gives 4.3 days as D.

But the average size of transactions reported by the New York Federal Reserve Bank survey differed among categories as follows:

Spots	$4 million
Outright forwards	$23 million
Swaps	$32 million
Options	$40 million

The weighted average size of the combined swaps and the less-than-seven-day forwards was thus $(0.473/0.812)$ x $4 + (0.339/0.812)$ x $32 = $15.7 million, compared with the weighted average size of the forwards greater than seven days but less than year, $32 million. Dividing the turnover of the first group by $32/15.7$ reduces its turnover from 84.7 to $84.7/2.03 = 41.7$. Dividing 41.7 into 365 gives an average D of 8.75 days for the first group. Dividing the overall turnover of 42.1 into 365 gives a weighted average D of 8.67 for all transactions. Clearly, short round trip trading determined the global average.

Notes

1. Felix (1995) contends that "putting sand in the well-greased gears of the international financial market mechanism" is now unavoidable if broader macroeconomic stabilization policies are to be workable and feasible. He also claims that the Tobin tax is the most "market friendly" means of fulfilling that prerequisite. See also Eichengreen, Tobin and Wyplosz (1995).

2. The 1992 and 1995 BIS surveys (BIS 1993, 1995a) are compilations of national survey data provided by the central banks of 26 countries, including all the financial-centre countries.

3. The increase of daily 1995 turnover over 1992 is reported to be 60% in the United Kingdom, 46% in the United States, 34% in Japan and 40% in Germany (Bank of England 1995, Federal Reserve Bank of New York 1995). In 1992, the United Kingdom accounted for 27%, the United States for 17%, Japan for 11% and Germany for 5% of global foreign exchange turnover (BIS 1993; table IV). Applying these 1992 shares to the above 1995 volume increase produces a 45% increase of 1995 global foreign exchange volume over 1992. But since the United Kingdom's share in 1995 is undoubtedly higher than in 1992, current-year shares would give a higher estimate for the 1995 global volume increase. We have thus picked 48% as a reasonable projection.

4. This figure excludes daily trades in cross-currency derivatives. The notional value of derivatives traded daily over-the-counter in 1995 was around $688 billion. See table A.9 in the Statistical Appendix, and BIS (1995b). The market value can be estimated at $55 billion.

5. Interdealer trading made up 75% of the London foreign exchange volume in 1995 (Bank of England 1995).

6. Dealer banks are "market-makers", which obliges them to transact continuously in foreign currency with all creditworthy counter-parties. Since supply usually deviates from demand for individual currencies, bank dealers chronically find themselves long or short in specific currencies and hence incur currency risk. Closing their positions to stay within the exposure volume and time limits imposed on the dealers by their bank thus involves speculating on short-term exchange rate movements (Grabbe 1986, chapter 5). "Rogue traders" that make headlines are dealers who have skirted the limits, guessed wrong and piled up large losses from their speculating.

7. This information comes from the chief trader of a major US bank, who must remain nameless.

8. The volume of MNC funds far outstripped that of hedge funds in the September 1992 currency runs (Group of Ten 1993).

9. In the BIS survey, official transactions are buried in the category "Other Financial Institutions", which also includes foreign exchange transactions by mutual and pension funds, leasing companies, securities companies and non-reporting banks. The entire category accounted for 13% of net global turnover in 1992. Allotting 10% of that turnover to official transactions is probably erring on the high side.

10. Walmsley is quoting from an internal Salomon Brothers document, which he cites.

11. This information comes from the same nameless source cited in foot-note 7.

12. It is also a journalistic finding (McGee 1995).

13. Hedge funds also speculate in other assets, such as commodities, when their price volatility is high enough to create attractive speculative opportunities.

14. Swaps, the most rapidly growing category of foreign exchange turnover, which in 1995 overtook spot transactions (see table A.3 in the Statistical Appendix), typically involve a spot and a forward leg. However, in the BIS net foreign exchange estimates, the spot leg of swaps is netted out. It is added to neither the spot nor the swap totals (BIS 1993, p.31).

15. A relevant analytic distinction should be made between liquidity traders and information-based traders, in which "liquidity traders' transactions are dri-ven by the needs for buying and selling goods and services and financial assets internationally". These "do not speculate, but buy or sell currencies due to the financing needs of their normal business activity. Informed traders profit by intermediating the demands and supplies of foreign exchange for the liquid-ity traders" (Bollerslev and Melvin 1994, p.357).

The interdealer chaining does not mean that dealers merely pass along the small Tobin tax multiplied by the number of links, since the links of each chain diminish progressively in size. In the New York branch of the Federal Reserve's 1992 survey of foreign exchange trading in US markets, the average size of pri-mary transactions ranged from $23 million for outright forwards, to $32 million for swaps, to $40 million for options, compared with an average size of $4 million for spots (Federal Reserve Bank of New York 1993). Since almost three-fourths of the spots were interdealer, a plausible inference is that each chain of inventory adjustments forms a diminishing series, implying that interdealer chaining would apply only a moderate multiplier of the tax rate to the transaction fees.

16. By including Singapore and Hong Kong among developing countries, we are following the UN's current classification.

17. Other studies using a broad definition of transaction costs include Demsetz (1968), Frenkel and Levich (1977), Overturf (1982) and Bahmani-Oskooee and Das (1985).

18. Walmsley reports that hedging a one-year foreign government bond, with the hedges rolled over every three months, would result in transaction costs ranging from 0.25% to 0.75%, not including risk premia (Walmsley 1991, pp.122-23).

19. Another researchable issue whose resolution would modestly improve the accuracy of revenue estimates is to ascertain the number of global foreign exchange trading days per year. Frankel uses 240 days, we use 250.

20. Frankel speculates that the sizable shrinking of interdealer trading from a 0.5% tax might lead the foreign exchange market to transform itself from being a decentralized "dealer-driven, over the counter and non-transparent market" to a centralized, customer-driven transparent market resembling the organized stock exchanges. He recognizes that such a denouement has its merits, but views the transitional disruption as too great to justify the effort.

We are sceptical that such a denouement would be likely, for three reasons. First, foreign exchange markets were decentralized in the early 1980s, when turnover was a small fraction of today's volume. Second, the Tobin tax will not tilt in favour of brokered transactions if such transactions are also subject to the tax, as would surely be the case. Third, organized stock exchanges require market-makers to help keep them liquid. The obvious candidates for such market-makers would be the dealing banks with their deep pockets. Since they benefit from the informational advantages the current non-transparent foreign exchange system provides them, it is difficult to see why they would want to, or how they could be impelled to, affiliate with an organized market.

21. However, Walker's revenue estimate of $8.4 billion from a 0.003% tax is much too high. He took the 1992 foreign exchange volume to be $280 trillion, whereas the total, net of double counting, was only $220 trillion. He also makes no deductions for exemptions, tax evasion, and collecting costs. The $4.3 billion estimate in table 9.5 tries to allow for these deductions.

References

Aiyagari, S. Rao and Mark Gertler. 1991. "Asset Returns with Transactions Costs and Uninsured Individual Risk." *Journal of Monetary Economics* 27(13): 331–2.

Argy, Victor. 1991. "The Design of Macroeconomic Policy in the World Economy." In Jacob Frenkel and Morris Goldstein, eds., *International Financial Policy: Essays in Honor of J.J. Polak*. Washington, D.C.: International Monetary Fund.

Bahmani-Oskooee, Mohsen and Satya Das. 1985. "Transactions Costs and the Interest Parity Theorem." *Journal of Political Economy* 93(4):793–9.

BIS (Bank for International Settlements). 1993. "Central Bank Survey of Foreign Exchange Market Activity in April 1992." Basle. March.

———. 1995a. "Central Bank Survey of Foreign Exchange Market Activity in April 1995: Preliminary Global Findings." *Press Communiqué.* Basle. October 24.

———. 1995b. "Central Bank Survey of Derivatives Market Activity: Release of Preliminary Global Totals." *Press Communiqué.* Basle. December 18.

Bank of England. 1995. "The Foreign Exchange Market in London." Press notice. September 19.

Blundell-Wignall, Adrian and Frank Browne. 1991. "Macroeconomic Consequences of Financial Liberalization: A Summary Report." Working Paper 98, Department of Economics and Statistics of the OECD. Paris.

Bollerslev, Tim and Michael Melvin. 1994. "Bid-Ask Spreads and Volatility in the Foreign Exchange Market: An Empirical Analysis." *Journal of International Economics* 36(3–4):355–72.

Calian, Sara. 1995. "A Latin Fund Manager's Bumpy Ride Reflects the Sector's Zigzag Fortunes." *Wall Street Journal.* July 7.

Calvo, Guillermo, Leonardo Leiderman and Carmen Reinhart. 1993. "Capital Inflows and Real Exchange Rate Appreciation in Latin America: the Role of External Factors." *IMF Staff Papers* Vol 40. Washington, D.C.

Camdessus, Michel. 1995. "The IMF in a Globalized World Economy." *IMF Survey.* June 19.

Clinton, Kevin. 1988. "Transactions Costs and Covered Interest Arbitrage: Theory and Evidence." *Journal of Political Economy* 96(2):358–70.

Demsetz, Harold. 1968. "The Cost of Transacting." *Quarterly Journal of Economics* 82(February):33–53.

Dixit, Avinash. 1992. "Investment and Hysteresis." *Journal of Economic Perspectives* 6(1):107–32.

Dolde, Walter. 1993. "The Use of Foreign Exchange and Interest Rate Risk Management in Large Firms." University of Connecticut School of Business Administration Working Paper 93-042. Storrs, Conn.

———.1995. "Hedging, Leverage, and Primitive Risk." *Journal of Financial Engineering* 4(2):187–216.

D'Orville, Hans and Dragoljub Najman. 1995. *Toward a New Multilateralism: Funding Global Priorities.* New York: United Nations.

Eichengreen, Barry, James Tobin and Charles Wyplosz. 1995. "Two Cases for Sand in the Gears of International Finance." *The Economic Journal* 105(January):162-72.

Federal Reserve Bank of New York. 1993. "Summary of Results of the U.S. Foreign Exchange Market Turnover Survey Conducted in April 1992 by the Federal Reserve Bank of New York."

―――. 1995. "April 1995 Central Bank Survey of Foreign Exchange Market Activity." Press Release. September 19.

Felix, David. 1994. "The Tobin Tax Proposal: Background Issues and Prospects." *Futures* 27(2):195-213.

―――. 1995. "Financial Globalization vs. Free Trade: The Case for the Tobin Tax." *UNCTAD* Discussion Paper No. 108. New York.

Ffrench-Davis, Ricardo, Manuel Agosin and Andras Uthoff. 1995. "Movimientos de Capitales, Estrategia Exportadora y Estabilidad Macroeconomica en Chile." In Ricardo Ffrench Davis and Stephany Griffith-Jones, eds., *Las Nuevas Corrientes Financieras Hacia América Latina*. Mexico/Chile: Fondo de Cultura Económica.

Frankel, Jeffrey. 1989. "International Financial Integration, Relations Among Exchange Rates and Interest Rates, and Monetary Indicators." In Charles Pigott, ed., *International Financial Integration and U.S. Monetary Policy*. New York: Federal Reserve Bank of New York.

―――. 1992. "Measuring International Capital Mobility: A Review." *American Economic Review* 82(2):187–202.

Frenkel, Jacob and Richard Levich. 1975. "Covered Interest Arbitrage: Unexploited Profits?" *Journal of Political Economy* 83(2):325–38.

―――. 1977. "Transactions Costs and Interest Arbitrage: Tranquil versus Turbulent Periods." *Journal of Political Economy* 85(6):1209–26.

Grabbe, J. Orlin. 1986. *International Financial Markets*. New York/Amsterdam: Elsevier.

Group of Ten. 1993. "International Capital Movements and Foreign Exchange Markets: A Report to the Ministers and Governors by the Group of Deputies." Rome. April.

Guth, Wilfried. 1993. "The Liberalization Trap: How the Free Flow of Capital is Undermining Multilateral Trade." *The International Economy* (May/June):56–9.

Hubbard, R. Glenn. 1993. "Security Transactions Taxes: Tax Design, Revenue and Policy Considerations." *Tax Notes*. November 22, pp.985-1000.

International Monetary Fund. 1995. "Benefits of Capital Flows Tied to Strong Risk Management." *IMF Survey*. June 19.

Kenen, Peter. 1996. "The Feasibility of Taxing Foreign Exchange Transactions." This volume.

Kiefer, Donald. 1990. "The Securities Transactions Tax: An Overview of the Issues." *Tax Notes*. August.

McGee, Suzanne. 1995. "Volatility is Making Hedges Grow." *Wall Street Journal*. June 12.

Overturf, Stephen F. 1982. "Risk, Transactions Charges, and the Market for Foreign Exchange Services." *Economic Inquiry* 20(April):291–302.

Reisen, Helmut. 1993. "Capital Flows and Their Effect on the Monetary Base." *CEPAL Review* (51):113–22.

Tobin, James. 1978. A Proposal for International Monetary Reform. *Eastern Economic Journal* 4(July–October):153–59.

Wachtel, Howard A. 1995. "Taming Global Money." *Challenge* (January-February):36–40.

Walmsley, Julian. 1988. *The New Financial Instruments: An Investor's Guide.* New York: John Wiley & Sons.

———. 1991. *Global Investing: Eurobonds and Alternatives.* New York: St. Martin's Press.

Walker, Martin. 1993. "Global Taxation—Paying for Peace." *World Policy Journal* 10(2):7–12.

10

Potential Uses of the Revenue from a Tobin Tax

Inge Kaul and John Langmore

Recent turbulence in the financial markets of Europe, the United States, Mexico and other developing countries has rekindled debate over the proposal for a levy on international currency transactions—the Tobin tax. The levy would be beneficial not only in creating an incentive for longer-term capital flows and reducing the risk of unwanted financial volatility. It would also generate a large amount of revenue. Not surprisingly, then, both financial market experts and public finance—notably development—specialists are contributing to the debate. The latter see the Tobin tax (and other, similar global policy measures) as an innovative way to mobilize resources and alleviate budgetary constraints of both nation-states and international organizations.

Although the revenue-raising aspect of the Tobin tax has recently received considerable attention, it has not yet been systematically analysed. Here, we explore different dimensions of this topic and suggest issues requiring further research and policy discussion.

The Tobin tax is often referred to as a global tax, the term "global" sometimes being equated with "supranational". But, as we discuss in the first section, individual governments would collect the tax and control

The views expressed here are those of the authors and do not necessarily reflect those of the organizations with which they are affiliated.

its proceeds. The tax is characterized as global because its implementation would be based on an international treaty. As we suggest in the second section, governments are likely to keep a substantial portion of the yields for domestic use—reducing budget deficits, meeting growing needs for public outlays or reducing national taxes. The major recipients of the tax proceeds would be the United Kingdom, the United States, Japan, Singapore and Hong Kong, followed by a number of industrial countries (primarily European). Industrial countries would receive about 86% of the total revenue, and developing countries about 14%.

But as we point out in the third section, greater resources are also needed at the international level. Growing interdependence among countries generates growing needs for joint action—to safeguard the environment, maintain peace and security and end global poverty. Because these "global public goods" affect all countries, it would be inadequate and inappropriate to finance them from existing funds designated for official development assistance (ODA), that is, finance them through an income transfer from richer to poorer countries. It would be more logical and effective to finance global public goods through levies and fees on international activities, such as international currency transactions.

In the fourth section, we propose possible formulae for sharing the Tobin tax proceeds between domestic and global uses. We also comment on institutional mechanisms and on the importance of ensuring compliance with "no taxation without representation".

We conclude by stressing that the justification for the Tobin tax is twofold. First, it lies in the tax's capacity to improve the functioning of financial markets by reducing short-term speculative flows and the consequent risk of excessive volatility. Second, it lies in the tax's revenue potential and the need for additional resources, nationally and internationally, that it could help meet. While revenue considerations should always be secondary to the use of the tax as a global incentive policy, it is nevertheless important to note that economic liberalization and the internationalization of markets, especially that of financial markets, have affected the taxation capacity of nation-states. Global taxes such as the Tobin tax, applied across all countries, could help restore some of the taxation power governments have lost in these globalization processes. But this topic is only one of a longer list of policy issues that the paper recommends for further study and debate.

Proceeds from the Tobin tax: who collects, who controls?

Studies on the technical feasibility of the Tobin tax have shown that a practical way of implementing the tax is to collect it on a market basis and at the dealing site.[1] In other words, the Tobin tax would be introduced through an international agreement, giving it its global character. But revenue collection would be a national responsibility. Tax yields would accrue on a country-by-country basis, raising the question of how much revenue each country would be likely to collect.

Although few countries today are without a foreign exchange market, several are dominant in international currency trading, particularly the United Kingdom, the United States and Japan.[2] Consequently, the amount of revenue accruing to each country would also vary greatly, although the incidence of the tax would be the same for all. Revenue estimates show that the United Kingdom—having a turnover volume greater than the combined total of the United States and Japan—would receive the largest share of the proceeds: more than one-fourth of total revenue. Assuming a 0.1% tax rate, this would amount to $44 billion (table 10.1). The United Kingdom is followed by the United States, with a share of 15.5%, or $23 billion, and Japan, with a share of 10.2%, or $15.1 billion.

Among developing countries, the main recipients would be Singapore and Hong Kong, receiving about 7% and 6% of the total revenue, respectively. Developing countries as a group would claim a share of about 14%, amounting to about $21 billion. With more developing countries entering the international financial market and increasing their participation therein (as seen, for example, in the emerging markets of Latin America and Asia), a more even distribution of yields could emerge over time.

The Tobin tax would thus not weaken national taxation power (as some commentators have argued), but strengthen it—in some cases substantially. And since the tax would be collected nationally, governments would control the uses of its proceeds. Three criteria in particular, could guide them in determining these uses: their domestic resource requirements, international financing needs and the balance between domestic and international resource demands required to ensure that the revenue is used efficiently and welfare is maximized.

Table 10.1 Annual revenue from a Tobin tax by collecting country
(1995 foreign exchange volume, billions of US dollars)

	Tax Rate			
	0.25%	0.10%[a]		0.05%
Industrial countries				
United Kingdom	89.0	43.7	(29.5)	26.6
United States	46.8	23.0	(15.5)	14.0
Japan	30.8	15.1	(10.2)	9.2
Switzerland	16.4	8.0	(5.4)	4.9
Germany	14.4	7.0	(4.7)	4.2
France	11.3	5.5	(3.7)	3.3
Australia	7.4	3.6	(2.4)	2.2
Denmark	5.7	2.9	(2.0)	1.7
Canada	5.5	2.6	(1.8)	1.6
Netherlands	4.7	2.2	(1.5)	1.3
Sweden	3.6	1.8	(1.2)	1.1
Other OECD	25.1	12.3	(8.3)	7.6
Group total	260.7	127.7	(86.2)	77.7
Developing countries				
Singapore	20.0	9.8	(6.6)	5.9
Hong Kong	17.1	8.4	(5.7)	5.1
South Africa	0.9	0.4	(0.3)	0.3
Bahrain	0.5	0.2	(0.1)	0.1
Other LDCs	2.9	1.7	(1.1)	1.0
Group total	41.4	20.5	(13.8)	12.4
Global total	302.1	148.2	(100.0)	90.1

a. Figures in parentheses are percentage of total.
Note: Based on the assumption that pre-tax transaction costs amount to 0.5%.
Source: The table is based on data presented in Felix and Sau (1996) and the following sources: BIS (1993); Federal Reserve Bank of New York (1995); and Bank of England (1995).

Potential national uses

Current statistics reveal that most governments are severely constrained by budgetary deficits or by an inadequate revenue base, which cannot be significantly increased for either economic or political (electoral) reasons. Therefore, most countries would probably welcome an additional source of revenue. But even countries not affected by these problems may want to use the proceeds nationally—to extend and improve human services and infrastructure or reduce existing national taxes.

Improving fiscal positions

It is becoming increasingly evident that while the 1980s was the decade of external debt crises in developing countries, the 1990s are emerging as a decade of fiscal crises in industrial countries. In 1994, the financial government balances in all OECD countries were negative, with budget deficits averaging about 3.9% of nominal GDP.[3] In 1995, Norway was the only country estimated to have had a positive balance, of 0.6%. Japan, which in 1991 still had a budget surplus of 3% of its GDP, is estimated to have had a deficit of about 4% in 1995.

Sluggish economic growth is one factor that has led to the present fiscal crisis in industrial countries—which would be the primary recipients of Tobin tax proceeds. It has shrunk governments' tax bases and at the same time increased demands for spending on unemployment benefits and related support services. In fact, these outlays have been one of the main forces driving recent spending increases in OECD countries (OECD 1995, pp.24–6). Upward pressure on government outlays has also come from demographic changes, notably the ageing of populations. In order to cope with rising spending pressures, governments have allowed debt to increase. A number of European countries have more than doubled their net public debt during the last 15 years, raising it on average to more than half of their total GDP in 1995. A similar trend has occurred in the United States. Increased public debt coincided with higher interest rates. Real long-term interest rates in the United States, for example, have, since the beginning of the 1980s, averaged around 5%. During the preceding three decades, they had averaged only 2% (Norman 1995). As a result, interest payments on general government net debt in OECD countries now amounts to about 3% of GDP, accounting for the major part of the average budget deficit of 3.9%. Although interest rates have recently been reduced marginally, debt-service costs are expected to remain high in the years to come.

General government outlays in OECD countries have increased from about 36% of GDP in 1979 to 41% in 1994. But this trend is soon to be halted, if not reversed, in many countries. Governments are facing stronger demands than ever before to maintain market credibility.[4] Because of the ease with which private capital funds can be withdrawn or inflows discouraged, they are hesitant to introduce new taxes or to increase existing ones that make either a direct or indirect impact on financial markets. In the eyes of financial markets, a credible government is one that keeps public expenditure and taxation levels low and avoids large fiscal deficits. Meeting these requirements entails difficult political choices concerning where expenditure cuts should fall. The debate in the United States about how to balance its budget is the most potent of many examples illustrating how acrimonious negotiations about deficit reduction can be.

An additional motive for reducing public expenditures in the European countries is the concern about meeting the Maastricht conditions of fiscal convergence: budget deficits below 3% of GDP and public debts below 60%. Additional revenue from the Tobin tax or other similar policies could enable governments to reduce their budget deficits at lower economic, social and political cost.

Improving services and infrastructure, and lowering national tax burdens

For at least two of the major revenue recipients shown in table 10.1, the attraction of Tobin tax revenue might be different from the one analysed above. These are Singapore and Hong Kong. For many years, the two countries have maintained a budget surplus (as have some other South-East Asian countries). As we will discuss later, Singapore in particular is likely to maintain a surplus in the coming years as well. Its interest in Tobin tax revenues (as that of other countries with balanced budgets) might thus lie in further improving the coverage and quality of government services and infrastructure or lowering the rates of existing national taxes.

In all recipient countries, tax cuts could benefit both companies and private households. Depending on the specific conditions prevalent in the country, they could, for example, help improve the competitiveness of national enterprises and enhance the overall investment climate. And reducing taxes on wage incomes could provide an incentive for greater labour utilization, thereby increasing employment.

Economic impact

Because of the modest tax rate, the Tobin tax proceeds would generally have a small impact on recipient economies. Yet it is plausible to guess that the impact would be positive—improved national savings, the opportunity to lower interest rates and possibly employment and income expansion.

Yet in order to determine more precisely the impact of tax proceeds, country-specific studies must be undertaken. The impact will vary not only depending on each country's economic and financial situation, but also depending on the amount of proceeds collected and the uses to which they are put. The impact on the UK economy would, for example, be proportionately greater than that on any other country. The addition to its revenue of about $44 billion (29 billion pounds) would be close to the UK's public sector borrowing requirement—about 30 billion pounds—estimated in the budget issued in November 1995 (*Financial Times,* November 29, 1995). But the stimulus from this resource would be partly offset by the slightly increased costs for dealers, traders and investors that the Tobin tax would entail.

With its daily turnover of foreign exchange transactions averaging $244 billion in April 1995, the United States would collect revenue of about $23 billion. This amount is about one-seventh of the estimated federal budget deficit ($160 billion) in the same year. Thus the fiscal benefit scarcely needs reiterating at a time when balancing the budget is a principal issue of national political debate in the United States.

The Japanese fiscal position has changed dramatically during the current recession, with the budget deficit expected to be about 3.9% of GDP in 1995. Revenue from the Tobin tax would be of the order of $15.1 billion, a little more than 10% of the budget deficit, and hence a useful additional source of revenue.

As stated, the fiscal position of Singapore and Hong Kong is far stronger than that of other major financial-centre countries. Both have habitually maintained budget surpluses, though that in Hong Kong has fallen and in 1994 was down to 0.8% of GDP.[5] Presumably, the policy approach of the Chinese government would determine the impact of a Tobin tax on Hong Kong, following the return of the colony in 1997. But would the strength of Singapore's fiscal position—with a surplus of 6.8% of GDP in 1994—preclude interest in the tax? Or would rising expectations for services and infrastructure or for tax cuts lead citizens to welcome an additional source of revenue, particularly when part of the revenue would be paid by non-residents? Given the large inflows of foreign currency and the high level of savings—Singapore has the highest savings ratio in the world, about 48% of GDP in 1994—authorities there might welcome a global foreign exchange levy more for its role in financial stabilization than for the revenue it would generate.

Each of the other major recipients of revenue—Australia, France, Germany and Switzerland—had significant fiscal deficits as a proportion of GDP in 1994 (4.4%, 6.0%, 2.6% and 3.0%, respectively). To them, the tax's revenue contribution would be very useful, but do no more than allow deficit reduction, or some modest fiscal stimulus.

As table 10.1 shows, only a few developing countries have readily available statistics on international currency transactions, although several (notably Brazil, Chile, Colombia, India, the Republic of Korea, Malaysia and Venezuela) are beginning to develop substantial foreign exchange markets. The same holds true for the economies in transition. Since the resource needs of these two groups of countries are considerable (with the exception of Malaysia), a Tobin tax would probably constitute a modest, but welcome, source of additional revenue. The only possible negative effect could be that the short-term financial flows, which constitute the bulk of private capital flows to emerging markets, would decrease without a corresponding increase in longer-term flows. The existence and extent of this impact must be rigourously assessed. However, country experiences—such as those of Chile and Colombia—suggest that controls can have positive effects on the maturity structure of capital flows without reducing the total volume of recorded flows (IMF 1995, pp.38–46).

Implementing a new tax at a time of tax reduction

The Tobin tax would thus not necessarily add to total revenue collections. Also, it would not necessarily affect the government's relative ranking in terms of tax burden—and hence its rating by fund managers and investors—because the tax would be applied to all countries, or at least to the countries with major foreign exchange markets. Hence, the anti-tax arguments currently being advanced with respect to national taxes do not hold in the case of the Tobin tax. But, as the following discussion will show, there are not only compelling and attractive domestic purposes for which governments might want to use the proceeds from new global funding sources. Some of the unmet international financing requirements are just as urgent and critical.

Potential international uses

Existing national budgetary constraints have undoubtedly affected the financing of international organizations and programmes in recent years. But they are not the only cause of today's widening international financing gap. Additional factors include the growth in international cooperation needs and the lack of a persuasive rationale for that cooperation.

Allocations of ODA have been relatively stable during the past decades, ranging from around 0.3% to 0.36% of the combined gross national products (GNPs) of donor countries (see OECD/DAC 1992 and 1994). But assistance needs have been rising, especially during the 1990s. New countries—the transition economies—have been added to the list of aid recipients; new security challenges have arisen in Somalia, Rwanda and Bosnia, drawing ODA funds out of longer-term development and into short-term relief and peacekeeping operations; the rebuilding of war-torn societies, such as Angola, Mozambique and Nicaragua, has required massive investment efforts; and the accumulating cross-border spillover effects of environmental degradation and poverty have, in many instances, assumed critical proportions, calling for urgent corrective action.

"Agenda 21", the action programme that emanated from the 1992 UN Conference on Environment and Development in Rio de Janeiro, estimates that tackling the environmental challenges facing the international community would cost about $125 billion per year in terms of external concessional financing alone (United Nations 1993). The World Summit for Social Development, held in Copenhagen in 1995, considered among other things, a poverty eradication programme, which would entail additional external costs of about $40 billion per year (UNDP and others 1994). This amount would also cover the external assistance needs for reproductive health identified at the 1994 International Conference on Population and Development in Cairo. In addition, there are other important needs, such as those for infrastructure. According to World Bank estimates, external concessional funding of about $20 billion per year may be required for this purpose (World Bank 1994). Hence in these three areas, external funding requirements could reach as much as $200 billion annually. Yet ODA allocations in 1994 stood at only $56 billion (OECD/DAC 1994). Adding the costs for international peacekeeping, the figure would grow to approximately $60 billion.

The need for a new rationale for cooperation

There is broad consensus among donor countries that it would be extremely difficult, if not impossible, for them to increase existing allocations in order to bridge the present gap between international funding needs and available resources. The fiscal crisis existing in these countries has something to do with this hesitation. But the more basic issue is that, today, aid is the only rationale for international development cooperation—and the aid rationale has lost much of its persuasiveness. Three factors have contributed to that loss:

- While there are many examples of effective aid projects, aid has always been too small a factor to significantly affect the macroeconomy. As a result, many problems that it set out to resolve persist, causing loss of confidence in the effectiveness of aid and "aid fatigue" among policy-makers and the general public.[6]

- While the present rationale for development assistance emphasizes moral and ethical considerations, many developing countries have become strong competitors of donor countries in international markets. This has created ambivalence towards helping developing countries.
- Many critical problems today require coordinated action of both industrial and developing countries, and thus go well beyond aid. They concern the restoration and maintenence of global economic, social, political and environmental balances—such as controlling air pollution, preserving biodiversity, maintaining international peace and security, avoiding excessive international migration pressures or preventing the spread of contagious diseases. Effective and efficient management of these processes would benefit all countries and all people. It could be described as the provision of global public goods, rather than as aid. But there is no well-defined cooperation rationale that would explain this concept to the general public and policy-makers in developing and industrial countries, demonstrating why ensuring the provision of these goods is in the mutual interest of all and constitutes a shared responsibility.

Funding for global public goods

Applying the theory of public goods to international problems yields important new insights in international cooperation issues.[7] As Paul Streeten noted, the fact that so many identified problems remain unaddressed arises from a combination of the free-rider problem and the prisoner's dilemma (Streeten 1989, p.1,352). A public good is one from whose supply all will benefit, irrespective of whether they have contributed to its costs. Although all governments and people probably have an interest in maintaining global climatic conditions, air pollution and deforestation nevertheless continue at unsustainable rates, because everyone waits for others to act, hoping for a free ride. While this behaviour is rational from the viewpoint of each actor, all end up being worse off because of their inaction—the prisoner's dilemma.

Avoiding getting caught collectively in a prisoner's dilemma should become a new rationale for international cooperation. Given the continuing problem of poverty and the growing inequity in international income distribution, there is still a need for aid, that is, income transfer from richer countries (including richer developing countries) to poorer countries. But in addition, there must be a clearly defined second strand of cooperation to ensure the provision of global public goods, in particular, international security and global sustainable development.

It would be inappropriate to finance this new strand of international cooperation with ODA resources, which constitute an income transfer from richer to poorer countries and are meant to help individual countries and regions to attain their developmental goals. It would also be inappropriate to continue relying on ad hoc financing mechanisms for the provision of global public goods, as is often the case today. For example, the United Nations is forced to launch special fundraising efforts for each peacekeeping mission it is called upon to undertake. This has frequently impeded the speediness and effectiveness of the organization's response to critical situations. It would be more logical to tap international economic activities in order to generate the funding required for the provision of global public goods. International currency transactions would be one possible source. Others include international air travel, the stationing of satellites in orbit, the crossing of high seas, seabed mining, air pollution or exports of arms. The justification would be that international economic activities depend on global stability for their proper functioning. Measures such as the Tobin tax or fees for the use of global commons would help achieve this stability in two ways: through their respective incentive and disincentive effects and through the revenue they would generate for complementary investments in maintaining global balances—security, environmental regeneration, market stability and equity.[8]

Sharing tax yields between national and international purposes

Given the urgent, unmet funding needs lingering both nationally and internationally, the question arises whether—and according to what formula—governments would divide the Tobin tax revenue between these two competing uses. Before addressing this issue it is important to answer another question: Could governments legitimately argue that all proceeds should be retained nationally?

Sharing or not sharing

It might be difficult to sustain such a proposition. After all, the Tobin tax could be effectively implemented only if based on a collective decision. Nation-states would simply be implementing agents. Moreover, the tax would fail if other states (including those that might derive only marginal benefits) did not collaborate. The United Kingdom alone could not apply a tax on capital inflows and outflows. If it did, foreign exchange trading would migrate, and the United Kingdom's role as a world financial centre would be at risk. It is the joint effort of and the cooperation among countries that would make policy measures such as the Tobin tax feasible; therefore, the revenue-collecting countries could not legitimately claim that the yields should be totally theirs.

On the contrary, the global cooperative effort involved in making the Tobin tax feasible fully justifies sharing the proceeds between national and international uses. Moreover, the portion of the proceeds destined for international purposes does not constitute a loss to the contributing countries—the proceeds are to be used for global public goods. In fact, the contributing countries could probably maximize their welfare through a well-balanced distribution of the tax yields between national and global purposes.

Formulas for sharing the proceeds

Proceeds could of course be shared according to different formulas. There are many alternatives, some simple, some complex. Each would probably have different effects. Important principles that should be embodied in the formula include:
- Ensuring that agreed global tasks are adequately and appropriately funded.
- Maximizing the overall cost-effectiveness with which the funds are used.
- Recognizing each country's relative importance as a foreign exchange market, and distributing the benefits of international action to reduce financial risk.
- Ensuring equitable burden-sharing among countries, taking into account such factors as income and population size.

It would be difficult to ensure recognition of these principles in a simple percentage formula. However, in order to start the dialogue on this point, one could, for example, suggest the following:

- Developing countries with low incomes and lower-middle and middle-level incomes would retain 100% of the proceeds.
- Developing countries in the higher-middle-income bracket could retain 90% of the proceeds.
- High-income countries could retain 80% of the proceeds.

Assuming a 0.1% Tobin tax, this allocation formula would generate about $27 billion for international purposes. This amount would sharply increase the resources currently available to multilateral organizations. In 1994, the multilateral part of ODA from DAC countries represented 30% of the total assistance funds, or about $17 billion. However, a large portion of this amount was used for traditional aid purposes. The new, additional funds would thus be the money available primarily for global purposes.

A further refinement of the simple formula suggested above could be to cap the contribution to be made by countries with major financial markets. After all, serving as a financial centre often entails costs for the country concerned. For example, the United Kingdom government has had to be unusually attentive to avoiding sudden movements in the exchange rate and to keeping the exchange rate up. This has principally been ensured by keeping interest rates higher than they might have had to be otherwise, thereby depressing economic activity and reducing potential employment and income. One benefit of the Tobin tax proceeds for the United Kingdom would thus be the opportunity to offset the effects of such monetary restraint through fiscal stimulus. Accordingly, one could suggest that no country's international portion of the Tobin tax proceeds should exceed a certain US dollar amount, say, $2 billion. This would lower the international portion of the revenue by about $3 billion—from approximately $27 billion to $24 billion.

Institutional aspects

As discussed elsewhere (see, for example, Kenen 1996), the introduction of a Tobin tax would require an international treaty among all countries or at least among the countries hosting the major foreign exchange markets. This treaty could also provide the framework for negotiating the apportionment of proceeds. The agreed upon formula could be renegotiated periodically to ensure proper alignment among revenue capacity, funding needs and resource allocations.

In order to minimize the loss of national sovereignty, governments could allocate the international portion of the proceeds in much the same way as they today allocate ODA resources: for the amount they are committed to transfer to the international level, they could set their own expenditure priorities, bearing in mind established global objectives. An alternative would be to create a new international cooperation fund, which could function as a kind of international Treasury to which all multilateral organizations, including the Bretton Woods institutions, would submit their budget proposals for consideration and approval. But if we were to agree on the latter option, it would be important to organize the fund's intergovernmental supervisory body around the principle of "no taxation without representation" and provide avenues for consultation with representatives from the private sector, especially financial services, and civil society.

A new cooperation fund would be a useful means for harmonizing global policy priorities with global budgetary priorities (a task in which the present system of international cooperation is seriously deficient). The disadvantage would be that yet another entity would be added to the already quite elaborate framework of international organizations. But this may be unavoidable—and a small price to pay—in order to usher the international community into a new era of cooperation.

Conclusion

It may be appropriate to end this paper with a cautionary remark. The potential for resource mobilization gives the Tobin tax added importance and attractiveness. But the revenue aspect should not outweigh the primary purpose of the tax—to pose an incentive for longer-term capital flows and promote greater financial stability. While it is extremely important that there is an adequate provision of global public goods, their financing does not depend on the Tobin tax alone. As the foregoing discussion stresses, there are other global incentive policies that also need to be explored. In fact, for each of them, careful studies should be undertaken to assess their economic desirability as an incentive policy, technical feasibility, revenue potential and institutional implications. Only those qualifying in terms of economic desirability and technical feasibility should be seriously considered for eventual adoption.

In fact, many of the points raised in this paper will require more detailed study. Chief among them are questions concerning the net impact of the Tobin tax—in terms of its incentive-policy role and its revenue-raising role—on selected countries; the costs—in terms of efficiency and global equity—of underproviding global public goods; the legal implications of the Tobin tax; the effects of the internationalization of markets, especially financial markets, on the capacity of national governments to tax; the institutional framework for managing the global use of the proceeds from the Tobin tax and other similar measures; and the lessons to be drawn from national and regional (such as the European Union's) experiences in revenue collection and reallocating proceeds among different levels of government.

This present paper is therefore only a contribution to the beginning of the policy dialogue on the uses of the Tobin tax proceeds. Reliable findings and firm conclusions are not yet available. But to have identified some of the issues on which further work and debate will be required has undoubtedly brought us one step forward.

Notes

1. See, in this connection, Garber (1996) and Kenen (1996).

2. For statistics on foreign exchange turnovers by country, see table A.4 in the Statistical Appendix.

3. Data on the fiscal position of OECD countries are taken from OECD (1995), unless indicated otherwise.

4. For a more detailed discussion on this point, see Eatwell (1996) and Langmore (1995).

5. The data for Hong Kong and Singapore are taken from Asian Development Bank (1995).

6. For a more detailed discussion on these points see, for example, UNDP (1994, pp. 61–89); Kaul (1993); Speth (1995); Griffin and McKinley (1996); Riddell (1996).

7. Pioneering work in this area has been undertaken by Mendez (1992).

8. A more detailed discussion on the future of international cooperation and the importance of global incentive policies can be found in Kaul (1995).

References

Asian Development Bank. 1995. *Asian Development Outlook 1995 and 1996*. New York: Oxford University Press.

Bank of England. 1995. "The Foreign Exchange Market in London." Press Notice. September 19. London.

BIS (Bank for International Settlements). 1993. "Central Bank Survey of Foreign Exchange Market Activity in April 1992." Basle. March.

Eatwell, John. 1996. "Unemployment on a World Scale." In John Eatwell, ed., *Global Unemployment: Loss of Jobs in the 1990s*. New York: M.E. Sharpe.

Federal Reserve Bank of New York. 1995. "Central Bank Survey of Foreign Exchange Market Activity." Press Release. September 19.

Felix, David and Ranjit Sau. 1996. "The Revenue Potential and Phasing-in of the Tobin Tax." This volume.

Garber, Peter. 1996. "Issues of Enforcement and Evasion in a Levy on Foreign Exchange Transactions." This volume.

Griffin, Keith and Terry McKinley. 1996. "New Approach to Development Cooperation." ODS Discussion Paper 7. New York.

International Monetary Fund. 1995. *Capital Account Convertibility; Review of Experience and Implications for IMF Policies*. Washington, D.C.

Kaul, Inge. 1993. "A New Approach to Aid." *Development and Cooperation* 3(May–June):17–21.

————. 1995. "Effective Financing of Multilateral Development Cooperation: Proposals for a New Policy Framework." UNDP/Office of Development Studies. New York. Processed.

Kenen, Peter. 1996. "The Feasibility of Taxing Foreign Exchange Transactions." This volume.

Langmore, John. 1995. "Restructuring Economic and Financial Power. The Potential Role of a Foreign Exchange Transaction Levy." *Futures* 27(2):189–94.

Mendez, Ruben. 1992. *International Public Finance*. New York: Oxford University Press.

Norman, Peter. 1995. "What Makes Debt So Special?" *Financial Times*. January 16. p.18.

OECD (Organisation for Economic Co-operation and Development). 1995. *OECD Economic Outlook 58*. Paris.

OECD/DAC (Development Assistance Committee). 1993. *Development Co-operation*. Paris.

————. 1994. *Development Co-operation*. Paris.

Riddell, Roger. 1996. "Aid in the Twenty-First Century." ODS Discussion Paper 6. New York.

Speth, Gustave. 1995. "Development Cooperation in Peril: Defining Decisions for the United States." Address to the Council on Foreign Relations. March 22. New York.

Streeten, Paul. 1989. "Global Institutions for an Interdependent World." *World Development* 17(9):1,349–59.

United Nations. 1993. *Earth Summit Agenda 21; The United Nations Programme of Action from Rio.* New York.

UNDP (United Nations Development Programme). 1994. *Human Development Report 1994.* New York: Oxford University Press.

UNDP, UNESCO, UNFPA, UNICEF and WHO. 1994. *The 20/20 Initiative.* New York.

World Bank. 1994. *World Development Report 1994.* Oxford University Press: New York.

———. 1995. *World Development Report 1995.* Oxford University Press: New York.

Conclusion

The Tobin Tax:
What Have We Learned?

Barry Eichengreen

It is unrealistic to expect that the contributors to a first scholarly study of a global tax on foreign exchange transactions would agree on all issues. The purpose of this project is better thought of as an opportunity to pose the relevant questions and identify those on which economists have reached a broad consensus. In this chapter I attempt to do just that: I list the central issues identified in the course of the project and characterize the extent of consensus on each. I then describe the remaining agenda for research.

Arguments for a Tobin tax

Contributors offer three justifications for a Tobin tax. The reason offered by the development community, articulated by Inge Kaul and John Langmore, is to raise revenue for multilateral development assistance. With the end of the cold war and mounting problems of fiscal imbalance in the high-income world, industrial countries have grown increasingly reluctant to provide official development assistance. At the same time the proliferation of "failed states" has created a pressing need for foreign aid. Kaul and Langmore suggest that the pro-

ceeds from a Tobin tax could be shared between national governments and multilateral institutions in a way that rendered the tax
attractive to all.

Specialists in international finance suggest that a Tobin tax would
reduce exchange rate volatility. This justification is understandably controversial. To those who believe in the efficiency of markets and the
rationality of expectations, a transactions tax will only hinder market
efficiency and could even increase exchange rate volatility by driving
out stabilizing speculators. If it is necessary to take steps to reduce
exchange rate volatility, the argument goes, then the problem should
be attacked at its source—by reducing the volatility of the monetary and
fiscal policies in response to which speculative sales and purchases of
foreign exchange are made.

In the view of others, the rationality of expectations and the efficiency of markets is a more dubious proposition.[1] In this volume, Jeffrey
Frankel uses survey data to show that expectations of exchange rate
movements over short horizons tend to be extrapolative, while investors
expect exchange rates to revert to previous levels over long periods of
time. Because a Tobin tax would fall disproportionately on transactions
motivated by movements over short horizons, it would tend to drive participants with extrapolative expectations from the market, leaving the
price of foreign exchange to be governed mainly by traders with stabilizing expectations. Frankel presents a simple model of short-term speculators and long-term investors in which a Tobin tax, operating through
this channel, reduces exchange rate volatility.

It is not surprising that the generality of this result is a subject of
debate. The efficiency of markets and expectations are disputed issues
in macroeconomics. The evidence on connections between financial
transactions taxes and market volatility is weak.[2] Scholars make very different assumptions about market efficiency depending on their pre-
disposition and training. But even if Frankel's example remains only
that, an example, it nonetheless lends rigour to the debate by identifying conditions under which a Tobin tax can reduce exchange rate
volatility.

A third justification for a Tobin tax is to enhance the independence
of action taken by monetary and fiscal policy-makers, and the defensibility of the exchange rate system. James Tobin's (1978) original
rationale for a foreign exchange transactions tax was to enhance policy autonomy in a world of high capital mobility. Tobin argued that
currency fluctuations often have very significant economic and political costs, contrary to the views of the early proponents of floating

rates. Although it is theoretically possible for the government of a financially open country to pursue autonomous monetary and fiscal policies, assuming it is prepared to accept exchange rate fluctuations, in practice, such fluctuations disrupt the allocation of resources and disproportionately burden producers and consumers of traded goods. Governments are thus reluctant to exercise their macroeconomic independence. A Tobin tax, by breaking the interest-parity condition (the condition that domestic interest rates may differ from foreign interest rates only to the extent that the exchange rate is expected to change), will allow authorities to pursue different policies than those prevailing abroad without exposing them to large exchange rate movements.

The papers collected here raise some questions about the practical relevance of this justification. Their authors suggest that the rate at which foreign currency transactions are taxed could not exceed 25 basis points, for otherwise the tax would create an irresistible incentive for evasion. If this argument holds, macroeconomic policy autonomy will be enhanced only modestly. Over the horizon of a year, for example, a 25 basis point Tobin tax would allow authorities that are concerned with maintaining nominal exchange rate stability to pursue only policies that would have otherwise led to a 0.5% change in the exchange rate. This is not a very impressive increase in macroeconomic policy autonomy.[3]

But even a low tax rate can discourage transactions that involve moving in and out of currencies for short periods. Having to pay a 25 basis point tax twice a week (once when selling the domestic currency and again when buying it back) can dissuade speculators from betting on small currency fluctuations (or on large exchange rate changes that have a low probability of occurring in the coming week). This is the rationale for using the Tobin tax to strengthen the defensibility of the exchange rate regime. Chapter 3 develops this point. But the argument should not be overdrawn: in a world of highly liquid foreign exchange markets, a modest transactions tax will not save the authorities from having to realign when monetary and fiscal policies are out of equilibrium and the exchange rate is overvalued. But in order to prevent speculative pressure from quickly exhausting their reserves and provoking the collapse of the exchange rate system itself, governments need breathing space to meet and negotiate orderly realignments. A Tobin tax can provide just that. Charles Wyplosz and I suggest that the efficacy of such policies is evident from the 1992 crisis in the European Monetary System (EMS). Spain and Portugal, with controls in place, succeeded in negotiating realignments and remaining in the EMS, while Italy and the United Kingdom, with no such shelter, were driven from the system.

Reservations about a Tobin tax

Scholars have also voiced three reservations about implementing a Tobin tax. The first is political feasibility. In an era of rampant anti-tax sentiment, it is by no means clear that governments and constituencies will agree to implement the tax. Financial interests have considerable political influence and will lobby in opposition. Also, the international distribution of tax liabilities will not match the willingness and capacity of national governments to contribute development assistance. For example, although London is the world's largest foreign exchange market, the United Kingdom cannot be expected to be the largest donor of development aid. As we will see, individual countries may have an incentive to resist imposing the tax in order to capture the bulk of the world's foreign exchange business, and there is no obvious enforcement mechanism by which governments tempted to free ride can be compelled to cooperate. The imposition of the tax could be made mandatory through an amendment to the International Monetary Fund (IMF) Articles of Agreement, but such amendments are difficult to pass (requiring the support of 85% of IMF members).

This resistance points to a second obstacle to effective implementation: market migration. In its most extreme form, the argument holds that the geographical coverage of the tax must be complete. If the Cayman Islands, to cite everyone's favourite example, fails to impose it, then the world's foreign exchange business will move to the Cayman Islands, and the volatility of exchange rates, the autonomy of macro-economic policies, and the development-assistance crisis will not be discernably affected.

Although market migration is an indisputable problem, Peter Kenen's careful analysis suggests that the argument, in its extreme form, is overdrawn. If foreign exchange transactions are taxed at the trading site rather than at the booking site or at the settlement site, then the high fixed costs of establishing a trading operation will generate a disincentive for migration.[5] The costs include those of setting up a dealing room, inducing traders with the relevant expertise to relocate there, and shifting the "good funds" needed to collateralize the transactions to what might not be an entirely secure location.

Although it is not impossible for banks and governments to defray the costs of accumulating the human, physical, and financial capital needed to establish a new trading site—as illustrated by Singapore's success—Kenen suggests that it may be possible to limit the incentive to establish a venue in which the tax can be avoided by levying it at twice the standard rate on transactions with tax havens. If those on both sides of a transaction conduct business in the tax haven, they will still escape the tax. But one partner will not have an incentive to shift his or her business to the haven unless the other does so at the same time. Indeed, a substantial number of banks and other traders will have to migrate simultaneously to provide the liquidity and scale economies enjoyed by the principal centres for foreign exchange trading.

Thus, Kenen's analysis suggests that to prevent significant tax avoidance through market migration, it may suffice to secure the cooperation of, say, the eight countries that are home to the eight largest foreign exchange markets.[6] Still, this is no easy feat when the countries concerned are as heterogeneous as Hong Kong (soon to be China, of course), Singapore, Switzerland, the United Kingdom and the United States.

A third and even more serious obstacle to implementation and enforcement is asset substitution. A tax limited to spot transactions would encourage the substitution of short-dated forwards and futures; Kenen therefore recommends applying the tax to spots, forwards and futures alike.[7] Peter Garber suggests that, in its most extreme form, the tendency to substitute tax-exempt for taxable instruments could eliminate all effects of the tax. If the exchange of dollars for yen is taxed, then there is an incentive to exchange a US Treasury bill maturing in three days for a Japanese Treasury bill maturing in three days, assuming that these instruments are tax-free. If the authorities tax purchases and sales of US and Japanese Treasury bills maturing in three days, currency speculators will turn to exchanging futures contracts for delivery of wheat in three days denominated in dollars for futures contracts for delivery of wheat in three days denominated in yen. And if the authorities tax purchases and sales of commodity futures contracts, currency speculators may begin exchanging a derivative whose value in dollars is a function of the value of the Standard and Poor's index for a derivative whose value in yen is a function of the Standard and Poor's index. To be effective, the foreign exchange transactions tax will have to be generalized to other financial instruments.

The counter-argument is not that asset substitution is impossible, but that its scope will be limited. A transaction that promises delivery of foreign exchange in three days is not a perfect substitute for one that delivers foreign exchange today. And in any case, there is not a perfectly elastic supply of US and Japanese Treasury bills with the relevant characteristics.[8] The difficulty of synchronizing the component transactions exposes the parties concerned to interest rate risk. This suggests that there will be some avoidance of a Tobin tax through asset substitution—as there is avoidance of virtually all taxes—but that avoidance will be less than complete. The tax will bite precisely in periods of intense speculative pressure, when the excess demand for particular currencies is greatest relative to the supply of assets that are potential substitutes.

Still, there is a danger that financial engineers will create new derivative instruments that are closer and closer substitutes for a simple foreign exchange transaction, encouraging growing amounts of asset substitution over time. The question, then, is how strong is their incentive to do so. On the one hand, foreign exchange is a multi-trillion dollar business, creating a lucrative market for the talents of financial "rocket scientists". On the other hand, a tax of 5 basis points, as suggested by Kenen, would provide market participants with little incentive to engage in complicated financial shenanigans on any particular transaction. While some avoidance will undoubtedly occur, it is not clear that asset substitution will become so extensive that it neutralizes the economic effects of the tax.

The importance of market structure

Few discussions of the Tobin tax have paid much attention to the structure of the foreign exchange market. Yet, as Frankel's paper emphasizes, its structure and evolution could have major implications for the amount of revenue earned from a foreign exchange transactions tax. The famous "trillion dollars a day" of foreign currency transactions, which is commonly cited as the base for the tax, are conducted in a decentralized, dealer-driven, over-the-counter market. A third of these transactions are settled by brokers whose business is matching buy and sell orders from dealers (most of whom are banks), a second third are settled by automated dealer systems (including electronic order matching and automated direct trading) and the final third are executed by speaker phone. A single retail transaction in which an individual or corporation places an order for foreign exchange with a dealer close at hand typically gives rise to a chain of subsequent interdealer transactions until a dealer willing to hold the asset associated with the other side of that transaction is found. Estimates of the ratio of transactions to customer orders are as high as ten to one.

Frankel raises the possibility that a Tobin tax might cause this decentralized dealer-based system to give way to a centralized structure. Were foreign exchange to be traded in a centralized market, in which prices and quantities are public information, brokers themselves take no positions and customers are matched electronically, the ratio of transactions to customer orders might fall dramatically. Conventional calculations of the yield of a Tobin tax that are based on the assumption of a constant elasticity of transactions with respect to the tax, as in the chapter by David Felix and Ranjit Sau, may therefore be inappropriate: there will be a discontinuity in the demand curve at the point where the market transforms itself in response to the tax.

At what point might such a reorganization take place? There are significant fixed costs involved in establishing a centralized venue for trading, and such a venue would become sufficiently liquid to attract customers only if a large number of market participants brought their business there simultaneously. These considerations lend inertia to currently prevailing arrangements. Working in the other direction are ongoing improvements in computing and communications technologies—which facilitate centralized trading. This trend is already evident in the growth of electronic order matching. Frankel suggests that there would be considerable incentive to reorganize and centralize the market in the face of a 0.5% or 1% Tobin tax. Whether there would also be significant pressure to move in this direction in response to a 5 basis point tax is less certain.

Public finance issues

The effects of a foreign exchange transactions tax are not just concerns of macroeconomics and international finance. They are also concerns of public economics. As such, insights from the literature on public finance can be brought to bear. A foreign exchange transactions tax can be thought of as one of a variety of global taxes designed to internalize non-pecuniary externalities that would otherwise spill across borders. Other possibilities include Pigouvian taxes on airlines and shipping, which would reduce congestion at airports and seaports and limit the pollution caused by the consumption of jet and tanker fuel; internationally tradable pollution permits to internalize the externalities associated with automobile travel and energy use in industry; and an international carbon tax targeted at fossil fuel consumption.

This approach raises the not-all-together-transparent question of the nature of the externality associated with foreign exchange transactions. One formulation holds that excess volatility in foreign exchange markets has negative externalities for the volume of international trade and investment, although the evidence that trade and investment are negatively affected is far from overwhelming (see Frankel, Wei and Stein 1994 on trade and Goldberg 1993 on investment). Another holds that foreign exchange transactions have negative externalities for the effectiveness of macroeconomic policy and the durability of the exchange rate regime, although these points are not usually articulated in terms of the theory of externalities.

Theories of optimal taxation imply that, absent externalities, deadweight loss is minimized when taxes are imposed on goods and services whose supply and demand are price inelastic. It is not clear that the market for foreign exchange satisfies these conditions. Certainly, the debate over market migration suggests that effective supplies and demands are more price elastic at the national level than globally; just as it would be more efficient to raise a given amount of revenue through a capital income tax levied globally rather than nationally, it would be more efficient to raise a given amount of revenue through a foreign exchange transactions tax imposed globally instead of nationally. Even globally, however, the foreign exchange market, like most markets, is surely characterized by a downward-sloping demand curve. Leaving aside externality-based arguments, whether a Tobin tax is an economically efficient means of raising revenue depends on the magnitude of the price elasticity of demand. In other words, the concerns about asset substitution raised in Garber's paper and about market organization raised in Frankel's can be formulated in terms of optimal taxation theory.

These theories also provide a way of thinking about the economic incidence of the tax (see, for example, Shome and Stotsky 1995). They suggest that those classes of traders in foreign exchange markets whose price elasticities of demand are lowest will bear the heaviest tax burden in an economic sense. If the financial services industry is competitive, for example, then the high elasticity of supply will lead to exit in response to the tax to the point where initial profit margins are restored. In the long run, the burden of the tax will be shifted to the ultimate users of financial services.

Lessons from country experience

Several countries have applied taxes and restrictions on capital inflows and outflows that serve some of the functions of a Tobin tax. Ricardo Ffrench-Davis and Manuel Agosin review Latin American experience, and Yung Chul Park reviews the experience of the Republic of Korea. The papers by Eichengreen and Wyplosz and by Frankel provide compendia of such measures.

The efficacy of taxes and controls on capital inflows and outflows has not been systematically examined from the vantage point of revenue-raising capacity. (Ffrench-Davis and Agosin do provide some information on the relatively limited revenue earned from the Chilean tax. Garber notes that the Japanese transfer tax on sales made by securities companies raised substantial amounts of revenue during the bubble economy period of the 1980s, but more limited amounts subsequently.) From the standpoint of currency instability, autonomy of macroeconomic policy and defensibility of the exchange rate regime, however, there is considerable evidence that such controls have had discernible effects. The Korean government has used such measures to limit the movement of the won in order to insulate Korean exporters from destabilizing exchange rate swings and to prevent the build-up of an excessively heavy external debt burden. Chilean policy-makers have used limits on capital inflows to insulate the economy from destabilizing shifts in sentiment about emerging markets. Ffrench-Davis and Agosin show that these measures influenced the composition of capital inflows into different Latin American countries. Wyplosz and Eichengreen generalize these points by showing that countries with such restrictions in place were able to ride out the "tequila shock" of early 1995 more smoothly than countries that left access to international capital markets unregulated.[9]

The question is how informative this experience is to the debate over the Tobin tax. Where domestic financial markets have been tightly regulated and access to international finance has been suppressed by capital controls, little can be inferred about the effects and effectiveness of, say, a 5 basis point tax on a lightly regulated market.

From experience with a financial market as tightly regulated as the Republic of Korea's, for example, it is hard to say much about the scope for evading a modest Tobin tax. And while requiring foreign investors in the Brazilian stock market to keep their money there for a minimum period may provide the same insulation against capital inflows (and therefore subsequent outflows) as a foreign exchange transactions tax, the economic effects of the two measures differ, again complicating attempts to draw inferences. Frankel compares Chile's deposit requirement on inflows with the Tobin tax and shows that the two measures differ depending on whether the tax or tax equivalent is applied to only capital inflows or to both inflows and outflows, whether the tax is paid by only foreign investors or by all of those purchasing and selling foreign exchange, whether the income associated with the tax accrues first to the central bank or to the fiscal authorities, whether the implicit tax rises with the interest rate in times of speculative pressure (which is true of deposit requirements but not the Tobin tax) and automatically declines with the time required for the investment project to mature (which is the case with the Tobin tax but not with the Chilean deposit requirements)[10] and whether the tax can be effective when imposed by one country (as with deposit requirements) or whether its coverage must be international (as with the Tobin tax). In other words, these measures differ in a sufficient number of dimensions that all but suggestive comparisons are problematic.

The agenda for research

The papers assembled here advance the state of knowledge. They also suggest an agenda for research.

Political economy issues

Whether dominant coalitions are likely to form in support of or against the imposition of a Tobin tax is a question for political scientists. This work should draw on the above-mentioned analysis of tax incidence: those on whom the tax is initially levied are not necessarily those on whom it falls in an economic sense. And it is the economic incidence of the tax that will presumably govern the lobbying of different economic interest groups.

A further justification for a detailed analysis is that the traditional distinction between Wall Street, which is likely to oppose the tax, and Main Street, which is more likely to support it, may be breaking down. As multinational production and sourcing become increasingly prevalent, leading a growing number of firms to hedge their foreign exposure, traditional distinctions between sectors with and without a stake in foreign exchange transactions begin to lose their force. And as increasing numbers of working-class households invest in foreign markets through mutual and pension funds, they too gain a stake in foreign exchange transactions. Thus, traditional assumptions about what sectors or factors of production should favour and oppose a tax on foreign exchange transactions may no longer apply.

Then there is the likelihood that coalitions will form transnationally. Financial interests in one country are almost certain to ally with financial interests in another, for example. Standard analyses of the political economy of trade and tax policy, which focus on coalition formation within countries, will have only limited relevance to the case of the Tobin tax.[10]

The impact on market volatility

Frankel has given an example of how the imposition of a Tobin tax can reduce the volatility of exchange rates by driving destabilizing speculators out of the market. But the generality of his result remains uncertain. In particular, this finding may be vulnerable to the Lucas critique: that the expectations of short- and long-term currency traders will not be invariant to the tax. Exchange rate movements depend on the real and monetary disturbances to which the underlying macroeconomic environment is subjected as well as on the expectations of currency traders about the market's response to those disturbances. Economic policy-makers operating behind the shelter of a newly imposed Tobin tax will pursue different policies than their predecessors, which in turn will alter the expectations of participants in foreign exchange markets. It would be desirable to analyse the implications in a general equilibrium setting.

Financial engineering issues

Additional research is needed on the extent to which asset substitution and the development of new financial instruments provide opportunities for tax avoidance. While it is certain that there will be some avoidance through asset substitution, it is much less clear that avoidance will be extensive. The prevalence of asset substitution will depend on the propensity of market participants to develop and use financial instruments that are close substitutes for spot foreign exchange transactions. Will banks and brokers begin to pre-package about-to-mature Treasury bills or commodity futures contracts denominated in different currencies that can be readily substituted for foreign currency? If so, will the market in such instruments gain the liquidity needed to constitute a viable alternative to the foreign exchange market? Will banks and brokers develop derivative instruments, combinations of which are equivalent to a spot foreign exchange transaction? If so, how liquid will the market in those instruments become?

Market migration

The likely extent of market migration remains in dispute. Here, there is a reservoir of evidence from experience with asset turnover taxes, reviewed by, among others, Campbell and Froot (1994). For several years prior to 1991, for example, Sweden levied a turnover tax, at rates between 0.15% and 1%, on the transfer of shares, bonds and other securities. This tax seems to have led to the large-scale migration of transactions to off-shore markets such as London and New York. In 1988, for example, only 27% of transactions in Ericsson, Sweden's most actively traded company, were conducted in Stockholm (Campbell and Froot 1994:282). The figure in 1989 was 23%. In response, tax rates were reduced, and ultimately, the Swedish turnover tax was abolished (on December 1, 1991). The share of Ericsson trades conducted in Stockholm recovered to 41% in 1992. Campbell and Froot similarly conclude that taxes on futures transactions in Tokyo led to the migration of trade to Osaka and Singapore and that taxes on stock transactions in Finland caused a substantial fraction of trade in the shares of local companies to move to London.

In contrast, other countries, such as Switzerland and the Republic of Korea, have levied duties of 0.15 to 0.5% on transfers of stocks, bonds, Treasury bills, bank notes and other securities without losing large amounts of business to foreign markets. The question is whether a relatively low turnover tax, on the order of 0.15%, can be imposed without creating irresistible pressure for market migration, or whether the absence of significant market migration in these cases is attributable to other factors, like the compensating advantages of security and anonymity in Switzerland and the prevalence of capital controls in the Republic of Korea.

Market structure and revenue-raising capacity

For those concerned with development assistance, it will be worth sinking the costs and hazarding the uncertainties of imposing a Tobin tax only if the tax will raise significant amounts of revenue. In addition to the problems of market migration and asset substitution described above, the amount of revenue generated will depend on how the structure of the foreign exchange market is affected by the imposition of the tax and, in particular, on the point at which the market will transform itself into a centralized, over-the-counter organization. Surveys and interviews of foreign exchange traders could shed valuable light on these issues.

Conclusion

At this stage, the feasibility and effects of a foreign exchange transactions tax remain open questions. But the papers assembled here go a long way towards identifying the research questions that remain to be answered. These include questions about the operation of foreign exchange markets: the scope for asset substitution, the feasibility of market migration and the possibility that foreign exchange transactions might be reorganized on an over-the-counter basis. They include questions about the political economy of taxation: about the economic as opposed to statutory incidence of the Tobin tax and about the political coalitions that are likely to form in favour and in opposition. Answers are needed if domestic and international policy-makers are to make informed decisions about whether a Tobin tax is even a partial solution to the crisis in development finance, to the problem of exchange rate volatility and to the difficulty of formulating a coherent national economic strategy in an environment of high capital mobility.

Notes

1. Rose (1994) shows that there does not appear to be a link between the volatility of the exchange rate and the volatility of the associated monetary and fiscal policies.

2. Roll (1989) provides evidence on stock market volatility for 32 countries from 1978 to 1989, finding little systematic connection with margin require-

ments and financial transactions taxes.

3. Frankel reaches similar conclusions. The 0.5% change in the exchange rate is equal to the 50 basis point tax that would be paid if it was levied on both halves of a round trip between domestic and foreign currency.

4. This can be thought of as an extension of the findings of Svensson (1994), who shows that even a narrow target zone that allows for limited exchange rate variability can enhance significantly domestic monetary autonomy. Jeanne's Tobin tax has the effect of widening the effective band, reinforcing this effect.

5. Taxation at the settlement site is not viable, as Kenen notes, because so many foreign exchange transactions are netted before they are settled and because of the difficulty of distinguishing their implications for cash flow from those of other transactions.

6. A further caveat is that the imposition of a substantial transactions tax on banks at the dealing site may encourage non-banks to arrange retail transactions among themselves to evade the tax. Kenen suggests that while the volume of such transactions would be low initially, it could grow significantly over time.

7. Kenen similarly recommends the taxation of swaps but at rates which avoid double taxation (since a swap is a combination of a spot and an offsetting forward). Options are a more difficult case whose treatment, Kenen suggests, depends on the purposes for which the tax is applied.

8. Garber notes that the supply of outstanding Treasury bills in Japan amounted to only 11 trillion yen in late 1994, far below the daily volume of foreign exchange transactions. On the other hand, it is conceivable that the market could be organized so that it would be necessary to use Treasury bills only to settle net rather than gross foreign exchange transactions.

9. This same conclusion is reached on the basis of analysis of a larger sample of developing countries by Frankel and Rose (1995).

10. There are few analyses focusing on the implications of transnational coalitions: see however Putnam (1988) and the contributions to Evans, Jacobson and Putnam (1993).

References

Campbell, John Y., and Kenneth A. Froot. 1994. "International Experiences with Securities Transaction Taxes." In Jeffrey Frankel, ed., The Internationalization of Equity Markets. Chicago: University of Chicago Press.

Eichengreen, Barry and Albert Fishlow. 1996. "Contending with Capital Flows: What is Different about the 1990s?" Council on Foreign Relations Occasional Paper 1. New York.

Evans, Peter B., Harold K. Jacobson and Robert D. Putnam, eds. 1993. Double-Edged Diplomacy: International Bargaining and Domestic Politics. Berkeley: University of California Press.

Frankel, Jeffrey, and Andrew Rose. 1995. "Exchange Rate Crises in Emerging Markets: An Empirical Treatment." Department of Economics. University of California, Berkeley. Processed.

Frankel, Jeffrey, Shangjin Wei, and Ernesto Stein. 1994. "APEC and Regional Economic Arrangements in the Pacific." Department of Economics. University of California, Berkeley. Processed.

Goldberg, Linda. 1993. "Exchange Rates and Investment in United States Industry." Review of Economics and Statistics 75(4): 575–88.

Putnam, Robert D. 1988. "Diplomacy and Domestic Politics: The Logic of Two-Level Games." *International Organization* 42(3): 427–60.

Roll, Richard. 1989. "Price Volatility, International Market Links, and Their Implications for Regulatory Policies." Journal of Financial Services Research 3(2–3):211–46.

Rose, Andrew. 1994. "Are Exchange Rates Macroeconomic Phenomema?" *Federal Reserve Bank of San Francisco Economic Review* 19(1): 19–30.

Shome, Parthasarathi, and Janet G. Stotsky. 1995. "Financial Transactions Taxes." IMF Fiscal Affairs Working Paper 95–77. Washington, D.C.

Tobin, James. 1978. "A Proposal for International Monetary Reform." Eastern Economic Journal 4(July–October): 153–9.

Statistical Appendix

David Felix

These tables summarize most of the statistical information on the trading of global foreign exchange used by contributors to this volume. The data for 1995 were obtained from preliminary estimates by the Bank for International Settlements (BIS). For 1986 through 1995, the data are based on triennial surveys by participating central banks of monthly foreign exchange turnover in their respective national markets. Collating the survey data and producing global estimates net of double reporting by the counter-parties has been the responsibility of the BIS.

Intertemporal comparisons face, however, two main complications. One is that while only the central banks of Canada, Japan, the United Kingdom and the United States conducted national surveys in 1986, the number of participating banks expanded to 21 in 1989, and to 26 in 1992 and 1995. The original four countries, however, have accounted for a steady three-fifths of global foreign exchange turnover in the broader-based, later-year estimates. Consequently, one can expand the 1986 survey data by 5/3 with reasonable confidence to obtain the 1986 global estimate. Blowing up the 1989 survey data requires a lesser act of faith, since the top nine countries alone supplied 84% of the 1992 global turnover. Prior to 1986, however, only the Federal Reserve Bank of New York published triennial surveys of its national foreign exchange trading. To extract global estimates for these earlier years (tables A.1 and A.2), we used 17% as the average US share of global turnover in the 1986 through 1995 surveys. This may overestimate global foreign exchange turnover for 1977, 1980 and 1983, since the US global share was probably higher during these periods.[1]

A second complication stems from the rapid rise of cross-currency derivatives. Tables A.8, A.9 and A.10 report preliminary 1995 findings of the first comprehensive central bank survey of global derivative trading. The notional amount of such derivative contracts at the end of March 1995 is reported at over $13 trillion, virtually all relating to "customized" over-the-counter contracts, while the gross market value of these contracts averaged 7.8% of the notional amount. The net notional amount of daily over-the-counter foreign exchange derivative trades in April 1995 is reported as $688 billion (see table A.9), which, when multiplied by 0.078, yields $54 billion as a plausible estimate of daily global turnover in cross-currency derivatives. Added to the $1,230 billion daily turnover and also taking into account exchange-traded foreign exchange derivatives, makes $1,300 billion the approximate total of daily foreign exchange turnover of all types in 1995 (table A.1). But since the 1992 and 1989 BIS global turnover data do not allow comparable treatment of derivatives, it seemed best to exclude derivatives altogether in the time series in table A.2.[2]

Notes

1.   The 1977 global foreign exchange figure in tables A.1 and A.2 is an overestimate for a separate reason. The New York Federal Reserve's estimate of US turnover for that year is a gross figure, whereas its subsequent US estimates were net of double counting.

2.   The $1,300 billion daily turnover, is, however, a more appropriate starting point for calculating Tobin tax revenue, which means that those estimates that are based on a $1,230 billion daily turnover should be raised 7% to 8%. This assumes, of course, that the technical problems of taxing the market value of "customized" derivatives, for which there is no open resale market to determine market values, can be handled.

References

BIS (Bank for International Settlements). 1993. "Central Bank Survey of Foreign Exchange Market Activity in April 1992." Basle. March.

———. 1995a. "Central Bank Survey of Foreign Exchange Market Activity in April 1995: Preliminary Global Findings." Press Communique. Basle. October 24.

———. 1995b. "Central Bank Survey of Derivatives Market Activity: Release of Preliminary Global Totals." Press Communique. Basle. December 18.

Bank of England. 1995. "The Foreign Exchange Market in London." Press Notice. London. September 19.

Federal Reserve Bank of New York. 1992. "Summary of Results of the U.S. Foreign Exchange Market Turnover Conducted in April 1992." New York. September.

Federal Reserve Bank of New York. 1995. "April 1995 Central Bank Survey of Foreign Exchange Market Activity." New York. September 19.

IMF (International Monetary Fund). Various years. *International Financial Statistics*. Washington, D.C.

Appendix Tables

Table A.1 Daily global foreign exchange turnover
(billions of US dollars)

	Excluding derivatives[a]	Including derivatives[b]
1977	18.3	..
1980	82.5	..
1983	119.0	..
1986	270.0	..
1989	590.0	620.0
1992	820.0	880.0
1995	1,230.0	1,300.0[c]

.. denotes not available.
a. Includes spot, outright forward, and swaps.
b. Includes in addition futures and options.
c. Approximately 1,300.
Sources: BIS (1993, 1995); New York Federal Reserve Bank (1992, 1995).

Table A.2 Global official reserves, foreign exchange trading and exports, 1977–95

A. Reserves vs. foreign exchange trading volume[a]
(billions of US dollars)

	Global official foreign exchange reserves	Reserves + gold holdings[b]	Daily global foreign exchange turnover	Reserves/daily turnover (days)	Reserves + gold/ daily turnover (days)
	1	2	3	1/3	2/3
1977	265.8	296.6	18.3[d]	14.5	16.2
1980	386.6	468.9	82.5[d]	4.7	5.7
1983	339.7	496.6	119.0[d]	2.8	4.2
1986	456.0	552.6	270.0[d]	1.7	2.0
1989	722.3	826.8	590.0[c]	1.2	1.4
1992	910.8	1,022.5	820.0[c]	1.1	1.2
1995[e]	1,202.0	1,330.0	1,230.0	1.0	1.1

B. Exports vs. reserves and foreign exchange trading volume

	Annual world exports	Annual global foreign exchange volume[f]	Exports/ foreign exchange	Reserves/ exports	Reserves+gold/ exports
	4	5	4/5	1/4	2/4
	(trillions of US dollars)			(percents)	
1977	1.31	4.6	28.5	20.3	22.6
1980	1.88	20.6	9.1	20.6	24.9
1983	1.66	29.8	5.6	20.5	29.9
1986	1.99	67.5	2.9	20.5	27.8
1989	2.91	147.5	2.0	24.8	28.4
1992	3.76	205.0	1.8	24.2	27.2
1995[e]	4.80	307.5	1.6	25.0	27.9

C. Memorandum items

	1961–65	1966–70
1. (Global foreign exchange Reserves + Gold)/Exports	43.5%	32.3%
2. (Reserve Position with IMF)/Exports	3.1%	2.8%

a. Foreign exchange excludes trading in foreign exchange options and derivatives.
b. Official gold holdings valued at 35 special drawing rights (SDRs) per ounce.
c. Net of double reporting of same transactions by intracountry and/or intercountry counterparts.
d. Estimated by dividing the reported US volume by 0.17, the US share of global foreign exchange turnover in 1989 and 1992.
e. Preliminary estimates of 1995 net foreign exchange turnover and world exports.
f. Daily global foreign exchange turnover multiplied by 250 trading days.
Source: BIS (1993) New York Federal Reserve Bank (1993, 1995); IMF (various years); Bank of England (1995).

Table A.3 Daily global foreign exchange turnover net of local and cross-border double counting and excluding derivatives
(billions of US dollars)

	1989		1992		1995	
	Amount	% share	Amount	% share	Amount	% share
Main categories						
Spots	350	59	400	49	535	43
Outright forwards[b, c]	..	..	58	7	99	8
Swaps[c]	184	31	324	40	596	49
Estimated reporting gaps	56	9	38	5	..	..
Total net daily turnover	590	99.9	820	100.1	1,230	100.0
Foreign exchange dealer transactions with:						
Other dealers	436	74	574	70	800	65
Other financial customers[d,e]	..	..	98	12	246	20
Non-financial customers[e]	154	26	148	18	184	15
Totals	590	100.0	820	100.0	1,230	100

.. 1995 data not fully available at time of going to press.
Note: Percentages may not add up because of rounding.
b. Over-the-counter transactions with cash settlement in more than two days plus exchange-traded futures. Latter includes double counting.
c. The 1989 survey does not separate outright forwards from swaps; $184 billion is the combined total.
d. Dealer transactions with private non-reporting banks and non-bank financial firms and funds as well as central banks and other official financial institutions.
e. The 1989 survey combined all dealer-customer transactions in one figure.
Source: BIS (1993, tables 1 and 1-A); BIS (1995a).

Table A.4 Daily average foreign exchange turnover by country
(billions of US dollars)

Country	April 1989		April 1992		April 1995	
	Amount	% share	Amount	% share	Amount	% share
United Kingdom	184.0	26	290.5	27	464.5	30
United States	115.2	16	166.9	16	244.4	16
Japan	110.8	15	120.2	11	161.3	10
Singapore	55.0	8	73.6	7	105.4	7
Hong Kong	48.8	7	60.3	6	90.2	6
Switzerland	56.0	8	65.5	6	86.5	5
Germany	..	..	55.0	5	76.2	5
France	23.2	3	33.3	3	58.0	4
Australia	28.9	4	29.0	3	39.5	3
Denmark	12.8	2	26.6	2	30.5	2
Canada	15.0	2	21.9	2	29.8	2
Belgium	10.4	1	15.7	1	28.1	2
Netherlands	12.9	2	19.6	2	25.5	2
Italy	10.9	1	15.5	1	23.2	1
Sweden	13.0	2	21.3	2	19.9	1
Luxembourg	..	..	13.2	1	19.1	1
Spain	4.4	1	12.3	1	18.3	1
Austria	..	..	4.4	0	13.3	1
Norway	4.3	1	5.2	0	7.6	0
New Zealand	..	..	4.2	0	7.1	0
Finland	3.4	0	6.8	1	5.3	0
South Africa	..	..	3.4	0	5.0	0
Ireland	5.2	1	5.9	1	4.9	0
Greece	0.4	0	1.1	0	3.6	0
Bahrain	3.0	0	3.5	0	2.6	0
Portugal	0.9	0	1.3	0	2.4	0
Total turnover	717.0	100	1,076.2	100	1,572.2	100

.. denotes not available.
Note: Countries participating in the BIS surveys. Turnover adjusted for local double counting only.
Total does not include the BIS adjustment for foreign exchange trading with non-participating countries and other data gaps.
Source: BIS (1995a).

Table A.5 Maturity breakdown of foreign exchange turnover
(percentage share of turnover)

| | Spot | | | | Forward | | | |
| | 2 days or less | | 3 to 7 days | | 8 to 365 days | | Over 365 days | |
Settlement	1992	1995	1992	1995	1992	1995	1992	1995
United Kingdom	49.3	40.5	34.9	42.0	15.2	17.0	0.6	0.5
United States	49.2	55.0	32.1	29.7	18.2	14.4	0.5	0.9
Japan	37.8	..	36.4	..	25.2	..	0.6	..
Singapore	49.1	..	..	..	..	..	..	..
Switzerland	..	..	..	..	..	..	..	..
Hong Kong	52.1	..	33.2	..	14.5	..	0.1	..
Germany	48.7	..	34.9	..	15.5	..	0.9	..
France	49.8	..	24.5	..	25.0	..	0.7	..
Australia	42.1	..	46.3	..	10.9	..	0.7	..
Denmark	37.3	..	..	..	..	..	..	..
Canada	34.2	..	43.4	..	21.2	..	1.2	..
Sweden	46.6	..	27.1	..	24.9	..	1.4	..
Netherlands	46.5	..	38.4	..	14.0	..	1.1	..
Belgium	33.3	..	29.1	..	37.3	..	0.3	..
Italy	69.3	..	16.8	..	12.6	..	1.3	..
Luxembourg	46.7	..	37.9	..	15.0	..	0.4	..
Spain	50.8	..	25.1	..	22.6	..	1.5	..
Finland	..	..	..	..	..	..	..	..
Ireland	77.3	..	9.9	..	11.7	..	1.1	..
Norway	38.2	..	42.0	..	19.0	..	0.8	..
Austria	87.4	..	4.6	..	7.6	..	0.4	..
New Zealand	46.9	..	39.9	..	12.9	..	0.3	..
Bahrain	..	..	..	..	..	..	..	..
South Africa	55.7	..	17.8	..	25.5	..	1.0	..
Portugal	90.5	..	6.7	..	2.8	..	0.0	..
Greece	93.8	..	0.3	..	5.9	..	0.0	..
Total	47.8	43.0	33.6	38.8	18.0	17.7	0.6	0.5

.. 1995 data not fully available at time of going to press.
Source: BIS (1993, tables 2-A, 3-B, 5-A); BIS (1995a); Bank of England (1995); New York Federal Reserve Bank (1995).

Table A.6 Currencies on one side of foreign exchange transactions
(percentage of gross global turnover)

Currency	1989	1992	1995
US dollar	90	82	83
Deutsche mark	27	40	37
Japanese yen	27	23	24
Pound sterling	15	14	10
French franc	2	4	8
Swiss franc	10	9	7
Canadian dollar	1	3	3
ECU	1	3	2
Australian dollar	2	2	3
Other EMS currencies	3	9	13
Other reporting country currencies	3	3	2
Non-reporting country currencies	19	8	8
All currencies	200	200	200

Source: BIS (1995a, table 2).

Table A.7 Share of local currency in foreign exchange turnover net of local double counting

(percents)

Country	1992	1995
United Kingdom	23.9	16.0
United States	88.7	86.0
Japan	73.9	..
Singapore	3.2	..
Switzerland	46.6	..
Hong Kong	14.4	..
Germany	83.4	..
France	49.0	..
Australia	41.6	..
Denmark	16.3	..
Canada	65.3	..
Sweden	50.7	..
Netherlands	47.3	..
Belgium	25.2	..
Italy	81.1	..
Luxembourg	4.5	..
Spain	71.1	..
Finland	51.9	..
Ireland	7.9	..
Norway	45.0	..
Austria	23.6	..
New Zealand	44.2	..
Bahrain	1.3	..
South Africa	62.7	..
Portugal	57.6	..
Greece	54.6	..
Overall average	47.3	..

.. 1995 data not fully available at time of going to press.
Source: BIS (1993, tables 2–A, 2–D); Bank of England (1995); Federal Reserve Bank of New York (1995).

Table A.8 Global notional amounts and gross market values of derivative contracts outstanding at end-March 1995
(billions of US dollars)

A. Over-the-counter contracts

	Foreign exchange[a]			Interest rates			Other[b]		
	Notional amounts	*Market values*	*Ratio[c]*	*Notional amounts*	*Market values*	*Ratio[c]*	*Notional amounts*	*Market values*	*Ratio[c]*
Deals[d]	13,153	1,021	0.078	26,645	646	0.024	916	78	0.085
Dealers with:									
Other dealers	7,221	515	0.071	15,732	349	0.022	277	30	0.108
Local	2,577	197	0.076	6,756	156	0.023	..	..	..
Cross-border	4,643	317	0.068	8,976	193	0.022	..	..	..
Dealers with:									
Fin. customers	2,798	177	0.063	6,566	156	0.024	..	..	..
Local	1,061	61	0.057	2,910	55	0.019	..	..	..
Cross-border	1,737	115	0.066	3,656	101	0.028	..	..	..
Dealers with:									
Nonfin. custom.	3,132	329	0.105	4,347	139	0.032	632	47	0.074
Local	2,044	189	0.092	2,583	69	0.027	..	..	..
Cross-border	1,088	140	0.129	1,763	69	0.039	..	..	..

B. Exchange-traded contracts
(Notional amounts)

	Foreign exchange[a]	Interest rates	Other
Deals outstanding[e]	120	15,674	787

.. 1995 data not fully available at time of going to press.
a. United Kingdom data on outright forwards and foreign exchange swaps are unavailable, hence both overall and foreign exchange totals are underestimates.
b. Equity indices and commodity-based derivatives.
c. Market values/notional amounts.
d. Net of local and cross-border double counting.
e. As reported by survey participants of the reporting countries, not by the exchanges. The data could not be adjusted for double counting for lack of information on counter-parties.
Source: BIS (1995b, table 1).

Table A.9 Daily average of global turnover in notional amounts of foreign exchange and interest rate derivative contracts in April 1995

A. Over-the-counter contracts

	Foreign exchange		Interest rates	
	Notional amounts (US$bn)	Share (%)	Notional amounts (US$bn)	Share (%)
Total reported turnover[a]	688	100	151	100
with other dealers	427	62	102	68
local	162	23	45	30
cross-border	265	39	57	38
with other financial institutions	149	22	32	21
local	74	11	16	10
cross-border	75	11	16	11
with non-financial customers	111	16	17	11
local	76	11	12	8
cross-border	35	5	5	3

B. Exchange-traded contracts

	Foreign exchange	Interest rates
Total reported turnover[b]	15	1,121

a. Adjusted for local and cross-border double-counting. Adjustments have been made by halving the positions with respect to other dealers.
b. As reported by survey participants of the reporting countries, not by the exchanges. The data could not be adjusted for double-counting for lack of information on counter-parties.
Source: BIS (1995b, table 4).

Table A.10 Shares of outstanding derivative contracts by type and risk category as of end-March, 1995

A. Over-the-counter-contracts[a]

	Notional amounts		Market value		Market value/ notional (%)
	Amount ($US 10⁹)	Share (%)	Amount ($US10⁹)	Share (%)[b]	
Foreign exchange[c]	13,153	100	1,021	100	7.8
Forwards and foreign exchange swaps	8,742	72	602	70	6.9
Currency swaps	1,974	11	345	22	17.5
Options	2,375	16	69	7	2.9
Single-currency interest rates[c]	26,645	100	646	100	2.4
Forward rate agreements	4,597	17	18	3	0.4
Swaps	18,283	69	560	87	3.1
Options	3,548	13	60	9	1.7
Equity and stock indices	599	100	50	100	8.3
Forwards and swaps	52	9	7	14	13.5
Options	547	91	43	86	7.9
Commodities	317	100	28	100	8.8
Forwards and swaps	208	66	21	78	10.1
Options	109	34	6	22	5.5

B. Exchange traded contracts[d]

	Notional amount ($US 10⁹)	Share (%)
Foreign exchange	120	100
Futures	39	33
Options	81	67
Interest rates	15,674	100
Futures	12,436	79
Options	3,238	21
Equity and stock indices	645	100
Futures	195	30
Options	450	70
Commodities	142	100
Futures	92	65
Options	56	35

a. Net of local and cross-border double counting.
b. Percentages computed with incomplete UK data excluded.
c. Shortfall of components from the totals due to exclusion of "other products".
d. See note d of table A.8.
Source: BIS (1995b).

About the Contributors

Manuel R. Agosin
Manuel R. Agosin is Director, Graduate School of Economics and Management, and Professor, Department of Economics, University of Chile. He has also been an adviser to Latin American Governments and consultant to the UN Comisión Económica para América Latina y el Caribe (CEPAL), the United Nations Conference on Trade and Development (UNCTAD) and the Inter-American Development Bank. His main publication areas include trade policy and foreign direct investment in Latin America.

Michael Dooley
Michael Dooley is Professor of Economics, University of California, Santa Cruz. He is also Research Associate of the National Bureau for Economic Research and Managing Editor of the *International Journal of Finance and Economics*. From 1983 to 1991, he served as Assistant Director of the Research Department of the International Monetary Fund. He has written extensively about capital controls, monetary economics and international banking.

Barry Eichengreen
Barry Eichengreen is the John L. Simpson Professor of Economics and Political Science, University of California, Berkeley. He is also Research

Associate of the National Bureau of Economic Research and Research Fellow of the Centre for Economic Policy Research. As a consultant, he has worked for the International Monetary Fund, the World Bank, the US Department of Labor and several other institutions. He has written numerous books and articles about international monetary systems and international economic cooperation, including *International Monetary Arrangements for the 21st Century* (The Brookings Institution 1994) and *Currency Convertibility: The Gold Standard and Beyond* (co-edited, Routledge 1995).

David Felix

David Felix is Emeritus Professor of Economics, Washington University in St. Louis. He has written extensively on economic development issues, both regional (Latin America) and global. In the past decade, his main focus has been on trends in international finance and their effects on the global and developing-country economies. He has also authored several studies on the Tobin Tax.

Ricardo Ffrench-Davis

Ricardo Ffrench-Davis is Principal Regional Adviser of the UN Comisión Económica para América Latina y el Caribe (CEPAL), Santiago de Chile. He has been Deputy Manager and Director of Research of the Central Bank of Chile, as well as Vice President and researcher at the Center of Economic Research on Latin America (CIEPLAN), Santiago de Chile. He has written and published extensively on international economics, development strategies, foreign financing and Latin American economies. His most recent publication is *Coping with Capital Surges—The Return of Finance to Latin America* (co-edited with Stephany Griffith-Jones; Lynne Rienner Publishers 1995.)

Jeffrey Frankel

Jeffrey Frankel is Professor of Economics, University of California, Berkeley, where he is also Director of the Center for International and Development Economics Research. In addition, he is Research Associate of the National Bureau of Economic Research, where he is also Director for International Finance and Macroeconomics. He recently served as Senior Fellow, Institute for International Economics, Washington, D.C. He is currently a member of the Presidential Economic Policy Advisory Board, of the Council of Economic Advisers in Washington, D.C. His recently published books include *Does Foreign Exchange*

Intervention Work? (Institute for International Economics 1993), *On Exchange Rates* (MIT Press 1993) and *Financial Markets and Monetary Policy* (MIT Press 1995).

Peter Garber

Peter Garber is Professor of Economics, Brown University, and has been Professor at the University of Rochester and University of Virginia. He has been a visiting scholar at the Board of Governors of the Federal Reserve and the Bank of Japan, and a consultant at the International Monetary Fund since 1989. He has published numerous articles and books on international capital markets, in particular on the economics of speculative attacks, speculative bubbles, financial crises and taxes on securities transactions. His most recent books include *Speculative Bubbles, Speculative Attacks, and Policy Switching* (co-authored with Robert Flood; MIT Press 1994) and *The Economics of Banking, Liquidity and Money* (co-authored with Steven Weisbrod; Heath 1992).

Stephany Griffith-Jones

Stephany Griffith-Jones is a Fellow at the Institute of Development Studies, Sussex University. As senior consultant on international capital flows, she worked in many international institutions, such as the UN Comisión Económica para América Latina y el Caribe (CEPAL), the World Bank, the Inter-American Development Bank and the United Nations Conference on Trade and Development (UNCTAD), as well as with several governments, including those of Brazil, Chile and the Czech Republic, and with Barclays Bank International. She has published many articles and books, the most recent being *Coping with Capital Surges—The Return of Finance to Latin America* (co-edited with Ricardo Ffrench-Davis; Lynne Rienner Publishers 1995).

Isabelle Grunberg

Isabelle Grunberg is Senior Policy Analyst at the Office of Development Studies of the United Nations Development Programme, New York. Previously, she was Associate Director of United Nations Studies at Yale University and a MacArthur Fellow and Lecturer at Yale. She was also a lecturer at the London School of Economics and the Institut d'Etudes Politiques in Paris. She received a French doctoral equivalent (agrégation) from the Sorbonne University and the Ecole Normale Supérieure. Her areas of publication include international political economy and theories of the international system.

Mahbub ul Haq

Mahbub ul Haq is President of the Human Development Centre in Islamabad, Pakistan. He has been Chief Economist of the Pakistan Planning Commission, Director of the World Bank's Policy Planning Department, Planning and Finance Minister of Pakistan and Special Adviser to the Administrator of the United Nations Development Programme, where he was the main author of the independent annual *Human Development Report.* He has also served as an Eminent Adviser to the Brandt Commission, as a Governor of the IMF and as a Governor of the World Bank. His latest books include *The UN and the Bretton Woods Institutions* (co-edited with Khadija Haq, Richard Jolly and Paul Streeten; Macmillan 1995) and *Reflections on Human Development* (Oxford University Press 1995).

Inge Kaul

Inge Kaul is Director, Office of Development Studies at the United Nations Development Programme. She has previously served as Director of the Human Development Report Office at UNDP, where she coordinated a team of authors producing the annual *Human Development Report* from 1990 to 1995. Before that, she held senior policy positions with UNDP. She has extensive research experience in developing countries and is the author of a number of publications and reports.

Peter B. Kenen

Peter B. Kenen is Walker Professor of Economics and International Finance at Princeton University. He is also Director of the International Finance Section at Princeton and has been a consultant to the Council of Economic Advisers, the Office of Management and Budget, the Federal Reserve Bank, the International Monetary Fund and the US Treasury. He has written and edited several books on international economics, exchange rates and monetary systems. The most recent include *Exchange Rates and the Monetary System* (Edward Elgar 1994) and *Managing the World Economy Fifty Years after Bretton Woods* (Institute for International Economics 1994).

John V. Langmore

John Langmore has been a member of the Australian House of Representatives since 1984. Positions held prior to his election included Lecturer in Economics at the University of Papua New Guinea and Economic Adviser to the Australian Treasurer. He has chaired several parliamentary committees and published widely on domestic and international economic policy, including a jointly authored book, *Work for All* (Melbourne University Press 1994).

Yung Chul Park
Yung Chul Park is Professor of Economics, Korea University, Seoul, and President of the Korea Institute of Finance. In addition, he is a member of the Ministry of Finance's Financial Development Committee and chair of its Financial Reform Subcommittee. He has served as Chief Economic Adviser to the President of Korea and as an academic member of the Bank of Korea's Monetary Board. He was also the Director of the Institute of Economic Research at Korea University and a visiting professor at Harvard University and the Institute for International Development, as well as a research economist at the International Monetary Fund.

Ranjit Sau
Ranjit Sau is Professor at the Indian Institute of Management, Calcutta, and currently a visiting professor at the School of Industrial Management, New Jersey Institute of Technology. He has held teaching positions in several universities in India and the United States. His main research interests include international finance and development economics. He has published several books on international investments and exchange rates.

James Tobin
James Tobin is Sterling Professor of Economics Emeritus at Yale University, where he retired from his teaching position in 1988. In 1961–62, he was a member of President Kennedy's Council of Economic Advisers in Washington. He was President of the Econometric Society in 1958, of the American Economic Association in 1971 and of the Eastern Economics Association in 1977. In 1981 he received in Stockholm the Prize in Economic Science, established by the Bank of Sweden in Memory of Alfred Nobel. He is author or editor of thirteen books and more than four hundred articles. His main professional subjects have been macroeconomics, monetary theory and policy, fiscal policy and public finance, consumption and saving, unemployment and inflation, portfolio theory and asset markets, and econometrics.

Charles Wyplosz
Charles Wyplosz is Professor of Economics, Graduate Institute for International Studies, Geneva. He has written extensively on monetary

policy exchange rates and capital movements. He has advised the European Commission on the effect of the Single Act on capital movements and then on the European Monetary Union. He is a frequent consultant to governments (currently Russia) and international organizations, such as the International Monetary Fund and the World Bank.

Further Reading on the Tobin Tax

Davidson, Paul. 1995. "Are Grains of Sand in the Wheels of International Finance Sufficient to Do the Job When Boulders Are Often Required?" University of Tennessee. Processed.

Dornbusch, Rudiger. 1995. "Cross-Border Payments Taxes and Alternative Capital Account Regimes." Report to the Group of Twenty-Four. UNCTAD. September.

Dornbusch, Rudiger and Jeffrey Frankel. 1987. "The Flexible Exchange Rate System: Experience and Alternatives." NBER Working Paper 2464. Cambridge, Mass.

D'Orville, Hans and Dragoljub Najman. 1995. *Towards a New Multilateralism: Funding Global Priorities*. New York: United Nations.

Eichengreen, Barry, James Tobin and Charles Wyplosz. 1995. "Two Cases for Sand in the Wheels of International Finance." *Economic Journal* 105 (January):162–72.

Felix, David. 1995. "The Tobin Tax Proposal: Background, Issues and Prospects." *Futures* 27(2):195–213.

———. 1995. "Financial Globalization vs. Free Trade: The Case for the Tobin Tax." UNCTAD Discussion Paper 108. New York.

Garber, Peter and Mark P. Taylor. 1995. "Sand in the Wheels of Foreign Exchange Markets: A Skeptical Note." *Economic Journal* 105(January): 173–80.

Hubbard, R. Glenn. 1993. "Securities Transactions Taxes: Tax Design, Revenue, and Policy Considerations." *Tax Notes* 61: 985–1,000. November.

Kelly, Ruth. 1993. *Taxing the Speculator: The Route to Forex Stability.* The Fabian Society Discussion Paper 15. London.

Shome, Parthasarathi and Janet Stotsky. 1995. "Financial Transaction Taxes." IMF Working Paper 95–77. Washington, D.C.

Spahn, Paul Bernd. 1995. "International Financial Flows and Transaction Taxes: Surveys and Options." IMF Fiscal Affairs Working Paper 60. Washington, D.C.

Summers, Lawrence H. and Victoria P. Summers. 1989. "When Financial Markets Work Too Well: A Cautious Case for a Securities Transactions Tax." *Journal of Financial Services Research* 3(2–3):163–88.

Tobin, James. 1978. "A Proposal for International Monetary Reform." *Eastern Economic Journal* 4 (July–October):153–9.

Index